Literacy Assessment of Second Language Learners

Sandra Rollins Hurley
Josefina Villamil Tinajero
The University of Texas at El Paso

Allyn and Bacon

Boston ▪ London ▪ Toronto ▪ Sydney ▪ Tokyo ▪ Singapore

Editor-in-chief: *Paul A. Smith*
Series editor: *Arnis E. Burvikovs*
Series editorial assistant: *Patrice Mailloux*
Marketing Manager: *Brad Parkins*
Composition and prepress buyer: *Linda Cox*
Manufacturing buyer: *Julie McNeill*
Cover administrator: *Brian Gogolin*
Production coordinator: *Mary Beth Finch*
Editorial-production service: *Modern Graphics, Inc.*
Electronic composition: *Modern Graphics, Inc.*

Copyright © 2001 by Allyn & Bacon
A Pearson Education Company
160 Gould Street
Needham Heights, Massachusetts 02494

Internet: www.abacon.com

Between the time Website information is gathered and then published, it is not unusual for some sites to have closed. Also, the transcription of URLs can result in unintended typographical errors. The publisher would appreciate notification where these occur so that they may be corrected in subsequent editions. Thank you.

Library of Congress Cataloging-in-Publication Data
Literacy assessment of second language learners / Sandra Rollins Hurley, Josefina Villamil Tinajero.
    p. cm.
    Includes bibliographical references and index.
    ISBN 0-205-27443-9 (pbk.)
    1. Language and languages—Ability testing. 2. Literacy—Ability testing. 3. Education, Bilingual. I. Hurley, Sandra Rollins. II. Villamil Tinajero, Josefina.

P53.4 .L58 2000
418'.0076—dc21

00-056916

Printed in the United States of America

10 9 8 7 6 5 4 3 2   05 04 03 02 01

To Tom, Ryan, Clay, and my students who are the inspiration for all I do.
Sandra Rollins Hurley

To second-language learners, whose richness and diversity enhance our schools and our nation, and to you, their teachers.
Josefina Villamil Tinajero

CONTENTS

PREFACE

In 1991, Saville-Troike wrote that bilingual education "has come a long way . . . however, not all areas have changed at the same rate, and there has been a 'cultural lag' in some areas, perhaps most notably in the area of assessment" (available on-line: www.ncbe.gwu.edu). Over the past ten years, much progress has been made in developing, implementing, and refining programs and strategies to support literacy, biliteracy, and content area instruction. The issue of assessment is still being resolved, however, particularly for second-language learners. Assessment dominates the educational reform dialogue in general. The demand for assessment alternatives to standardized testing and other paper-and-pencil-multiple-choice tests has grown among language educators as well (Short, 1999). Traditional assessment techniques are often incongruent with English-language-learner (ELL) classroom practice. Standardized testing is particularly antithetical to process learning (Bartolomé, 1998; Moya and O'Malley, 1994; Short, 1999). Thus in the last several years, educators have begun to explore alternative forms of student assessment known as authentic assessment practices for second language learners.

The contributing authors of *Literacy Assessment of Second Language Learners* take the position that teachers must skillfully connect teaching, learning, and assessment in meaningful ways. Assessment measures, therefore, need to be designed for use as an integral part of instruction—not as a separate, add-on procedure—so that assessment does not take away from instructional time. The authors also take the position that authentic assessment practices reflect a view of instruction that is more sensitive to the natural growth of students acquiring English. This new view of assessment becomes an integral part of instruction, is on-going and is based on everyday classroom activities. It is focused on both process and product. It acknowledges the fact that teachers are in a position to constantly observe and assess students in action, engaged in a wide range of procedures. The traditional tools of ethnography—observation, journals, and checklists—have been used successfully to accomplish these purposes. It follows, then, that in the classroom, just as in ethnographic research, the primary tool is the investigator—the teacher. It is the teacher who makes the decisions on which assessment measures to use and when and how to use them. The most important implication, therefore, is that teachers must be knowledgeable, well-informed individuals who can ask the critical questions, determine ways to find answers to questions, and then make wise instructional decisions. This book supports that preparation.

The editors and contributing authors value linguistic and cultural diversity. Just as various voices in a choir combine to make more beautiful music than a single voice, the contributing authors of *Literacy Assessment of Second Language Learners* bring rich and diverse experiences and their various voices add depth and breadth to the book. Our main goal is to provide teachers, particularly those within grade K to 8 settings, theoretical and practical information about assessment. By enhancing instructional performance, we increase the possibility of students' academic, social, and linguistic growth. To this end, each chapter in the book begins with a vignette, a snapshot of language learners and teachers in action, that reflects real life experiences in bilingual and ELL classrooms across the United States. The vignettes are followed by a synopsis of the research literature specific to the assessment issues that are the focus of that chapter. This research forms the theoretical base for the chapter and ultimately for the entire book, and it provides a meaningful and functional framework within which to design assessment and instructional practices. The research cited provides substantive evidence for the best and most promising practices for assessment and sets the stage for the application section of each chapter. The application part of each chapter provides state-of-the-art information, paradigms, and issues associated with effective teaching and assessment within dual language settings, taking into account how linguistic and cultural factors influence language and literacy development and academic outcomes. The authors recommend alternative assessment measures, such as checklists, portfolios, and performance-based tasks. In most cases, the authors provide assessment instruments that can be copied or adapted for use in the classroom. Our goal here is to enhance the confidence of teachers on the selection and use of the best or most promising assessment practices and measures in dual or multiple language instructional classes. Each chapter closes with final thoughts, bringing the readers back to the opening vignettes, composites of real-life experiences in the classroom.

Diane Lapp, Douglas Fisher, James Flood , and Arturo Cabello's chapter, "An Integrated Approach to the Teaching and Assessment of Language Arts," provides a comprehensive view of integrated teaching and assessment. They include a number of excellent assessment instruments for teachers and for student use in self-assessment. Included are a story retell inventory, a speaking checklist, holistic writing rubrics, and a writing portfolio conference record.

Josefina Villamil Tinajero and Sandra Rollins Hurley's chapter, "Assessing Progress in Second-Language Acquisition," chronicles children's language growth and development and provides teachers with ideas and instruments on how to assess that growth.

Kathy Escamilla and Maria Coady's chapter, "Assessing the Writing of Spanish-Speaking Students: Issues and Suggestions," provides an in-depth look at writing development in two languages through a case study approach. Assessment practices that look at second-language learners only in English, often underestimate the cognitive and academic strengths of students. Rubrics for assessing writing in the primary grades and in the intermediate grades are provided.

Lorraine Valdez Pierce's chapter, "Assessment of Reading Comprehension Strategies for Intermediate Bilingual Learners," considers ways to simultaneously enhance and assess reading comprehension. Included are prereading anticipation guides, observation checklists, reading and writing scoring rubrics, and student self-assessment forms.

Sandra Rollins Hurley and Sally Blake's chapter, "Assessment in the Content Areas for Students Acquiring English," is focused on upper elementary and middle schoolers. Content area reading is critical for students in the upper grades and academic language develops more slowly than social language. The chapter discusses ways to enhance comprehension of content area text while integrating instruction and assessment. The authors include a content reading and study skills inventory, samples of student-made graphic organizers, and examples of performance-based assessment.

Douglas Fisher, Diane Lapp, James Flood, and Lucy Suarez focus on the important topic of assessment policies for second language learners in the chapter, "Assessing Bilingual Students: When Policies and Practices Meet in the Classroom." A conversation between Mrs. Martinez who was introduced in Chapter 1 and Mr. Riley, her student teacher, culminates with a table of assessment accommodations for English-language learners.

The dilemma of distinguishing between language and learning difficulties is addressed by Jim Cummins. He explores ways of integrating standardized and informal assessment in the chapter, "Assessment and Intervention with Culturally and Linguistically Diverse Learners," in which he addresses the following important questions: How can we distinguish between language and learning difficulties that are a reflection of the normal process of learning English as a second language from those that may be reflective of intrinsic "genuine" learning or language disorders that require special education intervention? He describes the development of and use of the Bilingual Verbal Abilities Test (BVAT).

Sandra Fradd and Okhee Lee explore ways of integrating standardized and informal assessment in the chapter, "Needed: A Framework for Integrating Standardized and Informal Assessment for Students Developing Academic Language Proficiency in English." They examine academic language development in the context of fourth grade science and literacy instruction. Included is a reporting rubric for use in assessing students' writing in science classrooms.

Jill Kerper Mora's chapter, "Effective Instructional Practices and Assessment for Literacy and Biliteracy Development" provides a theoretical view and model of biliteracy development. The chapter presents an analysis of cross-linguistic interaction in the reading process for youngsters reading in two languages. An instrument for assessing biliteracy development is included to link strategies for instructional intervention with students' strengths and areas of difficulty in reading.

Finally Alma Flor Ada, F. Isabel Campoy, and Rosa Zubizarreta challenge all of us to assess our work with parents in their chapter, "Assessing Our Work with Parents on Behalf of Children's Literacy." They remind us that in addition to assessing our work in the areas of parent education and parent engagement, we also need to assess our everyday classroom curriculum regarding the inclusion of parents, family, and community. A framework for considering these issues is provided.

In these ten chapters we provide teachers with some of the information they need to make powerful choices for themselves and their students. *Literacy Assess-*

ment for Second Language Learners challenges us to use this information to create learning environments where learning is facilitated and stimulated by caring adults. We hope that in sharing this collection of best practices in assessment will be distributed across significantly more classrooms. Finally, we hope that the critical reading of this text will influence educators to view students' dual language and biliterate abilities as an asset, as an intellectual accomplishment, and as a nationally treasured resource. The realization of the promise of multiple languages and literacies is the basis for building a solid academic future for individual students from all groups in our society, and enhancing the welfare of our nation.

Sandra Rollins Hurley and Josefina Villamil Tinajero

References

Bartolome, L. I. (1998). *The misteaching of academic discourses: The politics of langauge in the classroom.* Boulder, CO: Westview Press.

Moya, S. S., & O'Malley, J. M. (Spring 1994). A portfolio assessment model for ESL. *The Journal of Education Issues of Language Minority Students. 65,* 13–36.

Saville-Troike, M. (1991). *Teaching and testing for academic achievement: The role of language development.* National Clearinghouse for Bilingual Education. Focus: Occasional Papers in Bilingual Education, No. 4. Available: *www.ncbe.gwu.edu*

Short, D. (1999). Assessing integrated language and content instruction. In I. A. Heath & C. J. Serrano (Eds.), *Annual editions: Teaching English as a second language* (pp. 129–141). Guilford, CT: McGraw-Hill.

CONTRIBUTING AUTHORS

Alma Flor Ada is a professor of International Multicultural Education at the University of San Francisco, where she has guided the doctoral research of numerous students. A leader in bilingual education and critical pedagogy, she works with schools and communities worldwide as an advocate for social justice and linguistic human rights. Her experience as a children's book writer fuels her commitment to helping teachers, children, and parents find their own voice and strength as authors.

Sally Blake earned her Ph.D. from the University of Mississippi in 1991. She was an early childhood teacher in a variety of states for seventeen years before returning to the university to complete her research. She is presently the Associate Director of Partners for Excellence in Science Education (PETE) and director of the Texas Prefreshman Engineering program. Her research focus is educational reform in mathematics and science education. Dr. Blake has published numerous articles and book chapters. She coauthored with Jean Shaw the text, *Mathematics for Young Children*. Dr. Blake received The University of Texas at El Paso's College of Education Outstanding Research and Outstanding Service Award.

Arturo Cabello is a language, speech, and hearing specialist in the Sweetwater Union High School District. He serves students whose heritage language is Spanish in grades seven to twelve. His interests focus on bilingual and special education and the service delivery systems for all students. Dr. Cabello is a frequent presenter at local, state, and national conferences in the areas of speech and hearing and special education.

F. Isabel Campoy offers seminars on education and empowerment through creative expression, including writing, theater, and strorytelling. Her professional work also includes antibias education. With an academic background in applied linguistics and a long career in educational publishing, she has produced numerous textbooks on language learning. In her creative capacity as an author, she has written books for young readers in the areas of poetry, theater, music, cultural history, and art.

Maria Coady is a doctoral student in Social, Multicultural, and Bilingual Foundations at the University of Colorado, Boulder. She has lived and worked in a variety of settings and locations in the United States, Argentina, and Ireland. Her area of emphasis is bilingual education and language policy.

Jim Cummins is currently a professor in the Modern Language Centre of the Ontario Institute for Studies in Education. He has published several books related to bilingual education and minority student achievement including *Bilingualism and Special Education: Issues in Assessment and Pedagogy* (Multilingual Matters, 1984), *Bilingualism in Education: Aspects of Theory, Research and Policy* (Longman, 1986, with Merrill Swain), *Minority Education: From Shame to Struggle* (Multilingual Matters, 1988, with T. Skutnabb-Kangas), *Empowering Minority Students* (California Association for Bilingual Education, 1989), and *Brave New Schools: Challenging Cultural Illiteracy through Global Learning Networks* (St. Martin's Press, with D. Sayers).

Kathy Escamilla is an Associate Professor in the Social, Multicultural and Bilingual Foundations Division at the University of Colorado, Boulder. She has been a bilingual teacher, program administrator, and professor of bilingual education. Her research has explored various topics related to educational programs and their impact on Spanish speaking students. She is particularly interested in literacy and biliteracy development in Spanish speaking students. She has served two terms as the President of the National Association for Bilingual Education.

Douglas Fisher, Assistant Professor of Teacher Education at San Diego State University, currently serves as the Director of Professional Development for the City Heights Educational Pilot. This pilot is a partnership between Rosa Parks Elementary School, Monroe Clark Middle School, Hoover High School, and San Diego State University focused on improving the educational experiences for five thousand public school children in three inner-city schools and improving the likelihood that these students attend college. In addition, Dr. Fisher is a teacher, teacher educator, and writer. His writing has appeared in *The California Reader, The Reading Teacher,* and the *National Reading Conference Yearbook.* In addition, he is the coauthor of four books focused on curriculum development and modification.

James Flood, who is a Professor of Reading and Language Development at San Diego State University, has taught in preschool, elementary, and secondary schools and has been a language arts supervisor and vice principal. He has also been a Fulbright scholar at the University of Lisbon in Portugal and the President of the National Reading Conference. Dr. Flood has chaired and cochaired many IRA, NCTE, NCRE, and NRC committees. Currently, Dr. Flood teaches preservice and graduate courses at San Diego State University. He has coauthored and edited many articles, columns, texts, handbooks, and children's materials on reading and language arts issues. These include the following, which were codeveloped with Diane Lapp: *Content Area Reading and Learning,* which is in its second edition and *The Handbook of Research on Teaching Literacy Through the Communicative and Visual Arts.* His many educational awards include being named as the Outstanding Teacher Educator in the Department of Teacher Education at San Diego State University, the Distinguished Research Lecturer from San Diego State University's Graduate Division of Research, and a member of the California Hall of Fame.

Sandra H. Fradd is a professor in the Department of Teaching and Learning at the University of Miami. A native speaker of English, Dr. Fradd grew up speaking Spanish in South Florida and in Latin America. She also has a working knowledge of Portuguese and Haitian Creole. She has directed more than twenty federal and state grants and published six books and more than fifty refereed journal articles and book chapters. During the past six years Dr. Fradd has directed research grants funded by the National Science Foundation to learn more about the relationship of language proficiency, literacy learning, and science instruction. In this context, she has been directly involved in many inner-city classrooms where most of the students are learning English as a new language. With the classroom teachers, she has cotaught and assessed students' language development and acquisition of content knowledge. Because the research sites use an inclusion model, a portion of most classrooms have students identified as having mild learning disabilities and communication disorders.

Sandra Rollins Hurley Associate Dean, Assistant Professor of Reading Education in the Department of Teacher Education, and is Program Director of the Literacy Education Center at The University of Texas at El Paso. She teaches in and collaboratively developed field-based preservice and graduate courses. She has designed and delivered graduate literacy courses by distance learning. Dr. Hurley has published numerous articles and book chapters on literacy and biliteracy and teacher education. She has taught elementary school children K to 5. Education awards include the College of Education's Outstanding Service Award and the College's Outstanding Teaching Award, a UTEP Teaching Effectiveness Award, El Paso County IRA's Outstanding Teacher of Reading for exemplary contributions to the teaching of reading in higher education, and was recently named a UTEP/American Association for Higher Education Faculty Teaching Scholar. She was a distinguished finalist in the International Reading Association's dissertation of the year competition in 1994.

Diane Lapp, Professor of Reading and Language in the Department of Teacher Education at San Diego State University, has taught in elementary and middle schools. Dr. Lapp, who codirects and teaches field-based preservice and graduate courses, spent her recent sabbatical team teaching in a public school first grade classroom. Dr. Lapp has coauthored and edited many articles, columns, texts, handbooks, and children's materials on reading and language arts issues. These include the following two, which were codeveloped with James Flood: *Teaching Reading to Every Child*, a reading methods textbook in its fourth edition; and *The Handbook of Research in Teaching the English Language Arts*, second edition. She has chaired and cochaired several IRA and NRC committees. Her many educational awards include being named as the Outstanding Teacher Educator and Faculty member in the Department of Teacher Education at San Diego State University, the Distinguished Researcher Lecturer from San Diego State University's Graduate

Division of Research, a member of the California Hall of Fame, and IRA's 1996 Outstanding Teacher Educator of the Year.

Okhee Lee is an associate professor in the School of Education, University of Miami, Florida. Her research areas include science education, culture and language, and teacher education. She was awarded a 1993 to 1995 National Academy of Education Spencer Postdoctoral Fellowship. She was also a 1996 to 1997 fellow at the National Institute for Science Education, Wisconsin Center for Education Research, University of Wisconsin–Madison. She has directed research and teacher training projects funded by the National Science Foundation, U.S. Department of Education, Spencer Foundation, and the Florida Department of Education. One of her current research projects funded by the National Science Foundation designs and implements instructional interventions to promote science learning and language development for students from diverse languages and cultures. Lee serves on editorial boards for major science education research journals and various advisory boards for science education reform projects.

Jill Kerper Mora is Assistant Professor of Teacher Education at San Diego State University. She specializes in preparing teacher candidates for the California Cross-cultural Language and Academic Development credential. Her areas of research and publications include English language development and biliteracy instruction with a focus on crosslinguistic transfer and language maintenance in bilingual education programs. Dr. Mora is active in teaching, research, and public service, advocating for policies and programs that support effective schooling practices for language-minority students.

Lorraine Valdez Pierce teaches courses on assessment, curriculum design, and literacy for teachers in the Graduate School of Education at George Mason University in Fairfax, Virginia. She holds a Ph.D. in linguistics from Georgetown University and is coauthor (with J. Michael O'Malley) of *Authentic Assessment for English Language Learners: Practical Approaches for Teachers.* Dr. Pierce has led a school-university partnership for improving assessment practices for ESL students in Grades K to 12 for the past eight years.

Lucy Suarez is currently a peer Coach/Staff Developer for San Diego City Schools assigned to Baker Elementary School. Ms. Suarez has taught in bilingual education and Reading Recovery classrooms. She holds a master's degree in reading education and is currently a doctoral student in a joint program of San Diego State University and the Claremont Graduate School.

Josefina Villamil Tinajero, Associate Dean of the College of Education and Professor of Bilingual Education at UT El Paso, is a noted author and featured speaker in the field of bilingual education and in the recruitment and retention of Hispanic students in higher education. Dr. Tinajero is the author of several comprehensive, multicomponent reading and language arts and ESL programs used throughout the United States. Her most recent publications include: *Educating Latino Students: A Guide to Successful Practice*; *The Power of Two Languages 2000: Effective Dual Language Use Across the Curriculum*; *Into English!*; *McGraw-Hill Reading*; and *McGraw-Hill Lectura*.

Dr. Tinajero has had an impact on the field of education at the state and national levels. She has served on numerous advisory committees focused on the development of standards and on improving the preparation of educators and our nation's schools. Most recently, she has served on the Texas Kindergarten Reading Academies as a Master Trainer, Texas Master Reading Teacher Standards Development Advisory Panel, the 21st Century Vision for Schooling Committee, The Reading Standards Working Group, the TEKS Panel of Experts, and the SBEC Teacher Education Cyclical Advisory Committee. At the national level, she has served on the New Standards Primary Literacy Standards Committee, the ENL (English as a New Language) Task Force of the National Board for Professional Teaching Standards, and the National Tests Advisory Panel. Dr. Tinajero is the current president of NABE. She is a fellow of the W. K. Kellogg National Leadership Program and was one of thirteen women from the United States selected to participate in the NGO Women's '95 Forum in Beijing, China, as a delegate of the W. K. Kellogg Foundation.

Rosa Zubizarreta has a professional background in educational reform, exploring practices that build community in the classroom, throughout the school, and beyond. In addition to relationships between schools and parents, she has focused on literature and conversation as avenues for critical thinking and moral development; conflict as an opportunity for social learning and collaborative decision-making; and diversity work as a doorway to a deeper sense of connection with and respect for all beings.

An Integrated Approach to the Teaching and Assessment of Language Arts

DIANE LAPP, DOUGLAS FISHER, JAMES FLOOD, AND ARTURO CABELLO

San Diego State University

In a recent discussion, we were asked whether public schools must adapt to meet the needs of a multicultural student population or the "minority" students must adapt to the school. Given the changing demographics in the United States, we were somewhat surprised with the question; however, we did not miss the real issue hidden as an easy or naive question. The person was really asking about our core values and what we saw as the fundamental purpose of schooling. We think school is about equity and excellence, and that the charge to a modern, diverse school is to develop a curriculum that is bilingual, multicultural, and option-filled. We know and believe that instructional practices can be modified to effectively emphasize strategies which are effective for all students. We further believe that, with appropriate curriculum and instruction, teachers and schools can provide students with the knowledge and skills necessary for the twenty-first century. Because, as teacher-educators, we are field-based in many schools, we are constantly in contact with classroom teachers who share these beliefs. One such teacher is Mrs. Martinez who teaches fourth grade.

From observing Mrs. Martinez as she teaches, assesses, groups, and regroups students, we realize the importance of integrated instructional and assessment practices. Her actions illustrate that students need to be engaged in their instruction to learn and that instructional decision-making occurs as a result of continuous assessment (Doyle, 1992; Shearer & Homan, 1994). Mrs. Martinez will share more of her perspectives on an integrated approach to the teaching and assessment of language arts in Chapter 6.

We believe that the majority of teachers are working diligently to provide such interactive instruction and assessment. The following section provides some background information that we think is useful when planning similar literacy instruction for all students.

Mrs. Martinez

Meet Mrs. Martinez. She is bilingual and has been teaching for six years. From watching Mrs. Martinez as she interacts with her students, we have learned a great deal about effective instruction. Nichole is a student in Mrs. Martinez's class. Nichole says that "not everyone in class knows Spanish, but everyone is learning it." Nichole's classroom could be labeled as a multicultural class with an emphasis on Spanish and English.

The Class
Within this classroom of twenty-five students, which is designated to be a supportive home base for each child, some additional services are also provided. Two students receive support from the resource specialist, and four students with limited English proficiency receive support services from a bilingual educator. This print-rich environment is filled with both Spanish and English words, phrases, books, etc. Spanish and English are not the only languages spoken in this class. Three students, Bevian, James, and Erica, speak Tewa, a Native American language of the region.

The Service Delivery Model
There is a part-time instructional assistant, a bilingual support teacher, and a special education resource teacher as well as Mrs. Martinez. All support the instruction of Nichole and all the children in the classroom.

Experiences in School
During the daily morning opening, students are encouraged to share their experiences. This oral tradition is a very important way of maintaining the traditions of the region, especially for the Tewa speakers in the class. During a recent morning discussion, Mrs. Martinez encouraged the children to share experiences from their cultures that were similar to the festival that was being planned for the nearby pueblo. As the children shared, Mrs. Martinez recorded their talk on a language chart which the children read and reread together, individually and in pairs. When the children returned to their tables, Mrs. Martinez encouraged them to talk and read about the festival either alone or with a partner and to write, illustrate, and share their thoughts about the festival. Throughout this activity, the children were grouped heterogeneously.

After the opening conversation and subsequent literacy activity, the students were again grouped heterogeneously for science. The science centers focused on the study of the human body. Each student had previously sketched his or her own body on a large piece of butcher paper. These were cut out and personalized by each child before they were hung around the room.

At the center of which Nichole was a member, the group was reading and talking about circulation and had retrieved their body sketches to label their heart and lungs. They had previously read about circulation in their science book and were now writing in their scientific journals about things other than blood that might circulate. Nichole chose to write in Spanish about circulating water in an aquarium. Miguel, another student in Nichole's group had decided to write about air circulating in air conditioning units. He had chosen to write in English and often looked up to the classroom word wall to check his spelling. When he didn't know a word in English, he used the Spanish-English dictionary on his desk. After science, students were invited to free read. Some chose to read selections related to their science experience. Others read about the experiences shared from the opening conversation, while others read novels, newspapers, etc. Students were encouraged to select books from the classroom library for this "sustained silent reading" time.

The classroom library contains books, magazines, and newspapers in both Spanish and English. Mrs. Martinez shares library books with other classroom teachers to provide her students some variety. In addition, the bilingual resource teacher adds many materials to the classroom library.

Later in the day after recess, students were invited to sit on the floor near Mrs. Martinez. She talked with them about poetry and the kinds of poems that they had been sharing. Mrs. Martinez regrouped students for their group poetry reading and writing. She explained to them that they would be reading poetry to each other, writing group poems, and then creating individual poems to share orally with the class. Ms. Martinez explained that the beauty of poetry is in both the oral and written version. During this time, Mrs. Martinez also met with small homogeneous groups of children who needed explicit instruction on a specific topic related to any of the daily literacy events, such as essay writing, taking notes, or reading strategies.

Nichole's group moved quickly to the floor near the classroom library where they began to look through poetry books and select ones they would like to read aloud. Mrs. Martinez had previously read poetry with the entire group and had modeled how to write various types of poems. This lesson inolved student choices of what poetry to read and in what poetic form they wished to share. After reading several poems by Jack Prelutsky (1983), Shel Silverstein (1996), and Brod Bagert (1997), Erica had an idea for the opening of the poem; however, she had difficulty explaining her idea to the group. She turned to the next group and interrupted James. They spoke in Tewa. Erica turned back to the group and suggested that they write a poem about new friends. Bevian suggested that they might want to reread a few poems from *I Like You, If You Like Me* by Livingston, a book that had been previosly shared by Mrs. Martinez. When the groups finished writing, illustrating, and sharing their poems, they hung them in the hallway for everyone to read.

Mrs. Martinez uses both heterogeneous and homogeneous grouping. She believes that by using flexible grouping, often changing membership, students have opportunities to interact with as many of their peers as possible. Mrs. Martinez uses flexible grouping because this provides her with the opportunity to group homogeneously children who have similar needs and to group heterogeneously children by interests and choice. Mrs. Martinez continuously assesses her children as she watches them perform independently or in groups. Based on these continuous assessments, she plans the "next steps" in instruction and group compositions.

Background Research

How Does Literacy Develop?

Literacy, of which reading and writing are parts, is a developmental process. Many researchers think about literacy as a continuum (Squire, 1987; Tinajero & Ada, 1993). Everyone is someplace on this nonhierarchial continuum, and as Farnan, Flood, and Lapp (1994) note, "there is no point on the continuum that denotes too much literacy or, for that matter, not enough. There are no good or bad places to be, only places informed by children's previous knowledge and construction of literacy concepts" (p. 136). In thinking about this perspective, we should not view children as having a deficit that must be corrected. Rather, we can focus on what they know and are able to do and build our literacy approach from there. Table 1.1 illustrates many of the behaviors exhibited by children as they become fluent readers and writers. This table includes some of the behaviors related to the child's attitude about reading, an understanding of text and reading, and making meaning of words and extended discourse. As children are observed in literacy events, this information can become a resource to help us informally assess growth and to plan appropriate instruction. This list should not be viewed as hierarchical or linear but as behaviors that most children exhibit as they become literate.

Are Language One and Language Two Complementary?

As we plan instruction for second language learners, we must consider if the development of literacy in a child's primary language impedes, facilitates, or complements the development of literacy in a second language. Research indicates that academic and linguistic skills acquired in the first language transfer relatively easily to the second (Baker, 1993; Hornberger, 1990). In other words, students may be "newly fluent" readers in Spanish and "emergent readers" in English. The implication from this research is that emerging fluency in the first language (to a certain point) shortcuts the normal developmental process in the second language (Lanauze & Snow, 1989). Even though it may seem obvious, it is important to underscore the fact that children who are to any degree bilingual, and subsequently biliterate, are not disadvantaged. In fact, they have the privilege of two languages!

In addition to teaching children a second language, there is evidence that teachers need to continue to foster children's primary language skills. For example, Vocano (1994) believes that if children are forced into English too early or without proper support, there is a likelihood that the child will develop what is known as semilingualism or subtractive bilingualism. The result is a young person who does not speak, read, or write either language well. Allowing for the sustained use of the child's native language for longer periods allows the student to experience the normal linguistic developmental milestones; therefore, the student is in a better position to successfully acquire the second language (Cummins, 1981; Filmore & Meyer, 1992). This perspective is grounded in other research (Ramirez, Yuen, & Ramey, 1991; Spangenberg-Urbschat & Pritchard, 1994) with similar findings and recommendations, for example, that prolonged exposure to the child's native language in school strengthens the foundation from which to build the acquisition of the second language.

What Are the Current Issues in Assessment for Bilingual Students?

The most pressing educational concern continues to be the lack of appropriate, valid, and reliable assessment measures for students acquiring English as a second

TABLE 1.1   Development of Reading and Writing

Emerging Readers—Students will:
- Understand that print contains a meaningful message.
- Exhibit curiosity about print.
- Demonstrate an understanding of concepts about print (e.g., left to right, top to bottom, starting point).
- Imitate reading-like behaviors.
- Reproduce language patterns orally from familiar books.
- Know some letters (names, sounds, [phonemic awareness and segmentation]).
- Use first letter sounds to identify signficant words.
- Use prior knowledge to make meaning.
- Retell text that is read to them.
- Use illustrations and prior experience to help predict and bring meaning to text.

Early Readers—Students will:
- Match spoken words to the written word.
- Know and use a number of high frequency words.
- Begin to use the cueing systems (phonics, meaning, and structure) to confirm the message of the text.
- Demonstrate an awareness of details of print (e.g., punctuation, bold print, variations in format, etc.).
- Begin to apply reading strategies in other text types.
- Retell and summarize text in order with details.
- Begin to self-monitor and self-correct while reading.
- Use illustrations and prior experiences to infer, deduct, predict, and make meaning from text.
- Compare texts with similar themes, pictures, authors, etc.
- Identify main topic and characters.
- Understand both narrative and nonnarrative texts.
- Rely on beginning letters and sounding out words.
- Recognize many words in multiple contexts.
- Enjoy listening to stories.
- Select favorite texts.
- Use knowledge of sentence structure and punctuation to aid meaning making.
- Self-correct if text doesn't make sense.

Newly Fluent Readers—Students will:
- Rarely interrupt flow of reading to decode words.
- Consistently integrate and use cueing systems (phonics, meaning, and structure) to confirm the message of the text.
- Use all of the information in text to confirm the message.
- Retell, summarize, and infer meaning.
- Self-monitor and self-correct while reading.
- Use inference, deduction, and prior experiences to predict and make meaning from text.
- Read flexibly and strategically from a variety of texts.
- Ask questions as an extension for further reading.
- Make inferences, predictions, and generalizations.
- Confirm and extend knowledge.
- Use word indentification strategies very effectively.

(continued)

TABLE 1.1   Continued

- Discuss point of view.
- Contrast text themes and types.

As the child becomes more fluent, reading independence will be exhibited and many of these behaviors will become automatic.

Emerging Writers—Students will:
- Dictate an idea.
- Use initial sounds in their writing.
- Use pictures, scribbles, symbols, letters, and/or known words to communicate a message.
- Understand that writing symbolizes speech.

Early Writers—Students will:
- Understand that a written message remains the same each time it is read.
- Utilize their knowledge of sounds and letters as they progress through the stages of spelling development.
- With modeling and assistance, incorporate feedback in revising and editing their own writing.
- Begin to use conventional grammar, spelling, capitalization, and punctuation.

Newly Fluent Writers—Students will:
- Use prewriting strategies to achieve their purposes.
- Address a topic or write to a prompt creatively and independently.
- Organize writing to include a beginning, middle, and end.
- Revise and edit written work independently and/or collectively.
- Consistently use conventional grammar, spelling, capitalization, and punctuation.
- Produce many genres of writing.

As fluency develops, students will exhibit independence and writing style preferences. Reading influences one's language and writing proficiency.

---

language (Valdes & Figueroa, 1994). Significant cultural considerations are also often overlooked when assessing students from traditionally underrepresented groups. For example, time and stress management have been identified as two variables that make a significant difference in test results, especially for Spanish-speaking students (Fichtner, Peitzman, & Sasser, 1994; Garcia, 1994). Lower test results may not be reflective of student achievement or ability level but of the cultural traditions that are not considered in testing. Lipsky and Gartner (1997) believe that this practice has led to an overrepresentation of students who are acquiring English as a second language in special education programs.

After reviewing traditional methods of assessment and their outcomes, Roseberry-McKibbin and Eicholtz (1994) and Leslie and Jett-Simpson (1997) have proposed a combined form of assessment. Each suggests the use of traditional forms of assessment that are combined with a more ecological approach, that is, an assessment system that is both ongoing and integrated within the instructional context of the classroom. For example, in Nichole's classroom, Mrs. Martinez regularly reviews student's journals as part of her assessment process. She then uses this information during individual conferences with students. For example, Mrs. Martinez recently noticed that a few of her students were not consistently using capital letters for proper names. This assessment information led Mrs. Martinez to review the English rules for capitalization with this small homogeneous group while modeling the use of capitals in the morning message and other shared writing with the entire heterogeneous class. Mrs. Martinez realized that all the rules do not directly transfer from Spanish. She had to be careful that students did not overgeneralize the lesson, as days of the week and months are not capitalized in Spanish but are in English. As educators, we must continually ask ourselves, "*why* are we assessing students and *how* are we using the acquired information to inform instruction?" Such self-scrutiny may help us to strengthen the connection between assessment and instruction.

Why Are Students Assessed?

One must understand that students can be assessed for a wide variety of purposes, including:

- Diagnosing individual student needs (e.g., assessing developmental status, monitoring and communicating student progress, certifying competency, determining needs)
- Informing instruction (e.g., evaluating instruction, modifying instructional strategies, identifying instructional needs)
- Evaluating programs
- Providing accountability information

Teachers often use assessment information to make instructional decisions. For example, Mrs. Martinez uses a "speaking checklist" (Figures 1.1 and 1.2) to ensure that her students have ample opportunity to develop oral literacy skills. Recently Mrs. Martinez noticed that in his oral presentation, James had not been delineating minor points that would support his primary thesis. During one of the learning centers that day, Mrs. Martinez was able to provide explicit instruction to James through modeling as they read together. She helped him realize the need for a logical flow of ideas and the need to support one's ideas to make the "point."

Informing and improving instruction, however, are not the only reasons that students are assessed. As the public continues to demand increased accountability from its schools and as school administrators, teachers, and policymakers increase their use of performance and outcome data for decision-making, people are paying more attention to who gets tested, what kinds of tests are used, and what the data mean. In other words, assessment information is receiving more attention from more people.

This presents a challenge for teachers. Fortunately, several recommendations exist to address these challenges (Beck, 1997). First, we believe that there are no inherently "bad" or "good" assessments. Assessments are only useful when teach-

FIGURE 1.1   Speaking Checklist

Name:_____

When _____ speaks in a group, he/she:

	Sept.	Dec.	Mar.	June
sticks to the topic.				
builds support for the subject.				
speaks clearly.				
takes turns and waits to talk.				
talks so others in the group can hear.				
speaks smoothly.				
uses courteous language.				
presents in an organized and interesting way.				
supports the topical thesis.				
answers questions effectively.				
is comfortable speaking publicly.				
maintains listeners' interest.				
volunteers to answer in class.				
speaks only to those who share the same native language.				

A = always, S = sometimes, N = never

FIGURE 1.2   My Speaking Checklist (Self-Assessment)

Name: _____

Please read each sentence. Answer by writing YES or NO in the box.

	Sept.	Dec.	Mar.	June
I stick to the topic.				
I build support for the subject.				
I speak clearly.				
I take turns and wait for my turn to talk.				
I talk so others in the group can hear me.				
I speak smoothly.				
I keep the interest of listeners.				
I listen to what others say.				
My talk is organized and interesting.				
I talk so everyone can hear me.				
I use courteous language.				
I answer questions about my talk.				
I am comfortable speaking publicly.				
I enjoy oral presentations.				
I like to talk with all of the other class members.				

ers understand the purpose and use of the tool. For example, statewide achievement assessments are not likely to inform classroom instruction any more than classroom-based portfolios are likely to inform accountability systems. Both are useful, but each provides a different type of information.

Second, we believe that no one assessment provides sufficient information for all decision making. Teachers and administrators should use a variety of information sources for diagnosing students, instructional planning, and accountability. Useful assessments confirm the information from other useful assessments. The more information a teacher has about students, the more confident he or she is in developing lessons that match the students' current educational needs.

We also believe that teachers should take every assessment they plan to administer to students. Having answered the questions, performed the activities, or thought through the instructions ensures that the teacher is fully aware of the measures and how content is being assessed. The only way to gain an understanding of the dynamics of the assessment is to become a tested student.

Finally, we believe that the assessment standards, shown in Table 1.2, that were jointly developed by the International Reading Association and the National Council of Teachers of English should guide our assessment practices.

What Measures Are Available That Promote Effective Instruction for Second Language Learners?

Assessment is a continuous process that we use to evaluate a student's progress toward their learning goals (Flood, Lapp, & Wood, 1997). Table 1.3 provides an

TABLE 1.2   Standards for the Assessment of Reading and Writing

Standard 1.	The interests of the student are paramount in assessment.
Standard 2.	The primary purpose of assessment is to improve teaching and learning.
Standard 3.	Assessment must reflect and allow for critical inquiry into curriculum and instruction.
Standard 4.	Assessments must recognize and reflect the intellectually and socially complex nature of reading and writing and the important roles of school, home, and society in literacy development.
Standard 5.	Assessment must be fair and equitable.
Standard 6.	The consequences of an assessment procedure are the first and most important consideration in establishing the validity of the assessment.
Standard 7.	The teacher is the most important agent of assessment.
Standard 8.	The assessment process should involve multiple perspectives and sources of data.
Standard 9.	Assessment must be based in the school community.
Standard 10.	All members of the educational community—students, parents, teachers, administrators, policy makers, and the public—must have a voice in the development, interpretation, and reporting of assessment.
Standard 11.	Parents must be involved as active, essential participants in the assessment process.

Source: Standards for the assessment of reading and writing. Prepared by the IRA/NCTE Joint Task Force on Assessment, (1994). Standards for the Assessment of Reading & Writing. IRA: Newark, DE and NCTE: Urbana, IL.

TABLE 1.3   Formal and Informal Assessments

Type	Purpose	Procedure
Formal Assessment		
Standardized testing	To measure a student's performance in a variety of skills and compare those scores to students in other geographic locations	Administered at set intervals; students answer questions from booklet on standard forms
Criterion-referenced Tests	To indicate attainment of mastery on specific instructional objectives, usually by answering a percentage of questions correctly	Administered with lesson plans; students read items and answer on separate paper
Informal Assessment		
Observations	To assess a student's use of language in a variety of instructional settings	Observe and record student's use of language, often written in logs or journals
Skills checklists	To track a student's development by noting which skills have become or are becoming part of a repertoire	Set up a checklist of desirable skills in language arts and periodically observe the student to determine which have been attained
Portfolio assessment	To document in a variety of ways how a student has developed as a language user	Teacher collects or student selects samples of work, including "published" writing, taped oral readings, conference notes
Conferencing	To provide opportunities for the teacher and student to discuss development	Student and teacher meet at set times to review performance and discuss instruction that may be required for student to progress
Peer reviews	To involve students in the evaluation process and to build their evaluative and interactive skills	Give students guidelines for evaluation; two or more meet to discuss one another's work; peer's grade is factored into final grade
Self-assessment	To empower students by making them responsible for and reflective of their own work	Students continually evaluate their performance and progress via checklists, interactions, inventories, conferences, and portfolios

Source: Adapted from Flood, J., Lapp, D., & Wood, K. D. (1997). *Staff development guide.* New York: Macmilllan/McGraw-Hill.

overview of formal and informal assessments, their purposes and procedures. These techniques can be used in a comprehensive literacy program that is based on the languages and cultures represented in the class. Every child needs to develop communicative and visual language processes: speaking, listening, reading, writing, and viewing in their culture because

> a language taught without its attendant culture is like presenting a body without a heart. Language and culture are entwined in the healthy functioning of a body. Therefore, developing heritage, cultural awareness, and multiculturalism alongside first language teaching is an important element in language minority education. (Baker, 1993, p. 197)

Implications for Practice

While there are many types of and uses for assessments, we will focus on processes that are useful to teachers in designing instruction that supports the development of biliteracy. The performance assessment measures we suggest may be collected while students are participating in a classroom literacy event. We suggest that performance samples be collected over an extended period of time, as an ongoing form of student-based evaluation. We also suggest that information gathered with these assessment strategies be used to guide instruction and flexible grouping practices. Assessment and instruction should be viewed as interactive processes. The following section contains assessment instruments that classroom teachers have found useful in planning instruction. While each may be used to assess more than one of the language arts, we have arbitrarily grouped them for organizational purposes. We have presented each in English; however, other versions may be required. This will depend on the classroom goals, the language spoken in the classroom, and the reading fluency of the students. In Mrs. Martinez's classroom, which is a bilingual setting, assessment and instruction occur in both English and Spanish.

Oral Language

Story Retelling Inventory.   This inventory is an informal checklist that can be used to assess a student's **comprehension, sentence structure knowledge**, and **vocabulary development** as they retell a specific piece of literature (see Figure 1.3). This inventory can be used continuously throughout the year to demonstrate a child's reading progress. This inventory may be used in two ways. First, many teachers hold individual conferences with students to discuss their reading and writing. During one of these conferences per month, the teacher may ask the student to read and retell a piece of literature. The retelling inventory provides a record-keeping format for this information that may also be maintained in the student's individual portfolio.

In addition, this inventory may also be used when working with a small group of children. For example, we recently observed a teacher providing small-group instruction based on the book *When I Am Old with You* (Johnson, 1990).

FIGURE 1.3   **Story Retelling Inventory**

Student _____   Date _____

Book Title and Author _____

Check each skill as: (1) weak, (2) average, (3) very good, (4) superior

		1	2	3	4

1. The student comprehensively retold the story
2. Comprehended the story line and plot
   - Understood roles played by the various characters
   - Understood implied as well as stated meanings
   - Comprehended author's intention
3. Understood the major ideas
4. Understood the minor ideas that built to the major ideas
5. Brought a background of information to the selection
6. Analyzed and made judgments based upon facts
7. Retold the selection in sentences that made grammatical sense
8. Retold the section in sentences that include correct usage of:
   - predicates (verbs)
   - adverbs
   - adjectives
   - phrases
   - compound sentences
   - conjunctions
   - complex sentences

9. Used a rich and meaningful vocabulary:
   Example: _____
   _____

10. Overused, slang and colloquial expressions:
    List: _____
    _____

11. Summary of retelling:
    Comprehension: _____
    Sentence Structure: _____
    Vocabulary: _____
12. Proposed instruction:_____
    _____
    _____
    _____

When the group finished reading the book, the teacher asked each student specific questions that encouraged retelling of a segment of the story. As the teacher listened, she recorded student responses on the inventory form.

This assessment information is useful in evaluating student progress and planning the next steps in instruction. One teacher may use this measure to check his students' knowledge of mechanics, such as subject (nouns), predicates (verbs), and compound sentences. Another teacher may use this information to assess students' knowledge of story comprehension and plot development, including such things as roles played by various characters, implied but not stated meanings, and comprehension of the authors' intentions. Still another teacher may use this measure to assess student syntax and oral language patterns. Once the student information is collected all of these teachers can plan appropriate learning experiences that provide opportunities for students to expand their knowledge base.

Speaking Checklist.   As we have noted, literacy involves viewing, reading, writing, listening and speaking. Public speaking, however, is often forgotten or neglected, especially for students acquiring English as a second language. To focus more attention on the use of oral language skills in the classroom, we suggest that teachers use a speaking checklist similar to the one in Figure 1.1. Teachers use this in a variety of ways. In some classrooms, teachers require students to do presentations while being evaluated by their peers. These students have time during class to work on their presentations, receive feedback on the development of content and process from their teacher, and incorporate information into their sessions. Other teachers encourage their students to present information to younger grades. For example, a sixth grade teacher may arrange for her students to present to third and fourth graders. The speaking checklist, therefore, would be completed by the teacher of the younger students and provided to the presenter. In other classrooms, this assessment is much less formal and is conducted on an individual basis. Students may receive feedback on their speaking skills during small group lessons, class interactions, and interactions on the playground or in various other communicative settings. As shown in Figure 1.2, this assessment measure can also be used for student self-assessment. When using these measures, teachers and students should add the additional behaviors they wish to observe and expand. Self-assessment measures should be designed at the independent reading level of the student. We have included a variety of forms that can be altered according to the reading and writing fluency of a student.

Writing

Writing Portfolios.   Writing portfolios of ongoing and completed work are a normal part of classrooms where a process writing approach is used. Samples of student work should be gathered because they provide exceptionally good evidence regarding student progress. Daily work samples and journal entries provide rich information about students' developing knowledge, craft as writers, skill, and attitude. We believe, however, that before samples are assessed, students should be exposed to lots of great writing and should be given effective instruction in writing. In other words, "rough drafts" should not be used as part of the evaluative procedure. This is not to say that common errors in the writing process cannot be used in designing instructional lessons, but that student performance should be measured on final, "published" versions.

We recommend that writing assessment consist of portfolio reviews by teachers and students together or individually, if they are able to read it alone, periodically throughout the year. In asking students to complete an observation of their portfolio, it may be helpful to reflect on the questions found in Table 1.4. Once completed, the teacher can also jot down some notes about the student's writing. This can be followed by a teacher-student conversation. During this conversation, the "next steps" in instruction should be planned together.

These overall trends and patterns in the students' writing behaviors are very important in designing instruction. In addition to this general overview, teachers often need and want to evaluate each student's individual writing samples more

TABLE 1.4   Writing Portfolio Conference Record

Name: _____   Date: _____

Questions	Student Thoughts	Teacher Thoughts
1. What types of writing are you working on?		
2. What types of writing are you comfortable doing?		
3. What type of writing do you like most? Why?		
4. What topics seem to motivate you to write?		
5. Do you have a pretty good use of vocabulary?		
6. What type of writing help do you think you need?		
7. Do you like to write on the computer or with paper and pencil?		

closely. For very young children, we suggest teachers use the developmental model presented in Table 1.1. As students' writing gets more sophisticated, teachers may wish to provide more detailed feedback through the use of holistic and primary trait assessment.

Holistic Scoring for Writing.   Holistic assessment or scoring is often referred to as a general impression score. When teachers use this type of assessment system, they examine the total piece of writing as a product, not as a group of separate parts. In holistic assessment, the parts are not separated. These scores are based on guides, called rubrics, which are the standards against which each piece of writing is evaluated. As shown in Table 1.5, teachers can choose among a 9-point, 6-point, and 4-point scoring scale. These numbers are purposely used in rubrics to avoid an "average" score. After all, "average" provides very little information for either the teacher or the student. Neither has a clear idea whether the guidelines were addressed adequately or inadequately. The choice of the rubric scoring system depends on the teacher's objective. The 9-point scale offers the most flexibility and finest distinction in quality. The 6-point scale also offers a range of scores with less variation. The 4-point scale is used to make broader evaluations of writing and easily becomes a pass-fail evaluation of a paper.

Primary Trait Assessment.   Primary trait assessment is a quick and efficient method of scoring based on the objectives on individual writing assignments. The question asked in primary trait scoring is "Does the writing fulfill the objectives of a particular writing task?"

Before this scoring system can be used, students and teachers must understand that writing is a purposeful activity and that its primary trait is to communicate effectively. As illustrated in Table 1.6, once the criteria have been established, this method of scoring provides a clear message to both writers and teachers—either the piece does or does not, to some degree, meet the goals of the writing task. Following the assessment of a piece of writing, reasons for the score can be explored. If several writers are unsuccessful, the teacher should question the instruction, the writing prompt, or perhaps the scoring guide.

Several process steps should be followed when using the primary trait scoring system. First, the writing task must be clearly defined. For example, the class may be studying ways to save the environment. The writing prompt may be to pursuade more adults to recycle. After establishing the purpose, in this case persuasion, the means for meeting that purpose must be clearly stated. In this case, providing reasons and rationale that would appeal to specific adults in order to increase their recycling efforts. The primary traits for this writing activity could be stated as follows: **Present a clear position statement followed by sequentially stated thoughts and reasons that exhibit logical appeal as a means of persuasion.**

Then, what remains is the actual writing of a scoring guide, or rubric. Most primary trait scoring guides include four levels of skill. Level 1 indicates a paper that would provide little or no evidence. A level 2 paper would provide very few appropriate reasons. Level 3 would show some thought as evidenced by some

TABLE 1.5   Holistic Writing Rubrics

9-point scale	6-point scale	4-point scale
9–8 Excellent paper. A 9 is reserved for papers that are nearly perfect in content, organization, mechanics, and language use. Both 8 and 9 are excellent papers in areas of form and content, with 9s being definitely of higher quality.	**6–5** Excellent paper. A 6 is reserved for papers that are nearly perfect in content, organization, mechanics, and language use. Both 5 and 6 are excellent papers in areas of form and content, with 6s being definitely of higher quality.	**4** An excellent paper that is well organized and displays facile use of language, content, and mechanics.
7 Still an excellent paper, but not quite so well organized, creative, and articulate.	**4** A passing paper judged adequate in terms of content, organization, mechanics, and style. It may lack imagination and creativity.	**3** A paper that demonstrates adequate organization, content, language use, and handling of mechanics. It may lack imagination and creativity.
6–5 An adequate paper, but deficient in its organization, use of content, style, and / or mechanics.	**3** A lower-half paper that is weak in content, organization, style, and / or mechanics.	**2** A lower-half paper that is weak in content, organization, style, and / or mechanics.
4–3 A lower-half paper that is weak in content, organization, style, and / or mechanics.	**2** A very weak paper that addresses the topic but is only loosely organized with serious faults in organization, content, language use, style, and mechanics.	**1** An unacceptable paper that addresses the topic but is weak in organization, content, and language use and is full of errors in mechanics.
2 A very weak paper that addresses the topic but is only loosely organized with serious faults in organization, content, language use, style, and mechanics.	**1** A paper that addresses the topic but is disorganized, inarticulate, and full of errors.	
1 A paper that addresses the topic but is disorganized, inarticulate, and full of errors.		

appropriate reasons. Level 4 represents a well-organized paper with convincing reasons and evidence supporting the case.

As in holistic scoring, the rubrics or scoring guides are criterion-referenced and need to be adjusted for each writing task. Before writing takes place, class discussions should focus on the primary trait and scoring elements that are required. Students can be very helpful in articulating these elements and thus have a better understanding of how to fulfill the objectives of the writing task.

Reading

Reciprocal Questioning.   Reciprocal questioning is an interactive approach wherein two or more readers ask questions of each other to demonstrate an

TABLE 1.6   Primary Trait Writing Rubrics

Level 4	Position statement is clearly stated. Lines of argument and evidence are presented is systematic and convincing fashion.
Level 3	Position statement is both clearly stated and supported with several lines of argument. The lines of evidence and support are moderately well developed.
Level 2	Position statement is clear, but paper offers minimal evidence for support. The paper attempts to provide logical organization but falls short of unifying arguments presented.
Level 1	Position statement unclearly or inappropriately stated. Evidence is illogical and/or emotional or nonexistent. Paper lacks any clear organization scheme.

understanding of text. This strategy is especially useful for students who are learning a second language, as they often have greater ease with receptive language processing than with productive language use in the second language. To use this approach, select any reading material that you believe is at the student's independent reading level and model the following process with the student:

1. Examine the text and make predictions about the story. The teacher and student both look through the reading material. The teacher models questions and predictions and records responses from the student. For example, if the text is about the causes and effects of volcanos, you might say, "As I look through this book, I see pictures of volcanoes. I wonder what causes them and what happens to the people where they occur. I think from looking at the pictures and the headings that the author will answer my questions." Teachers often collect information at this stage of instruction on a format similar to the one found in Table 1.7. At this point, you would complete the first two columns of the table.
2. Read the story together orally or silently.
3. Summarize and make predictions. Once the story has been read, the student is encouraged to think aloud, share, and summarize all of the information gained and any difficulties encountered with the text. Again, the teacher records responses from the student on a chart similar to the one in Table 1.7. This time, the teacher focuses on the last two columns, "What I Learned" and "My Difficulties."
4. Create a question game. The teacher and student jot down questions on important information from the text. The teacher and student take turns asking each other questions, and the teacher continues to document student responses, for example, Where is Mount St. Helens? What causes volcanoes to erupt?

TABLE 1.7   Predictions and Questions During Reciprocal Questioning

What's This About?	My Questions	What I Learned	My Difficulties
Volcanos	Causes? Where they happen?		

We suggest this as an assessment strategy because it provides an opportunity to collect insights about a student's text processing and thinking. It is easy to see how instruction can follow such a conversation. Our example occurred between teacher and student but could easily occur among students as they interact together with the text. This classroom application builds on students' prior knowledge and will most likely improve their writing, oral language, and comprehension performance.

Cloze Reading Level Assessment Procedure.   Cloze is a measurement of comprehension or readability in which a reading selection is given and certain words are deleted. The student must then provide closure by inserting the proper words according to context clues. This informal, criterion-referenced assessment procedure is useful for teachers for two reasons. First, it is flexible enough to allow teachers to assess large groups of students at the same time or assess students individually. Second, the information gathered in the assessment procedure can be used to select reading material for students that is challenging but not frustrating. The procedure includes:

1. Selecting a student text, a passage of approximately 250 words. The passage should be in the language that the teacher wishes to assess.
2. Even if a 250-word passage ends in the middle of a sentence, just use the 250 words (see Figure 1.4 for example).
3. Delete every fifth word and insert a straight line in place of each missing word.
4. The passage should contain approximately fifty straight lines after deletions have been made (see Figure 1.4).
5. If you are unsure of text difficulty, select twelve 250-word passages that are approximately eight pages apart. This wide range of passages ensures a representative sample of text difficulty. If you have previously selected a passage that represents difficulty, administer it.
6. Give every student all of the passages.
7. Students are asked to insert the missing words. No time limits are set.
8. Responses are correct even if misspelled.
9. Each correct closure is worth two points.

FIGURE 1.4   Cloze Reading Level Assessment.
Passage from *The Hundred Dresses* by Eleanor Estes (1972)

Today, Monday, Wanda Petronski was not in her seat. But nobody, not even Peggy and Madeline, the girls who started all the fun, noticed her absence. Usually Wanda sat in the next to the last seat in the last row in room 13. She sat in the corner of the room where the rough boys who did not make good marks on their report cards sat; the corner of the room where there was most scuffling of feet, most roars of laughter, when anything funny was said, and most mud and dirt on the floor. Wanda did not sit there because she was rough and noisy. On the contrary she was very quiet and rarely said anything at all. And nobody had ever heard her laugh out loud. Sometimes she twisted her mouth into a crooked sort of smile, but that was all. Nobody knew exactly why Wanda sat in that seat unless it was because she came all the way from Boggins Heights, and her feet were usually caked with dry mud that she picked up coming down the country roads. Maybe the teacher liked to keep all of the children who are apt to come in with dirty shoes in one corner of the room. But no one really thought much about Wanda Petronski once she was in the classroom. The time they thought about her was outside of school hours, at noontime when they were coming back to school, or in the morning early before school began,

Today, Monday, Wanda Petronski _____ not in her seat. _____ nobody, not even Peggy _____ Madeline, the girls who _____ all the fun, noticed _____ absence. Usually Wanda sat in _____ next to the last _____ in the last row _____ room 13. She sat _____ the corner of the _____ where the rough boys _____ did not make good _____ on their report cards _____; the corner of the _____ where there was most _____ of feet, most roars _____ laughter, when anything funny _____ said, and most mud _____ dirt on the floor. _____ did not sit there _____ she was rough and _____. On the contrary she _____ very quiet and rarely _____ anything at all. And _____ had ever heard her _____ out loud. Sometimes she _____ her mouth into a _____ sort of smile, but _____ was all. Nobody knew _____ why Wanda sat in _____ seat unless it was _____ she came all the _____ from Boggins Heights, and _____ feet were usually caked _____ dry mud that she _____ up coming down the _____ roads. Maybe the teacher liked _____ keep all of the _____ who are apt to _____ in with dirty shoes _____ one corner of the _____. But no one really _____ much about Wanda Petronski _____ she was in the _____. The time they thought _____ her was outside of _____ hours, at noontime when _____ were coming back to _____ , or in the morning _____ before school began,

10. Score the assessment as follows: 58 to 100 points indicates an **independent** reading level for the student, 44 to 57 points indicates that this is the **instructional** level for the student, and less than 44 points indicates that the material is in the students' **frustrational** level. Once the results are tallied you will have a general idea of where to begin instruction in this or a similar text. By studying the type of error you can analyze the student's success in comprehending the passage. Although many educators may suggest that the exact word must be inserted, we believe that the inserted word should

be counted as correct if it is the appropriate part of speech and does not alter the text meaning. The child's performance rather than the score is the key to this successful integration of assessment and instruction.

As the child's responses are analyzed, the teacher must determine how he or she attempted to "make sense" of the passage. This type of scrutiny can help with planning appropriate instruction. While general scores can be easily calculated, many teachers want to ask each student to complete the information in Figure 1.5.

Self-Assessment

Students' Literacy Self-Evaluation.   Another informal way to collect information about the students' reading and writing behaviors involves the students reflecting on their own habits. This assessment is useful in determining instructional priorities and in providing the student the opportunity to develop self-monitoring skills. A form similar to the one shown in Figure 1.6 might be completed by each child three or four times throughout the school year. In doing so, students could be encouraged to respond to more specific questions and to analyze their approach to text. They might like to complete this alone or with a parent or teacher. Figure 1.7 provides some of the possible considerations that students can be taught to use in self-evaluation.

Teachers tend to keep these assessment results in student portfolios as a demonstration of continued development in language arts. Over time, teachers add strategies to the list and focus lessons on the strengths and needs exhibited by the students.

Linking assessment processes to curriculum and instruction is an important consideration for teachers. The information collected in assessments should be useful in planning instructional activities and lessons. Figures 1.8 and 1.9 are samples of assessment charts that many teachers attach to a manilla folder and use to make daily notes during instruction and observation. Teachers use information obtained from such observational assessments to plan objectives, to teach or reteach, and to determine appropriate materials.

FIGURE 1.5   **Making Sense of a Cloze Passage**

Name: _____ Please put an X on the correct answer:

When I read this passage, I tried to understand it by . . .

1. using what I already knew about this
        [prior knowledge]
2. reading beyond the blank to fill it in
        [context]
3. guessing a word that sounds right
        [syntax]

FIGURE 1.6 Student Assessment Record: How am I Doing on the Following Tasks?

Name: ____________ Date: ____________

Color the one most like you.

Talking in English.	I am	Super	Just OK	Needing practice
Talking in Spanish.	I am.	Super	Just OK	Needing practice
Writing in English.	I am	Super	Just OK	Needing practice
Writing in Spanish.	I am	Super	Just OK	Needing practice
Reading in English.	I am	Super	Just OK	Needing practice
Reading in Spanish.	I am	Super	Just OK	Needing practice

Name: ____________ Date: ____________

Color the one most like you.

Talking in English.	I am	Super	Just OK	Needing practice
Talking in Spanish.	I am.	Super	Just OK	Needing practice
Writing in English.	I am	Super	Just OK	Needing practice
Writing in Spanish.	I am	Super	Just OK	Needing practice
Reading in English.	I am	Super	Just OK	Needing practice
Reading in Spanish.	I am	Super	Just OK	Needing practice

FIGURE 1.7   Self-assessment Inventory

Name: _____   Date: _____   Grade:_____

How am I doing at:

- looking up words in the dictionary?

   Super   Just OK   Needing practice

- rereading portions of the story to help my comprehension?

  Super   Just OK   Needing practice

- writing a summary of the story?

  Super   Just OK   Needing practice

- taking notes while reading?

  Super   Just OK   Needing practice

- asking questions of teachers or friends to improve my comprehension?

  Super   Just OK   Needing practice

- underlining words for recall?

  Super   Just OK   Needing practice

- gaining comfort speaking English?

  Super   Just OK   Needing practice

What type of help do I think I need?

Practical Classroom Applications

What Instructional Strategies Promote Second Language Competencies and Emotional Security?

Nichole's classroom, which we visited in our opening vignette, is an example of an effective literacy program because it incorporates:

- Reading aloud to the students at their conceptual level
- Providing experiences for listening comprehension
- Encouraging oral language development
- Sharing reading between the teacher and students
- Modeling and guiding oral language and reading development

FIGURE 1.8   Assessment Record

Student Name	Date	Comments
Denise	8/27	
Michael	8/27	
LaShawn	8/29	
Andy	8/29	
Vic	9/2	

- Extending the shared reading through related pattern books, which invite the student to dictate to the teacher and then illustrate the book pages
- Guiding reading at the students' instructional level
- Using materials that are socially sensitive and culturally specific
- Providing time for students to choose and read books at their independent level
- Providing a wide range of reading materials of various genres, topics, and levels
- Modeling, encouraging, and guiding writing
- Inviting all voices to be heard
- Accepting and expanding everyone's knowledge
- Respecting students and promoting their choices

Clearly, children need to hear, see, and use language simultaneously so they can notice the connections between their thoughts, words, letters in printed words, and the way the words sound. Children need to be exposed to a print-rich environment to become aware of sound-symbol associations. This print-rich environment should reflect the range of languages represented in the class. As children interact with written and spoken languages, they begin to realize that certain sounds and letters are used in either or both languages. In addition, children

FIGURE 1.9   Summary of Student Assessments (Collected on 3 × 5 Cards)

Obverse side of 3 × 5 card

Informal teacher observations about _____ on_____
                                                                                 name   date

As a reader:

As a writer:

As a speaker:

In class behaviors:

Reverse side of 3 × 5 card

Plans for instruction based on observed strengths and needs.

improve vocabulary, learn decoding and encoding skills, attempt to share them and acquire reading comprehension and writing strategies in an environment that is accepting enough to provide the security one needs to "try on" a second language.

Foster Comprehension and Communication across Languages

In addition to learning sound-symbol associations, students need to develop strategies for making meaning of text and the basic concepts of sending and receiving messages and for sharing their thoughts through a variety of written genre. Failure to share or to comprehend text may occur because the reader does not have enough prior knowledge or does not use appropriate strategies. Background knowledge strongly influences one's ability to produce comprehensible written text and access to the meaning of the text for students learning a second language. Comprehension is likely to suffer when a student's background knowledge is substantially different from or culturally incongruent with the authors' perspective. This is often the case with bilingual learners. In fact, we believe that unfamiliar content may be as great an interference in comprehension as is unfamiliar form.

Based on these beliefs and our classroom experiences, we encourage teachers to use indirect and explicit instruction that is based on continuous student assessment to build the child's vocabulary, comprehension, and knowledge of how to share information through writing. Through explicit instruction, teachers can model oral language, reading, and writing for students. As students talk, read, and write, they encounter opportunities to enhance their language through words in the context of sentences or in their attempts to find the right word to share their ideas. Through such experiences they improve their reading fluency, comprehension, and effectiveness as writers.

DISCUSSION QUESTIONS

1. Why should assessment be linked to instruction?

2. What are the differences between formal and informal assessment techniques?

3. How can you use writing assessments in your classroom?

4. Describe when you would use the following assessment procedures: cloze, story retelling inventory, speaking checklist, and holistic writing rubrics.

5. Why should students be involved in self-assessment?

REFERENCES

Baggert, B. (1997). *The Gooch machine: Poems for children to perform.* Honesdale, PA: Boyds Mills.

Baker, C. (1993). *Foundations of bilingual education and bilingualism.* Philadelphia: Multilingual Matters.

Beck, M. (1997). The assessment conundrum. In J. Flood, D. Lapp, & K. Wood (Eds.), *Staff development guide for middle school teachers* (pp. 211–215). New York: Macmillan/McGraw-Hill.

Cummins, J. (1981). The role of primary language development in promoting educational success for language minority students. In California State Department of Education (Ed.) *Schooling and language minority students: A theoretical framework* (pp. 3–49). Los Angeles: California State Department of Education.

Doyle, D. (1992). Curriculum and pedagogy. In P. W. Jackson (Ed.) *The handbook of research on curriculum.* pp. 465–487. New York: Macmillan.

Estes, E. (1972). *The hundred dresses.* Orlando, FL: Harcourt Brace.

Farnan, N., Flood, J., & Lapp, D. (1994). Comprehending through reading and writing: Six research-based instructional strategies. In K. Spangenberg-Urbschat & R. Pritchard (Eds.) *Kids come in all languages: Reading instruction for ESL students* (pp. 135–157). Newark, DE: International Reading Association.

Fichtner, D., Peitzman, F., & Sasser, L. (1994). What's fair? Assessing subject matter knowledge of LEP students in sheltered classrooms. In F. Peitzman & G. Gadda (Eds.), *With different eyes: Insights into teaching language minority students across the disciplines* (pp. 114–123). Menlo Park, CA: Addison-Wesley.

Filmore, L. W., & Meyer, L. M. (1992). The curriculum and linguistic minorities. In P. W. Jackson (Ed.) *The handbook of research on curriculum* (pp. 626–658). New York: Macmillan.

Flood, J., Lapp, D., & Wood, K. D. (1997). *Staff development guide.* New York: Macmillan/McGraw-Hill.

Garcia, G. E. (1994). Assessing the literacy development of second-language students: A focus on authentic assessment. In K. Spangenberg-Urbschat & R. Pritchard (Eds.), *Kids come in all languages: Reading instruction for ESL students* (pp. 180–205). Newark, DE: International Reading Association.

Hornberger, N. H. (1990). Creative successful learning contexts for bilingual literacy. *Teachers College Record, 92*(2), 212–229.

Johnson, A. (1990). *When I am old with you.* New York: Orchard.

Lanauze, M., & Snow, C. (1989). The relation between first and second language writing skills. *Linguistics in Education, 1,* 323–339.

Leslie, L., & Jett-Simpson, M. (1997). *Authentic literacy assessment: An ecological approach.* New York: Longman.

Lipsky, D. K., & Gartner, A. (1997). *Inclusion and school reform: Transforming America's classrooms.* Baltimore: Paul H. Brookes.

Livingston, M. C. (1987). *I like you, if you like me: Poems of friendship.* McElderry.

Prelutsky, J. (1983). *The Random House book of poetry.* New York: Random House.

Ramirez, J. D., Yuen, S. D., & Ramey, D. R. (1991). Final report: Longitudinal study of structured English immersion strategy, early-exit, and late-exit programs for language-minority children. Report submitted to the US Department of Education. San Mateo, CA: Aguirre International.

Roseberry-McKibbin, C., & Eicholtz, G. (1994). Serving children with limited English proficiency in the schools: A national survey. *Language, Speech, and Hearing Services in Schools, 25,* 156–164.

Shearer, A. P., & Homan, S. P. (1994). *Linking reading assessment to instruction.* New York: St. Martin.

Silverstein, S. (1996). *Falling up.* New York: HarperCollins.

Spangenberg-Urbschat, K., & Pritchard, R. (Eds.). (1994). *Kids come in all languages: Reading instruction for ESL students.* Newark, DE: International Reading Association.

Squire, J. R. (Ed.). (1987). *The dynamics of language learning: Research in reading and English.* Urbana, IL: ERIC Clearinghouse on Reading and Communication Skills.

Tinajero, J. V., & Ada, A. F. (Eds.). (1993). *The power of two languages: Literacy and biliteracy for Spanish-speaking students.* New York: Macmillan/McGraw-Hill.

Vacano, M. V. (1994, May). Using the home language in the education of language-minority children. *NABE News, 17,* 27.

Valdes, G., & Figueroa, R. A. (1994). *Bilingualism and testing: A special case of bias.* Norwood, NJ: Ablex.

2 Assessing Progress in Second-Language Acquisition

JOSEFINA VILLAMIL TINAJERO AND
SANDRA ROLLINS HURLEY
The University of Texas at El Paso

The early childhood years are a remarkably active period for acquiring language and for learning about its written form. Classroom environments have a significant effect on children's language and literacy development. This is especially true for emergent readers and writers who are also acquiring English as a second language. The physical and social environment of the classroom, teacher beliefs, and attitudes about language acquisition and emergent literacy, the types of activities planned, and the assessment strategies and techniques used by teachers all affect the opportunities children have to acquire a new language and emerge as readers and writers. When working with young English language learners, therefore, teachers must know that children acquire English in a natural progression of stages. As language is acquired, literacy in the new language develops. When planning activities for young English language learners, teachers must be aware of the levels of receptive and productive language children bring to the task. They must also be able to monitor children's progress as they move through the stages of English acquisition to determine instructional needs. In short, teachers must skillfully connect teaching, learning, and assessment in meaningful ways to support language growth. As field-based teacher-educators, we work closely with a number of teachers who possess this expertise. One such teacher is Mr. Sierra, a first grade bilingual teacher in one of our partnership schools.

By observing Mr. Sierra for several weeks during ESL time, we gained some valuable insights into how authentic assessment practices can be linked to instruction that is sensitive to the natural growth of emergent readers and writers learning English as a second language. We were able to observe how this view of assessment thrives on the concept of performance assessment; that is, how assessment becomes an integral part of instruction, and in Mr. Sierra's case, how it is based on classroom activities that are appropriate for second language learners.

Mr. Sierra

Meet Mr. Sierra, a first grade bilingual teacher who has been teaching for eleven years. From watching Mr. Sierra we have learned a great deal about how skillful teachers connect teaching, learning, and assessment during English-as-a-second-language (ESL) time. We arrived on a Monday morning in early March just in time for the closing activities of a Spanish reading lesson and the introduction of a new ESL unit, Life on the Farm. Mr. Sierra began the unit by focusing on a number of activities he called Language Builders. He explained that these activities, which were part of the school's ESL curriculum (Tinajero & Schifini, 1997), built unit concepts and vocabulary vital to the language acquisition process. During this time, he said, he taps prior knowledge and builds vocabulary essential to understanding important concepts in the unit. He began by introducing the concept of farms by displaying several picture cards and pointing to the pictures as he explained, "A **farm** is a place where people have **animals** like this **goat** and this **rooster**. People grow **vegetables** like **corn** on a farm, too. Most of the food we eat comes from farms."

Next, to tap prior knowledge about farms, Mr. Sierra encouraged students to draw pictures or to select other picture cards to show and/or tell what they knew about farms—animals, crops, types of buildings, etc. He then had the children set the cards or drawings in the chalkboard tray and used various strategies to check students' understanding. With students with very limited levels of proficiency (Level 1, Preproduction), he used total physical response (TPR)-style directions and modeling, "I am pointing to the goat. Now you point to the goat." With students with higher levels of proficiency (Level 2, Early Production and Level 3, Speech Emergence), Mr. Sierra asked yes or no questions with embedded answers: "Is this a goat or a rooster? Is this a cow?" Finally, with students with near nativelike fluency (Levels 4 and 5, Intermediate and Advanced Fluency), Mr. Sierra elicited elaboration with open-ended prompts, "Tell us what you know about one of the animals on the farm." To conclude this activity, the children taped their pictures on chart paper and drew a farm scene around them.

The next day, Mr. Sierra explained that he would be working with the children to build vocabulary (vegetables, broccoli, carrots, corn, etc.) and that he would be conducting several performance assessment activities. First, he displayed a poster as he played the first verse of a chant by Sarita Chavez Silverman on audiocassette.

Pass the Vegetables

Pass the celery and broccoli, too.
Pass the squash—it's good for you!
Pass the carrots, if you please.
And don't forget to pass the peas! (Tinajero & Schifini, 1997, p. 191)

Mr. Sierra pointed out the picture of each vegetable as it was named. When the children were familiar with the chant, he had them do a choral rendition. First, he organized the class into three groups. Group 1 chanted the first line, group 2 the second line, and group 3 the third line. Everyone joined in on the last line. After the children heard and practiced the song several times, Mr. Sierra observed another rendition of the chant as an assessment opportunity. He used a rubric signaled by the numbers 1, 2, 3, 4, and 5 to assess fluency. These numbers indicated the way students with beginning, intermediate, and advanced levels of English proficiency participated in the activity. The scoring rubrics helped him relate what he observed to the language proficiency levels.

For example, he later explained that Mikaela chimed in on all of the chant but omitted the verb and produced another minor error when she said, "And no [don't] [forget] to pass the peas!" So, Mr. Sierra circled box 4 of the Student Progress Form for Fluency (Figure 2.1). That is, Mikaela recited an almost complete chant with few errors. For pronunciation and intonation, Mr. Sierra noted that Mikaela's language did not yet approximate native English. He then assessed other children using the same rubric. For those children who participated through body language only (clapping, making gestures, marking rhythm, etc.) while reciting the chant, he circled box 1. For those children who repeated key elements of memorable language or longer phrases he circled box 2 or 3. Others, like Mikaela, received a 4 because they recited an almost complete chant with few errors. None of the children received a 5 (recited the chant comparably to native-speaker peers).

Later in the week, Mr. Sierra conducted several other activities (Language Through Literature) using the district's ESL curriculum. The children made clay story characters for the story *The Goat in the Chile Patch* and used them in a dramatic group retelling activity. After the children practiced their retellings, Mr. Sierra observed their final retellings as the assessment opportunity. As Mikaela manipulated her clay bull, she said, "Next come bull. He say, 'I moo,' Rigo say, 'OK.' But Goat kick bull." Mr. Sierra circled box 3 for Language Functions of the Student Progress Form, because Mikaela produced phrases with story details (see Figure 2.1). Mr. Sierra explained that he selected a few children each week to assess their progress as they acquired higher and higher levels of proficiency in English. This week, he was focusing on five children, including Mikaela.

The following day, in a mathematics activity for the unit, students sorted vegetables and described the groups. Mr. Sierra observed their descriptions as the assessment opportunity. Mikaela sorted the vegetables by size and pointed to one sorting mat as she said, "These all big." As she pointed to the second mat, she said, "These not big." Mr. Sierra circled box 3 in the Student Progress Form for Critical Thinking (see Figure 2.1) because Mikaela used longer phrases to describe how she classified the vegetables. Mr. Sierra explained that if Mikaela had described the groups with language like *This one big and this small*, he would have circled box 4 because she would have produced connected discourse using the language of classification with only a minor error. Had Mikaela said *Big* he would have circled box 2 because she would have used only one word to describe a group.

On Friday, Mr. Sierra assessed the children's writing. He reviewed samples from Mikaela's journal and other products of her unstructured writing. Her writing contained a few drawings and mostly short phrases and sentences with invented spelling. Some of the text reflected symbols and structures of her home language, Spanish. Coherent narratives were not discernible; therefore, Mr. Sierra circled box 2 in Writing on the Student Progress Form (see Figure 2.1). We noticed that other children's writing included mostly drawings with some isolated words or phrases that reflected the structures of the home language, Spanish. Mr. Sierra had circled box 1 for them. Others used connected text with conventional English spelling and more extensive vocabulary as well as few grammatical errors. These children received a 4.

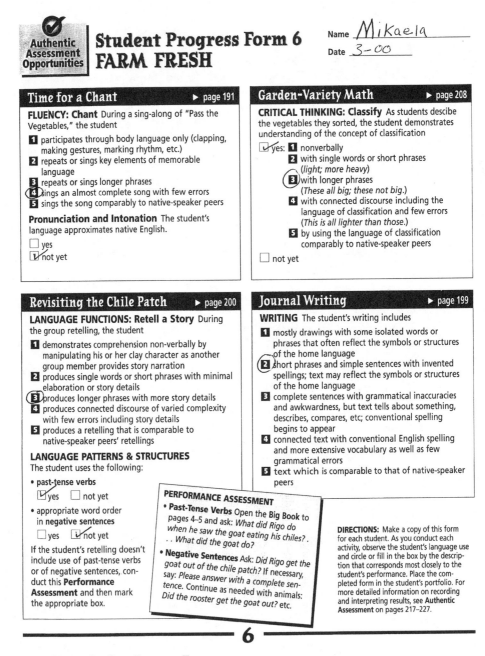

Authentic Assessment Opportunities

Student Progress Form 6
FARM FRESH

Name *Mikaela*
Date *3-00*

Time for a Chant ▶ page 191

FLUENCY: Chant During a sing-along of "Pass the Vegetables," the student

1 participates through body language only (clapping, making gestures, marking rhythm, etc.)

2 repeats or sings key elements of memorable language

3 repeats or sings longer phrases

4 sings an almost complete song with few errors *(circled)*

5 sings the song comparably to native-speaker peers

Pronunciation and Intonation The student's language approximates native English.

☐ yes
☑ not yet

Garden-Variety Math ▶ page 208

CRITICAL THINKING: Classify As students descibe the vegetables they sorted, the student demonstrates understanding of the concept of classification

☑ yes: **1** nonverbally

2 with single words or short phrases *(light; more heavy)*

3 with longer phrases *(circled)* *(These all big; these not big.)*

4 with connected discourse including the language of classification and few errors *(This is all lighter than those.)*

5 by using the language of classification comparably to native-speaker peers

☐ not yet

Revisiting the Chile Patch ▶ page 200

LANGUAGE FUNCTIONS: Retell a Story During the group retelling, the student

1 demonstrates comprehension non-verbally by manipulating his or her clay character as another group member provides story narration

2 produces single words or short phrases with minimal elaboration or story details

3 produces longer phrases with more story details *(circled)*

4 produces connected discourse of varied complexity with few errors including story details

5 produces a retelling that is comparable to native-speaker peers' retellings

LANGUAGE PATTERNS & STRUCTURES
The student uses the following:

• **past-tense verbs**
☑ yes ☐ not yet

• appropriate word order in **negative sentences**
☐ yes ☑ not yet

If the student's retelling doesn't include use of past-tense verbs or of negative sentences, conduct this **Performance Assessment** and then mark the appropriate box.

Journal Writing ▶ page 199

WRITING The student's writing includes

1 mostly drawings with some isolated words or phrases that often reflect the symbols or structures of the home language

2 short phrases and simple sentences with invented spellings; text may reflect the symbols or structures of the home language *(circled)*

3 complete sentences with grammatical inaccuracies and awkwardness, but text tells about something, describes, compares, etc; conventional spelling begins to appear

4 connected text with conventional English spelling and more extensive vocabulary as well as few grammatical errors

5 text which is comparable to that of native-speaker peers

PERFORMANCE ASSESSMENT

• **Past-Tense Verbs** Open the **Big Book** to pages 4–5 and ask: *What did Rigo do when he saw the goat eating his chiles?* . . . *What did the goat do?*

• **Negative Sentences** Ask: *Did Rigo get the goat out of the chile patch?* If necessary, say: *Please answer with a complete sentence.* Continue as needed with animals: *Did the rooster get the goat out?* etc.

DIRECTIONS: Make a copy of this form for each student. As you conduct each activity, observe the student's language use and circle or fill in the box by the description that corresponds most closely to the student's performance. Place the completed form in the student's portfolio. For more detailed information on recording and interpreting results, see **Authentic Assessment** on pages 217–227.

6

FIGURE 2.1 Student Progress Form

Finally, by observing language development across language functions, we were able to gain a better understanding of how to assess young children's progress in acquiring language forms in their second language.

The next section provides some background information that we think will be useful when planning similar instruction and assessment activities for English language learners.

Background Research

New Perspectives in the Teaching and Assessment of Early Literacy

Current understanding of how children learn has had an impact on instruction and assessment in the beginnings of reading and writing, known as emergent literacy, for both first and second language learners. Instead of treating skills and objectives (which teachers feel are important to language and literacy development) as discrete entities, these skills are now developed and assessed in an integrated, holistic manner through content themes (Strickland, 1989). From the beginning of school, children participate in genuine reading and writing activities in ways that help them not only to be able to read and write but also to want to read and write as they go through life (Martinez & Teale, 1993). Instructional practices and materials for young children are based on a set of beliefs that according to Martinez and Teale are the foundations of emergent literacy: (1) learning to read and write begins very early in life as children participate in activities in the home, community, and school that involve literacy; (2) reading and writing develop concurrently and interrelatedly rather than sequentially; (3) the functions of literacy are a critically important part of learning to read and write; (4) in becoming literate, young children develop knowledge and strategies in many different aspects of reading and writing; and (5) although early literacy learning can be described in terms of generalized benchmarks of progress, children become literate at different rates and take a variety of different paths to literacy. Because teaching, learning, and assessment must be connected in meaningful ways, assessment practices must be compatible with and complementary to an instructional plan that integrates these beliefs. That is, as the conceptualization of early literacy has changed, so have the views on assessment. For this reason, you will find that Mr. Sierra's assessment plan parallels and complements his more holistic, integrated approach to literacy.

The Connection between L_1 and L_2 Literacy

For children learning English as a second language, literacy instruction often begins in the native language. This is the case in Mr. Sierra's class. The children begin formal reading instruction in Spanish while they develop oral English language skills. Mr. Sierra and his colleagues have reviewed the research literature concerning how the native language plays a critical role in promoting literacy, and ultimately, in the overall success of Limited English Proficient (LEP) students. A number of researchers (Krashen & Biber, 1988; Ramirez, Yuen, & Ramey, 1991; Cummins, 1989, 1991; Snow, Burns, & Griffin, 1998) have found that literacy instruction in the native language is the most pedagogically sound way to teach students acquiring English about the relationship between meaning and print in both the native language and English. Literacy in the native language has been found to be the most stable predictor of English literacy (Pardo & Tinajero, 1993). In fact, research shows that those students with high levels of literacy proficiency in the L_1 perform better on tasks of academic English than do students with low levels of language and literacy proficiency in their native language (Lindholm & Zierlein, 1991; Snow, 1990). Therefore, "there is good reason to support reading in both first and second language. Free reading in the first language may mean more reading, and hence more literacy development in the second language" (Krashen, 1995, p. 8). Many of the assessment measures included in this chapter, therefore, can also be made available in other languages as needed.

The Connection between Oral Language and Literacy Development

According to Hiebert, Pearson, Taylor, Richardson, and Paris (1998), "oral language is the foundation on which reading is built, and it continues to serve this role as children develop as readers" (p. 1). Oral language abilities, therefore, are interwoven with learning to read and write. Comprehension of written text depends on the readers' oral-language abilities (Snow, Burns, & Griffin, 1998). For young English language learners, this means that they must learn both the oral and written forms of the new language—English. Both are difficult tasks. In bilingual classrooms, children develop literacy skills in their first language, most often Spanish, the language they speak and understand while acquiring oral proficiency in English and then subsequently taught to extend their skills to reading in English. Developing literacy skills in children's first language facilitates and accelerates learning to read in the second language (Thomas & Collier, 1997; Snow, Burns, & Griffin, 1998).

During ESL instruction, second language learners develop the oral proficiency, vocabulary, and other language skills that are crucial foundations for success in English reading. According to Snow, Burns, and Griffin (1998), learning to speak English before introducing the written text "contributes to children's eventual fluency in English reading because it provides a foundation to support subsequent learning about the alphabetic principle. . . . Hurrying young non-English speaking children into reading in English without ensuring adequate preparation is counterproductive" (p. 324).

A primary need of both bilingual and ESL teachers, like Mr. Sierra, is methods of assessing and evaluating students' acquisition of English, both oral and written. Such assessments yield valuable information for informing day-to-day instructional decisions, communicating progress to students and their parents, identifying students who need additional support, and evaluating program effectiveness. Teachers, then, must have the skills and tools to effectively assess language growth.

Facilitating Language Growth across the Stages

English language learners move through a series of predictable stages as they progress in their language development toward native-like fluency in English. As language is acquired, literacy in the new language develops. Just as each individual acquires the home language at his or her own pace, English learners also acquire their new language at individual rates. In fact, second-language acquisition is characterized by predictable phases, beginning with a silent period, or preproduction stage, when learners are busy listening to and assimilating the sounds and structures of English. Other features characterize progress through the stages of early production, speech emergence, and intermediate and advanced fluency as learners move toward the goal of native-like fluency.

Though the stages of language acquisition themselves are predictable, individual language acquisition varies as students develop at their own pace (Thomas & Collier, 1997). Progress along the pathway to fluency is not always signaled by forward movement alone. Rather, students who show a growth spurt in acquiring new vocabulary, for example, may exhibit less control in using it grammatically. Such spurts and lags in language development are highly individual and are a normal part of the language acquisition process (Tinajero & Schifini, 1997). Teachers can create language growth across the stages by using the instructional strategies and techniques suggested in Table 2.1. The assessment measures used should provide teachers with valuable information to make sound instructional decisions.

Current Issues in ESL Assessment

Traditional assessment techniques are often incongruent with ESL classroom practices. Standardized testing is particularly antithetical to process learning (Moya & O'Malley, 1994; Short, 1999; Bartolome, 1998). In the last several years, therefore, educators have begun to explore alternative forms to student assessment, known as authentic assessment practices, for second language learners. As the conceptualization of ESL has become more holistic and integrated, so have the views on assessment. For this reason, we find that the assessment plan in Mr. Sierra's class parallels and complements a more holistic, integrated approach to language teaching.

According to Pierce and O'Malley (1992) authentic assessment practices reflect a view of instruction that is more sensitive to the natural growth of students acquiring English. This new view of assessment thrives on the concept of performance assessment. That is, assessment becomes an integral part of instruction, is ongoing and is based on everyday classroom activities. It is focused on process as well as product. It acknowledges the fact that teachers are in a position to constantly observe and, thus, assess students in action, engaged in a wide range of behaviors. Authentic assessment has at least three advantages over formal assessment procedures: (1) it does not take away from instructional time because

TABLE 2.1   Teachers can create language growth across the stages by using these instructional strategies and techniques

Stages of Language Acquisition	Student Behaviors/Strategies
1. Preproduction	Students have very few oral skills; may be able to respond nonverbally by pointing, gesturing, nodding, or drawing.
	Students at this stage benefit when teachers provide abundant opportunities for active listening, utilizing visuals and real objects.
2. Early production	Students listen with greater understanding and can produce some English words, phrases, and simple sentences related to social, everyday events.
	Students at this stage benefit when teachers ask yes/no, either/or, and listing-type questions; they show reading ability in English if illustrations support text.
3. Speech emergence	Students can understand written English accompanied by concrete contexts, such as picutres, objects, actions, and sounds. They can understand ideas about events within the range of personal experience.
	Students at this stage benefit when teachers focus on communication, not language form, providing meaningful contexts in which students express themselves in speech and print for a wide range of purposes and audiences.
4 and 5. Intermediate and advanced fluency	At stage 4, students demonstrate increased levels of accuracy and correctness and are able to express thoughts and feelings. Students at this stage benefit when teachers provide opportunities for students to create oral and written narratives.
	At Stage 5, students produce language with varied grammatical structures and vocabulary, comparable to native English speakers of the same age. Students at this stage benefit when teachers continue ongoing language development through integrated language arts and content-area activities.

it is part of instruction; (2) it takes into account the learning context; and (3) it reflects individual student's progress (Garcia, 1994).

Although assessment is viewed holistically in an integrated approach to teaching language and content, teachers must have a clear understanding of grammatical and content knowledge as two separate (though interrelated) developments. That is, language issues can be separated from subject-area concepts (see Chapter 8; Short, 1999). In this way, teachers can monitor children's acquisition of the form of language and the use of specific discourse functions as they move through the stages of language acquisition. Teachers must determine in advance their assessment objective (language assessment versus content assessment) and select the appropriate assessment tools.

A number of assessment measures are now available to help teachers evaluate the form and function of language. The next section identifies some of these assessment measures and the processes that are useful to teachers in designing instruction that support English language development and other emergent literacy skills in young children. Our focus is on observing language development across language functions. Other chapters in this book focus on assessment of content knowledge and academic language (e.g., Chapter 5). Use of these assessment measures will help teachers get a global picture of where students stand, individually and collectively, on the continuum of language acquisition so that they may tailor instruction (Tinajero & Schifini, 1993).

Implications for Practice

Based on the research literature and on the classroom realities of ESL teachers like Mr. Sierra, some implications can be drawn for practice. Teachers need a variety of authentic assessment measures that can be used with relative ease and economy of time in the busy, complex world of bilingual and ESL classrooms. The measures need to be designed for use as an integral part of instruction—not as a separate, add-on procedure—so that assessment does not take away from instructional time. The measures also need to take into account the learning context of individual children as they work on their own and with other children. Finally, the assessment measures must chronicle children's language growth and development and their academic growth.

The traditional tools of ethnography, observations, journals, and checklists have been used successfully to accomplish these purposes. It follows, then, that in the classroom, just as in ethnographic research, the primary tool is the investigator—the teacher. The teacher makes the decisions on which assessment measures to use and when and how to use them. The teacher analyzes the data and uses them to inform instruction. The most important implication, therefore, is that teachers must be knowledgeable, well-informed individuals who can ask the critical questions, determine ways to find answers to the questions, and then make wise instructional decisions for each child. Knowledge of the steps in preparing for oral language assessment is important for teachers: identifying purpose, planning for assessment, developing (or identifying and selecting) rubrics or scoring procedures, setting standards, involving students in self- and peer assessment, selecting assessment activities, and recording information (O'Malley & Pierce, 1996). Some of these steps are discussed in the next section.

Practical Classroom Application

The matrix of Figure 2.2 is offered to language educators as a guide for selecting and using their assessment tools when monitoring children's growth in language proficiency. (The matrix is an adaptation of one developed by Short [1999] for use in assessment of integrated language and content.) This matrix examines what language might be assessed and how the assessment might be done.

FIGURE 2.2   Language Assessment: What and How

HOW

	Checklists	Teacher observation	Journal entry	Anecdotal record	Use of Manipulation
Communication skills					
Fluency					
Language functions					
Language patterns and structures					
Critical thinking					
Academic concepts and vocabulary					
Writing					
Individual behavior					
Group behavior					

WHAT

Source: Adapted from Short, D. (1999). Assessing integrated language and content instruction. In Heath, I. A., & Serrano, C. J. (Eds.), *Annual editions: Teaching English as a second language*, pp. 129–141. Guilford, CT: McGraw-Hill.

The objectives of a language development lesson can be divided into the following categories: communication skills (speaking), fluency, language functions, language patterns and structures, academic concepts and vocabulary, writing, individual behavior, and group behavior. These categories become the WHAT. These areas can then be assessed through some of the following authentic assessment measures or the HOW: checklists, teacher observations, journal entries, anecdotal records, and performance-based observations/use of manipulatives (Short, 1999). The key for teachers is to select the type of assessment carefully and to focus on the information that the assessment measures produce.

The matrix in Figure 2.2 distinguishes between individual and group work. Group work and cooperative learning activities that provide students with opportunities to use oral language to interact with others are optimal for assessing oral language (O'Malley & Pierce, 1996). Within this context, the areas of grammar, language functions, academic concepts, and vocabulary can be addressed. The next section briefly describes the skill categories in the matrix and some of the alternative assessment measures that teachers might use. The measures included in the matrix are only a few of the many options teachers have in assessing progress in language proficiency.

Skills Assessed

Communication Skills. Language is a social medium, spoken or written to express ideas for a specific purpose. English-language learners are motivated to use language when they have an authentic reason to communicate. Given such a reason, students experiment with language, revise their ideas about how it works, and move toward standard oral and written English in an effort to communicate successfully. Assessment includes teacher observations to determine if children speak in social and classroom settings with sustained and connected discourse. In the opening vignette, for example, Mr. Sierra conducted an authentic assessment activity using a checklist as the children participated in retelling their stories. He noted that some of the children simply manipulated their clay characters, demonstrating comprehension nonverbally, as another group member provided the story narration. Others produced single words or short phrases with minimal elaboration or story detail. Still others, produced connected discourse of varied complexity with few errors including story details.

In addition to checklists, teachers can also use anecdotal records to assess communication skills. That is, teachers can reflect on students' work or behavior during the day or over a short period of time and record impressions and anecdotes that pertain to the students' learning progress (Short, 1999).

Fluency. English learners must have ample opportunities to develop fluency in English. Poems, chants, songs, and raps are especially effective in involving students with language in a low-risk environment. Their simple rhythmic, rhyming text, often accompanied by gestures or movement, helps make language memorable, facilitating the internalization of vocabulary and language patterns and structures. Pronunciation and fluency develop naturally as students participate in these types of activities. Consider the example in the opening vignette. As children participate in reciting the chant, "Pass the Vegetables," they gain experience with a whole range of language skills. As they pass the vegetables or pictures of vegetables to the beat as they recite the chant, they are using sentences with present-tense verbs ("Pass the celery"). They are also using negative sentences ("And don't forget to pass the peas"). Students are also learning about and use vocabulary of vegetables (celery, broccoli, squash, carrots) (Tinajero & Schifini, 1997).

The authentic assessment measure might involve the use of a rubric such as the one used by Mr. Sierra. As Mr. Sierra observed the children's performance, he referred to the behaviors described on the Student Progress Form in the Fluency section (see Figure 2.1) and marked the one that most closely corresponded to the observation. The numbers in the boxes refer to the stages of language acquisition described in Table 2.1. Teachers can use this type of rubric as students are chanting or after the activity, on reflection.

The fluency observations also give teachers an opportunity to make a global evaluation of pronunciation and intonation. They simply note whether or not students' language approximates native English. Teachers must remember that nativelike pronunciation develops naturally over a long period of time and should not be a major factor in the assessment of proficiency levels.

Language Functions.   Young children have multiple opportunities in the classroom to use language functions to express meaning. Language functions refer to how children use language to accomplish specific tasks (Halliday, 1975) such as to describe or provide information or to express feelings. Consider an example in Mr. Sierra's class. During a book-talk activity that we observed, the children were encouraged to discuss what they thought about the story, *The Goat in the Chile Patch.* They shared their feeling about what they thought was the funniest part of the story. They also talked about whether or not they would recommend the book to a friend. Meanwhile, Mr. Sierra made mental notes, which he later added to the individual progress forms.

Language Patterns and Structures.   The teacher must assess young children on their ability to use a variety of language patterns and structures. In school, children participate in authentic communication activities in which the use of certain language patterns and structures occur naturally. As students participate in these activities, they often produce the target patterns and structures. In the opening vignette, for example, as students talked about the goat, they had multiple opportunities to use sentences with past-tense verbs and negative word order. During the retelling of the story about the goat, Mr. Sierra assessed the appropriate use of past-tense verbs and word order in negative sentences. These sentence patterns were connected to the plot of the story and were elicited naturally as the children retold the story.

Children's retellings, however, may not always include use of negative sentences. The teacher can still conduct a performance assessment activity designed to elicit a response that includes the negative form (see Performance Assessment in Figure 2.1). For example, the teacher might ask, "Did Rigo get the goat out of the chile patch?" (No, he didn't.) If necessary, the teacher may say, "Please answer with a complete sentence." The teacher may continue as needed with other animals: "Did the rooster get the goat out?" etc. Similarly, to retell the story *The Goat in the Chile Patch*, children must use the past-tense verbs. If the student's retelling doesn't include use of past-tense verbs, the teacher might ask the following questions to elicit a response: "What did Rigo do when he saw the goat eating his chiles?" "What did the goat do?"

Academic Concepts and Vocabulary. When students gather data, prepare, and present reports, they learn about and use vocabulary related to the topic at hand (e.g., weather, cloudy, sunny, rainy, etc.). In the vignette, the children used and developed concepts and vocabulary related to farm animals (cow, dog, goat, hen, horse), to the names of vegetables (broccoli, squash, pea), and to farms (animals, vegetables, field). Checklists, teacher observations, and anecdotal records can all be used to assess academic concepts and vocabulary development.

Individual Behavior. Although teachers often use cooperative learning activities to increase interaction among and between students, there are times when children must conduct and complete work individually. Individual behaviors that can be assessed include miming the retelling of a story and completing a journal entry.

Group Behavior. Here students complete group tasks or cooperative activities, such as participating in a story dramatization or building a sand castle.

Assessment Measures

Checklists, teacher observations, anecdotal records, use of manipulatives and journal entries can all be used to assess language development.

For second-language learners, however, growth in English acquisition is often demonstrated through oral production, creating no tangible "product" for collection. Nevertheless, a variety of formats in addition to checklists and structured observations can be used to document students' oral language development. Audio recordings can be used to document production during individual, partner, and group activities such as story retellings and project presentations. Video recordings can help isolate individual contributions during group activities such as dramatizations and discussions. They can also be used to capture interactions during unstructured time in the classroom, when students use language for their individual communicative needs. Photographs with accompanying anecdotal notes can document participation in puppetry, dramatics, content-area projects, and other group or individual activities (Tinajero & Schifini, 1997). Performance-based tasks that involve physical movement and manipulatives can also be used effectively to assess language development. Students can manipulate clay story characters, for example, to mime the events in a story following oral directions. Individual checklists or inventories can be completed for each child.

Many items often included in mainstream language arts portfolios can also be collected in the portfolios of students acquiring English: book logs that record self-selected listening activities (books on tape), drawings created in response to read-alouds, journal entries, etc. Products collected for the portfolio need not be limited to those created during independent work. Group and pair work also provide meaningful information about students' language use and often yield "collectible" products (Tinajero & Schifini, 1997).

Final Thoughts and Reflection

On the final week of our visit to Mr. Sierra's class, he explained that he has numerous opportunities throughout the day to observe and "collect" children's work for assessment purposes. He collects their work in a portfolio. He shared some of those portfolios with us. The ones we reviewed included a collection of students' work assembled from the beginning of the year that showed a variety of indicators of their progress in acquiring English. These indicators included documentation through logs, photographs, and students' drawings that indicated their participation in activities such as role playing or dramatizations (snapshots of children in costume or audio cassette tapes of dramatic interpretation, sing-alongs, interviews, and choral readings), drawings from guided visualization activities, pictures of anecdotal notes about children tracking text, participating in story retells, manipulating animals appropriately, and innovating on a story. All these were collected and placed in the students' portfolios.

The portfolios also included completed copies of the Student Progress Form (see Figure 2.1) for each unit. You may recall from the opening vignette that these forms identified opportunities to observe language use as children participated in authentic communication activities. The scoring rubrics for each observation helped Mr. Sierra relate what he observed to language proficiency levels. The numbers in the boxes, he explained, referred to the stages of languages acquisition described earlier in this chapter. Figure 2.1 shows the result of Mr. Sierra's observation of Mikaela. He noted that the Fluency observation also gave him an opportunity to make a global evaluation of pronunciation and intonation. In this way, he was able to tailor instruction to children's individual needs and to monitor their progress on their pathway to nativelike fluency.

On that last visit of the year to Mr. Sierra's class, he shared with us several Student Progress Forms that he had accumulated for each student, including Mikaela. He explained that as he reviewed the ratings since the beginning of the year, he could see a pattern emerge for each child. For example, there were students who were clearly at the preproduction stage of English development.

Box 1 was usually checked for most of the assessments at the beginning of the year. As students made progress in their language development, he noted that he was checking off box 2 more frequently. In this way the assessment process helped him monitor students' progress through the stages of English acquisition.

The Student Progress Form also helped him define profiles of individual strengths and areas requiring extra support. For example, he noted that box 1 and 2 were frequently circled for oral language activities for Sergio, another student, yet box 3 was circled most frequently for his journal sample. Such information helped him see that a reluctant speaker may actually have greater English proficiency than his oral performance indicated. Armed with such information, Mr. Sierra was able to adjust his teaching strategies to play to Sergio's strengths and to provide extra support in creating nonthreatening opportunities for practice with oral English. Armed with Mr. Sierra's ideas and expertise, we left his classroom ready to share them with our students at the university.

DISCUSSION QUESTIONS

1. List the five stages of language acquisition and describe student behaviors associated with each.

2. What instructional strategies are appropriate for use with youngsters at the early production stage? Provide specific examples of classroom activities.

3. Explain how assessment of student's second language acquisition can be integrated with instruction.

4. Describe the beliefs/assumptions that form the foundation of emergent literacy. What are some implications for practice?

5. Why is it important that students develop native language literacy as they are acquiring English as a second language?

REFERENCES

Bartolome, L. I. (1998). *The misteaching of academic discourses: The politics of language in the classroom.* Boulder, CO: Westview Press.

Cummins, J. (1989). *Empowering minority students.* Sacramento, CA: California Association for Bilingual Education.

Cummins, J. (1991). Interdependence of first- and second-language proficiency in bilingual children. In E. Bialystok (Ed.), *Language processing in bilingual children* (pp. 70–89). Cambridge: Cambridge University Press.

Garcia, G. A. (1994). Assessing the literacy development of second-language students: A focus on authentic assessment. In K. Spangenberg-Urbschat, R. Pritchard (Eds.), *Kids come in all languages: Reading instruction for ESL students.* pp. 180–205. Newark, DE: International Reading Association.

Halliday, M. A. K. (1975). *Learning how to mean: Explorations in the development of language.* London: Edward Arnold.

Hiebert, E. H., Pearson, P. D., Taylor, B. M., Richardson, V., & Paris, S. G. (1998). *Every child a reader: Applying reading research in the classroom.* Topic 1: Oral Language and Reading. University of Michigan. Ann Arbor, Michigan: Center for the Improvement of Early Reading Achievement (CIERA).

Krashen, S., & Biber, D. (1988). *On course. bilingual education's success in California.* Sacramento, CA: California Association for Bilingual Education.

Lindholm, K. J., & Zierlein, A. (1991). Bilingual proficiency as a bridge to academic achievement: Results from bilingual/immersion programs. *Journal of Education, 173* (2), 9–20.

Martinez, M., & Teale, W. (1993). *Emergent writing. Teacher's planning guide.* New York: Macmillan/ McGraw-Hill.

Moya, S. S., & O'Malley, J. M. (1994). A portfolio assessment model for ESL. *The Journal of Educational Issues of Language Minority Students. 13,* 13–36.

O'Malley, J. M., & Pierce, L. V. (1996). Authentic assessment for English language learners: Practical approaches for teachers. Reading, MA: Addison-Wesley.

Pardo, E. B., & Tinajero, J. V. (1993). Literacy instruction through Spanish: Linguistic, cultural and pedagogical considerations. In J. Tinajero & A. F. Ada (Eds.), *The power of two languages: Literacy and biliteracy for Spanish-speaking students.* pp. 26–36. New York: Macmillan/ McGraw-Hill.

Pierce, L. V., & O'Malley, J. M. (Spring 1992). *Performance and portfolio assessment for language minority students.* Washington, DC: National Clearinghouse for Bilingual Education.

Ramirez, J. D., Yuen, S. D., & Ramey, E. (1991). *Final report: Longitudinal study of structured English immersion strategy, early-exit and late-exit transitional bilingual education programs for language-minority children.* United States Department of Education, Contract No. 300-87-0156. San Mateo, CA: Aguirre International.

Short, D. (1999). Assessing integrated language and content instruction. In Heath, I. A., & Serrano, C. J. (Eds.), *Annual editions: Teaching English as a second language,* pp. 129–141. Guilford, CT: McGraw-Hill.

Snow, C. E. (1990). Rationales for native language instruction. In *Bilingual education: Issues and strategies.* In A. M. Padilla, H. H. Fairchild, & D. M. Valadez (Eds.), pp. 60–74. Alexandria, Virginia: Association for Supervision and Curriculum Development.

Snow, C. E., Burns, M. S., & Griffin, P. (Eds.). (1998). *Preventing reading difficulties in young children.* National Research Council. Washington, DC: National Academy Press.

Strickland, D. S. (1989). A model for change: Framework for an emergent literacy curriculum. In D. S. Strickland & L. M. Morrow (Eds.), *Emerging literacy: Young children learn to read and write.* pp. 135–146. Newark: International Reading Association.

Thomas, W. P. & Collier, V. (1997). *School effectiveness for language minority students.* Washington, D.C.: National Clearinghouse for Bilingual Education.

Tinajero, J., & Schifini, A. (1993). *ESL theme links program guide.* Carmel, CA: Hampton-Brown Books.

Tinajero, J., & Schifini, A. (1997). *Into English! Level B, teacher's guide.* Carmel, CA: Hampton-Brown Books.

3 Assessing the Writing of Spanish-Speaking Students

Issues and Suggestions

KATHY ESCAMILLA AND MARÍA COADY
University of Colorado, Denver
School of Education

In Feb. 1995, a graduate student brought Lupe's writing sample (Figure 3.1) to our university seminar on teacher education. She collected the writing sample as a part of an assignment in the class. When she brought it to our class, she reported that she had shared it with Lupe's English teacher. The English teacher had the following comments about Lupe's writing:

> The writing sample confirms every fear I have about Lupe. I think she may have a cognitive processing problem. She has poor vocabulary and grammar. She has a hard time expressing herself either orally or in writing. She has a hard time with logical sequencing. She has been here 7 months. She ought to be doing better. Maybe she needs a special program.

Lupe was in a school where there was limited support for second language learners. After discussing the Lupe sample in class, we asked the student to return to the school and collect a similar writing sample, this time in Spanish (Figure 3.2 A, B).

When Lupe's Spanish writing sample was discussed in our seminar, the students observed a stark contrast. Lupe did not have any of the "problems" with grammar, logical sequencing, or self-expression that she appeared to have when she was writing in English. Further, Lupe is a competent writer and thinker as evidenced by her ability to write about critical contemporary issues and relate them to her own personal experience.

There are many lessons to be learned from the story of the two Lupes. First, assessment practices that look at second language learners only in English often underestimate the cognitive and academic strengths of Spanish-speaking students. If we are truly going to develop bilingual and biliterate students in our schools, then we must assess Spanish-speaking students in both of their languages.

THE DAY I WAS SOMEONE EISE

I without the preccidant of Mexico I treat do morc works, and Not rob the moncy From the people, I use in arrange the alley and give food a people they are not have, money or work. I.

I DO morc good things to the country, better what go treatment with E.U. becqusc the E.U. give more problems go to Mexico.

I am so sorry I Not writing EUn.

FIGURE 3.1 Lupe's English Writing Sample

Assessment in both Spanish and English is important for students who have had formal schooling experiences before their arrival in the United States, even if they are not in bilingual education programs. It is equally important for students who are in schools where they are learning to read and write in Spanish and English.

Research Background

Holisitic writing assessment that utilizes writing rubrics is thought to be a more reliable means of assessing student writing progress than the use of traditional standardized tests (Fredericks & Rasinski, 1997; Hunter, Jones, & Randhawa, 1996; Rhodes & Shanklin, 1993). Many school districts are now using some form of holistic writing assessment and rubrics as a part of their assessment programs. This type of assessment is being used to document student growth, to determine whether students are meeting district and state writing standards, and as a way to examine how to improve writing instruction.

Districts implementing bilingual programs often assess students in both English and Spanish; however, it is frequently the case that the Spanish assessment

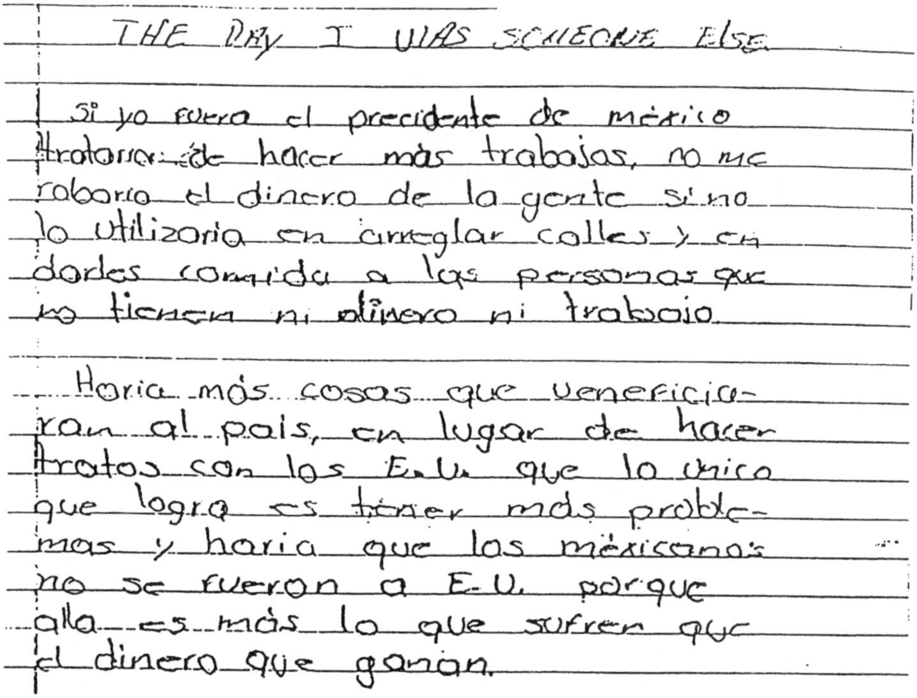

THE DAY I WAS SOMEONE ELSE

Si yo fuera el precidente de méxico
trataría de hacer más trabajos, no me
robaría el dinero de la gente si no
lo utilizaría en arreglar calles y en
darles comida a las personas que
no tienen ni dinero ni trabajo.

Haría más cosas que veneficia-
ran al pais, en lugar de hacer
tratos con los E.U. que lo unico
que logra es tener más proble-
mas y haría que los méxicanos
no se fueron a E.U. porque
ala es más lo que sufren que
el dinero que ganan.

FIGURE 3.2A   Lupe's Spanish Writing Sample

If I were the President of Mexico I would try to make more jobs, I would not rob money from people. Instead I would use it to fix streets and give food to people who don't have food or work.

I would do more things that would benefit the country instead of making treaties with the United States the only thing that that achieves is having more problems and I would make it so that Mexicans did not go to the United States because there you suffer more than any money you earn.

FIGURE 3.2B   Lupe's Spanish Writing Sample; English Translation

is not valued as highly as the English assessment. For example, many large city school districts regularly report the results of English assessments in newspapers and other popular media but not Spanish assessment data. Bilingual programs are judged based on student acquisition of English and not on the development of bilingualism or biliteracy. For assessment practices of Spanish and English students in bilingual programs to be more reliable, data presenting achievement in both languages must be gathered, analyzed, and reported. As seen in the case of "two Lupes," too often, only English data is presented for these students, making them look less competent than they really are. Recent research in bilingualism (Muñoz-Sandoval, Cummins, Alvarado, & Ruef, 1998) asserts that the bilingual student brings to learning a linguistic repertoire that cannot be measured in a single language; therefore, developing adequate assessments, in Spanish, for Spanish speaking students, and in English, is crucial.

Current practice in writing assessment for Spanish-speaking students is patterned after writing assessment for monolingual English speakers (Carlisle, 1989). There is an assumption that effective holistic writing assessment is universal and does not need to be modified when applied in languages other than English or when applied with students for whom English is a second language. As school districts develop writing rubrics and other authentic assessments to improve their writing programs and assessment practices, rubrics are often developed first, in English, for English speakers. They are then often used with second language learners but rarely modified. Further, these rubrics are then often translated into Spanish without consideration as to how they may need to be modified for Spanish writers.

Gersten and Jiménez (1998) and Goldenberg (1998) state that these notions of universal assessment practices are based on the logic that English and Spanish are both alphabetic languages and, therefore, share many conventions and traditions. They go on to say, however, that aside from logic, there is little actual research to support the universal application of writing assessment practices from English to Spanish or from English for native speakers to English for second language speakers. Gersten and Jiménez (1998) call attention to the need to develop literacy programs and assessment in ways that consider both universal notions of literacy and specific features and functions of particular languages. In short, it is important for assessments, in Spanish, to consider the forms and functions of Spanish as well as the features of appropriate assessment.

Research by Kaplan (1970) and Luther (1997) has established that speakers of languages other than English use discourse styles and patterns that vary greatly from English. These researchers have established that discourse patterns in non-English languages (specifically Spanish and Native American languages) is nonlinear. This is significant because it means that speakers of these languages are not likely to write narrative stories and other text that is linear in nature. Further, research by Montaño-Harmon (1991) has established that students writing in Spanish, as well as English-as-a-second-language (ESL) students writing in English, often use the discourse patterns of their native languages; therefore, a writing rubric that is based on the linear logic of English may have as a standard that good stories have a beginning, middle, and end. Students writing in Spanish may not use this linear logic when writing and, thus, be judged as noncompetent writers.

During the school year 1997 to 1998, research on writing assessment was conducted at an elementary school in the Denver area. This elementary school is an inner-city school of approximately 650 students. The majority of the school population at this school is Mexican, Mexican American, and Chicano (85%), with 60% of the students being labeled as limited English proficient. Ninety-six percent of the students at the school are on free and reduced lunch, and the majority are considered to be at risk for school failure.

The research study collected writing samples from 409 students in grades K to 5 in October 1997 and 353 in March 1998. Writing samples were collected in Spanish from students who are learning to read and write in Spanish (n= 205 fall; n=167 spring); in English from students learning to read and write in English (n=204 fall; n=186 spring); and from students who had begun their schooling in Spanish but have subsequently made the transition to reading and writing in English (n=29 fall; n=13 spring). Writing sample data were collected by giving all students a common prompt in English and Spanish. Students were given 30 minutes to write.

Writing samples were scored holistically using the Escuela Brillante Spanish / English writing assessment (see this chapter's Appendix). The Escuela Brillante writing assessment is an adaptation of the Gross Pointe, Michigan writing assessment, and the Greeley-Weld County School District #6 writing assessment (Weld County School District #6 Writing Assessment, 1993). In this case, the Spanish assessment is an equivalent of the English assessment system, including the same scoring rubric. Through scoring and discussing these writing samples with teachers and others at the school and by comparing English to Spanish writing samples, we discovered that Spanish writers and ESL writers write quite differently than their native English counterparts. Significant differences were noted in the following areas:

1. Spanish speaking students writing in Spanish and English often did not use English linear logic (see writing samples of Leticia and Brenda below).
2. Spanish speaking students, overall, wrote stories that were as complex and interesting as English speaking students; however, they had more problems with spelling, punctuation, and use of other conventions such as accents than English speakers did (see writing samples of Alfredo and Francisco below).
3. Because it was taken directly from English, the rubric used to score writing samples did not provide good feedback to teachers in how to improve writing in Spanish. In this case, assessment could not help to drive instruction.

Results of this research, together with the dearth of research dealing specifically with the creation of assessment tools and procedures in Spanish, has led us to conclude that English language writing rubrics must be modified when they are used to assess Spanish writing samples and when they are used to assess the writing of ESL students.

Implications/Applications for Practice

We suggest that writing rubrics for Spanish speaking students must be revised in both English and Spanish around three main considerations. Each consideration is presented and discussed here, and each includes samples of student writing to illustrate the issue in greater detail.

First, those writing rubrics in Spanish must consider the divergent rhetorical structures, discourse patterns, and learning styles used by Spanish speakers. The strict adherence to story structure that values the linear logic of English in which every story must have a beginning, middle, and end and not stray from that logic penalizes Spanish speaking students, both in their writing in Spanish and in English. Stories written using divergent discourse patterns are not less interesting or complex than those written using linear discourse patterns; however, because of the divergent patterns, they are often not judged to be good writing. Several examples, one in Spanish and one in English illustrate this point. (See Figures 3.3A and 3.3B)

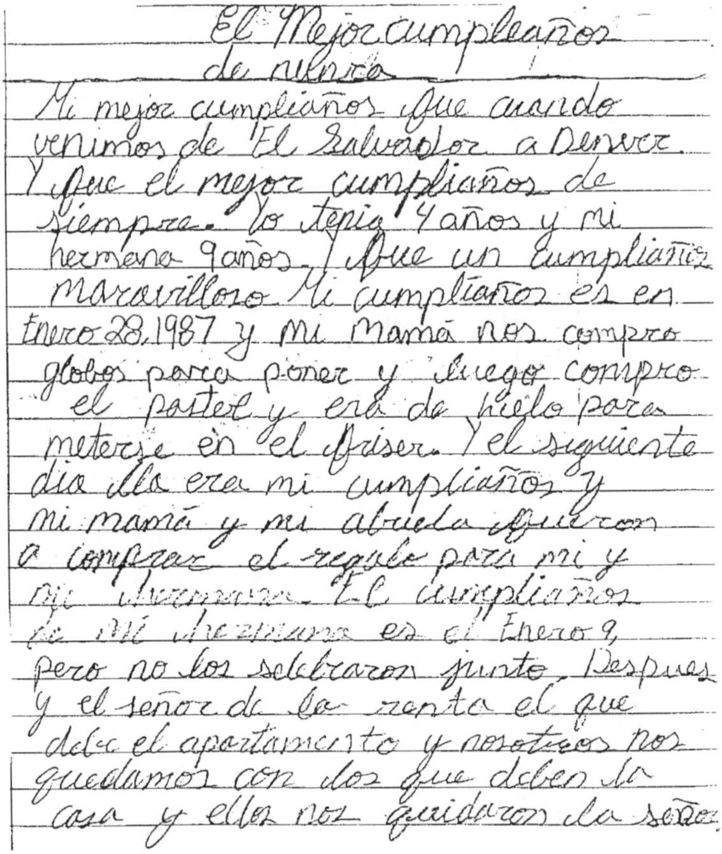

El Mejor cumpleaños
de niña
Mi mejor cumpliaños fue cuando
venimos de El Salvador a Denver.
Y fue el mejor cumpliaños de
siempre. Yo tenia 4 años y mi
hermana 9 años. Y fue un cumpliaños
maravilloso Mi cumpliaños es en
Enero 28, 1987 y mi Mamá nos compro
globos para poner y luego compro
el pastel y era de hielo para
meterse en el friser. Y el siguiente
dia lla era mi cumpliaños y
mi mamá y mi abuela fueron
a comprar el regalo para mi y
mi hermana. El cumpliaños
de mi hermana es el Enero 9,
pero no los selebraron junto. Despues
y el señor de la renta el que
deja el apartamento y nosotros nos
quedamos con los que deben la
casa y ellos nos quidaron la señor

FIGURE 3.3A Leticia's Spanish Writing Sample

Leticia's writing sample demonstrates clearly a divergent discourse pattern. Leticia's writing sample has several stories embedded within it, none of which are written in a linear way. She begins by setting the stage—talking about when her best birthday was and how her mother got ready for it (cake and balloons). She then tells us when her birthday is and that her mom and grandma went to buy presents for her that day. Then she switches topics to discuss her sister's birthday and that they celebrated their birthdays together. Then she switches to staying at the landlord's house while her mother and the landlord went to buy presents. She then switches back to the birthday party and what presents she received and what they ate.

While her story shows an ability to write in complete sentences using complex thoughts, it is not a linear accounting of her best birthday. Although reviewers of Leticia's story acknowledged her ability to write a story, they saw her story as disjointed and lacking in logical sequencing. Two raters (using the Escuela Bril-

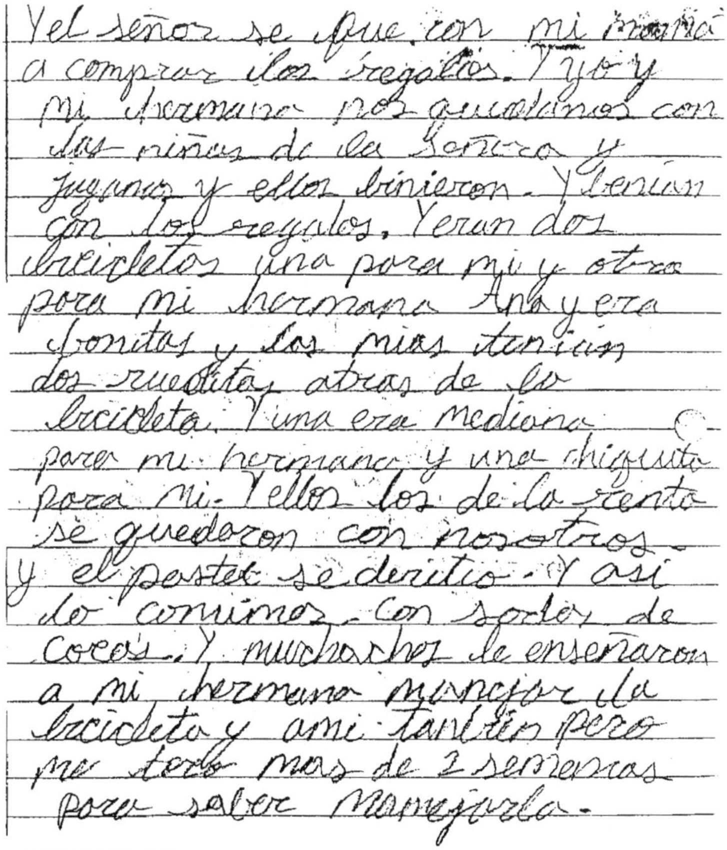
Y el señor se fue con mi mamá
a comprar los regalitos. Y yo y
mi hermana nos quedamos con
los niños de la Señora y
jugamos y ellos vinieron. Y venían
con los regalos. Y eran dos
bicicletas una para mi y otra
para mi hermana Ana y era
bonitas y las mias tenian
dos rueditas atras de la
bicicleta. Y una era mediana
para mi hermana y una chiquita
para mi. Y ellos los de la renta
se quedaron con nosotros.
y el pastel se derritio. Y así
lo comimos. Con sodas de
cocos. Y muchachos le enseñaron
a mi hermana manejar la
bicicleta y ami tanbien pero
me tardo mas de 2 semanas
para saber manejarla.

FIGURE 3.3A Continued

My Best Birthday

My best birthday was when we came from El Salvador to Denver and it was the best birthday ever. I was 4 years old and my sister was 9 years old. it was a marvelous birthday. My birthday is on the 28th of January, 1987 and my mother bought us balloons to hang up and then she bought cake and it was an ice cream cake to put in the freezer. And the next day it was my birthday and my mom and my grandmother went to buy a present for me and my sister. My sister's birthday is the 9th of January, but we celebrated it together. Then, the landlord, the one that owns the apartment, and us we stayed with the ones that live in the house and the wife of the landlord took care of us. The landlord went with my mom to buy the presents. And my sister and I stayed and played with the girls and they came home. And they came with the presents. And they were two bicycles, one for me and one for my sister Ana and they were pretty and mine had two wheels on back of the bicycle. and one was medium for my sister and one was small for me. And the two landlords stayed with us and the cake melted. And that's how we ate it with coca-cola. And boys showed my sister how to ride her bike and me too but it took me two weeks to learn how to ride it.

FIGURE 3.3B   Leticia's Writing Sample, English Translation

lante Writing Assessment Rubric in Appendix, model 4) gave her a score of 3 for this sample. A 3 score means that her writing is marginal and not competent.

We see a similar pattern in Brenda's writing (Figure 3.4). Brenda started school as a Spanish speaker and is now an English speaker and writer. She has been transitioned from Spanish reading to English reading, but her writing in English still reflects Spanish discourse patterns.

Brenda starts by telling us the story of Selena (the famous Mexican American singer who was murdered in 1995). In the middle of the story she starts to tell us about Selena's killer, a woman named Yolanda Saldivar, and then starts to tell Yolanda's story. In the end, she returns to the topic of Selena being a very popular singer. In Brenda's story we also see divergent discourse patterns. Raters of this writing sample also note that her story digressed from its original topic. Brenda was given a score of 3 on the English writing rubric (see Appendix, model 3) marking her as marginally competent in writing.

Using Kaplan's (1992) schema of Spanish discourse, we find that both Leticia and Brenda are really quite competent writers. Kaplan discusses Spanish discourse patterns as being divergent, often switching from one topic to another and then returning back to the first topic. Using Kaplan's schema, neither Leticia's nor Brenda's writing is disjointed and lacking in logical sequence. Instead, it is appropriate to the discourse style of Spanish speakers.

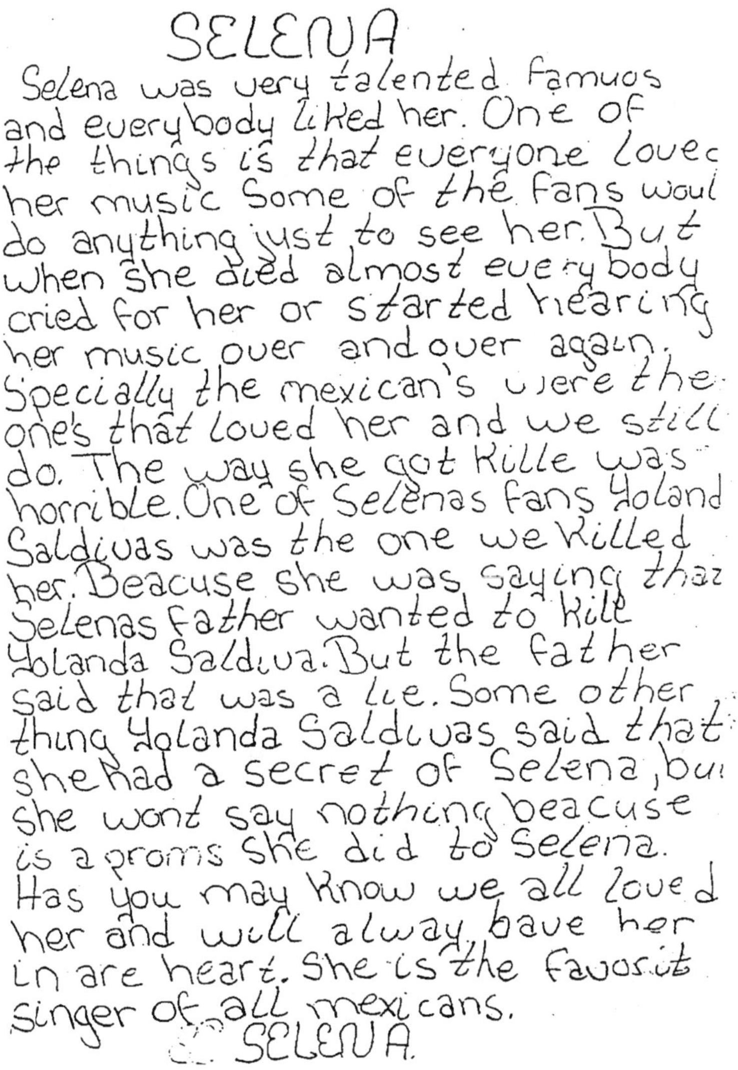

SELENA

Selena was very talented famuos and everybody liked her. One of the things is that everyone lovec her music Some of the fans woul do anything just to see her. But when she died almost every body cried for her or started hearing her music over and over again. Specially the mexican's were the one's that loved her and we still do. The way she got Kille was horrible. One of Selenas fans Yoland Saldivas was the one we killed her. Beacuse she was saying that Selenas father wanted to Kill Yolanda Saldiva. But the father said that was a lie. Some other thing Yolanda Saldivas said that she had a secret of Selena, but She wont say nothing beacuse is a promis She did to Selena. Has you may Know we all loved her and will alway bave her in are heart. She is the favorit singer of all mexicans.
SELENA.

FIGURE 3.4   Brenda's Writing Sample

The second issue related to the wholesale adaptation of writing rubrics from English to Spanish has to do with the balance between mechanics and content. At the intermediate level, many writing rubrics give equal weight to mechanics and content. This equal weighting is true of the Escuela Brillante Writing Rubric in the Appendix (all models in both English and Spanish).

This equal weighting may also penalize Spanish speakers. The phonetic regularity of Spanish facilitates learning to read; however, it makes learning to write more difficult. In Spanish, many letters share the same sound (e.g., b/v;

ll/y; c,s,z). Spanish writers must gain control of rules around the use of accents, tildes, and the dieresis. None of these conventions exist in English. English writing rubrics obviously do not account for Spanish writing conventions (see Appendix, models 2 and 4); therefore, they provide no direction for a teacher as to when a student should have control over them. Equal weighting of content and mechanics, and lack of directions for which mechanical conventions students should master by certain grade levels may once again serve to underestimate the writing ability of Spanish speakers. The following examples illustrate this point.

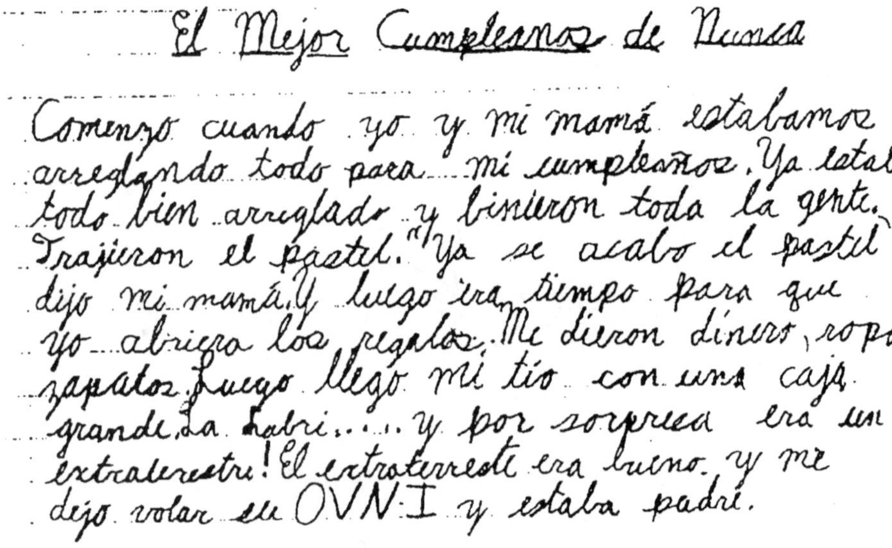

FIGURE 3.5A   Francisco's Writing Sample, Spanish Version

My Best Birthday

It started when my mom and I were getting everything ready for my birthday. Everything was ready and all of the people arrived. They brought a cake. "The cake is all gone" said my mom. Then it was time to open my presents. I got money, clothes, shoes. Then my uncle arrived with a big box. I opened it...........and what a surprise it was an alien from space. The extraterrestrial was great and it let me fly in his OVNI and it was awesome.

FIGURE 3.5B   Francisco's Writing Sample, English Translation

Francisco's writing sample (Figure 3.5A, B) clearly shows mature thinking. He uses complicated sentences and builds the reader up with the suspense of wondering what the "best present" might be. He lists presents he received that were "ok" but not exciting (money, clothes, shoes), and then he says his uncle came with a big box. He further shows knowledge of literary language when he uses the ellipsis (......) to indicate an incomplete sentence and to create more suspense. He then demonstrates great imagination when he talks about the best present being the alien and the ride in the space ship.

Francisco's score for this writing sample, using the writing rubric for intermediate students in the Appendix, was a 3* (Appendix, model 4). This score, 3*, represents a student who can compose a highly competent paper that is lacking in one or more basic skills. The raters said that his writing was competent from a content standpoint but had significant mechanical problems.

Francisco's writing demonstrated how mechanical issues in Spanish writing differ greatly from English. For example, Francisco does not yet apply the accent rule related to the third person preterite (e.g., *acabo* instead of *acabó* and *comenzo* instead of *comenzó*). In spelling he uses b when he should use v (e.g., *binieron* instead of *vinieron*), and uses h inappropriately (e.g., *habrí* instead of *abrí*).

The descriptors in the writing rubric (Appendix, model 4) say that competent writers (level 4) have spelling skills that are appropriate for the grade level; however, grade level spelling skills are different in Spanish than English. No direction is given to the rater as to what constitutes "good spelling" in Spanish for an intermediate student. When, for example, should students know the rule about accents as markers of the past tense? Or, when should a student have control over the use of h? H is a difficult letter to control in Spanish because it does not make a sound. Alfredo's writing sample further illustrates this issue.

Alfredo's writing sample (Figure 3.6A,B) illustrates some of the same issues as Francisco's. Alfredo demonstrates an ability to write an interesting and complex story about his best birthday. He skillfully uses foreshadowing to grab the reader's attention and to build up to his fabulous present. In terms of content, his story, on the Escuela Brillante writing rubric, is easily a level 5 or 6; however, Alfredo has some of the same mechanical problems that Francisco had. He uses descriptive vocabulary (e.g., *fábulo, fantástico*), and spells the words correctly, but he does not put accents on them. He does not use accent marks on verbs in the imperfect past tense (e.g., *quería*). Like Francisco, he does not know which words require h (e.g., he writes *echo* instead of *hecho* and *abía* instead of *había*). Alfredo's writing sample also received a score of 3* because of mechanics (Appendix, model 4).

As stated above, English writing rubrics give equal weight to content and mechanics. Our research has led us to observe many Spanish writers who are very competent story writers. In many cases, however, their mechanical skills are such that their overall score drops below the range of competent. While this phenomena also occurs in English, it occurs much more frequently in Spanish. These data suggest a need for different weighting of content and mechanics for

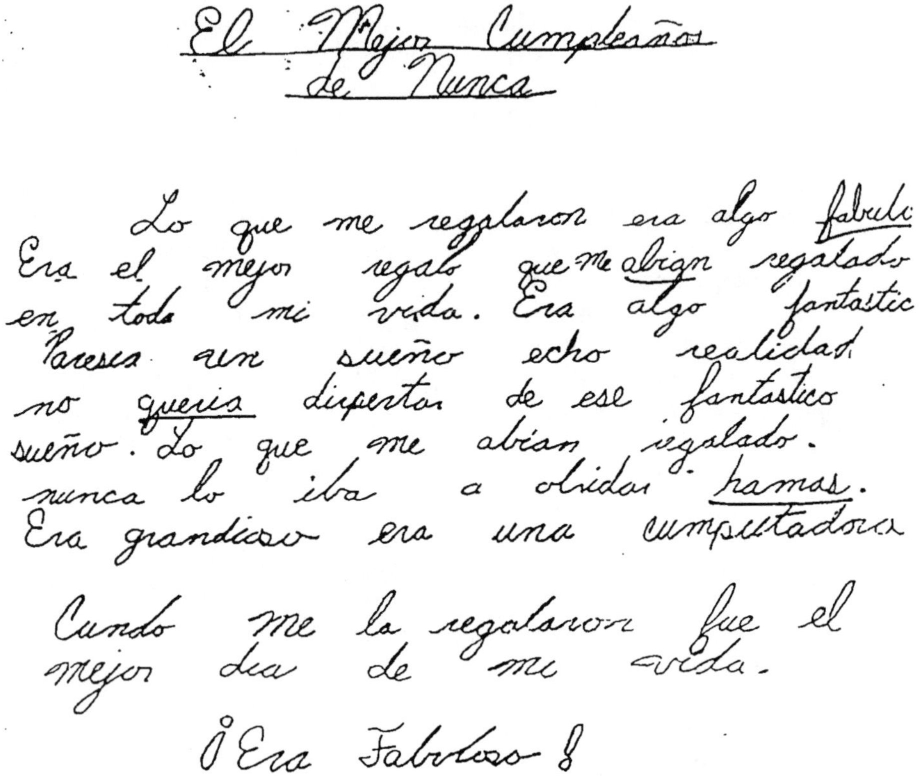

El Mejor Cumpleaños de Nunca

Lo que me regalaron era algo fabulo
Era el mejor regalo que me abian regalado
en toda mi vida. Era algo fantastic
Pareses un sueño echo realidad
no quería dispertar de ese fantastico
sueño. Lo que me abian regalado.
nunca lo iba a olvidar. hamas.
Era grandioso era una computadora

Cundo me la regalaron fue el
mejor dia de mi vida.

¡Era Fabuloso!

FIGURE 3.6A   Alfredo's Writing Sample, Spanish Version

My Best Birthday

What they gave me was fabulous. It was the best present that they had given me in my whole life. It was something fantastic. It was like a dream come true. I didn't want to wake up from this fantastic dream. I will never forget what they gave me. It was grandiose, it was a computer.

When they gave it to me, it was the best day of my life.

It was fabulous!

FIGURE 3.6B   Alfredo's Writing Sample, English Translation

Spanish writers. Spanish works differently than English, and these differences must be reflected on writing rubrics.

The third and perhaps the most important reason to use holistic writing assessment is to improve the teaching of writing. As was demonstrated above, however, Spanish writing rubrics developed directly from English cannot provide good feed-back to teachers in how to improve writing in Spanish. For assessment to drive instruction, Spanish writing assessments must help guide teachers so that they can help students become better writers.

Schools and teachers should develop Spanish writing rubrics that connect to writing instruction in Spanish. Both instructional practices and assessment must be developed from the standpoint of how the Spanish language works. This includes conventions such as punctuation and the use of accents, spelling issues and development, and the rhetorical structures of Spanish. Much can be learned by examining language arts texts in Spanish and studying methods used to teach reading and writing in Spanish-speaking countries (e.g., *Ficheros de Actividades Didácticas en Español* is the language arts program published by the Secretary of Education in Mexico). These books provide excellent guidance in how literacy in Spanish is developed and taught in Spanish-speaking countries.

When Spanish-speaking students are learning to write in English they must be explicitly taught English linear logic and the rhetorical and discourse patterns used in English writing. It is not enough to simply learn the mechanics of writing in English as a second language. Students must also learn how to "think" in English. The writing samples of Lupe (see Figure 3.1) and Brenda (see Figure 3.4) show us that this does not happen automatically.

Final Thoughts

The best kinds of assessment support the learning of both students and teachers (Townsend, Fu, & Lamme, 1997). Writing assessment in both English and Spanish that considers each language on its own structure and discourse patterns can help teachers learn about the nature of developing bilinguals and be more reflective of what two-language learners do as they learn to write in two languages.

Study after study has cautioned against assessment practices that do not look at students as a whole (Camp, 1993; Townsend, Fu, & Lamme, 1997). The case of the two Lupes presented at the beginning of the chapter provide concrete support for this research. If we only view Lupe in English, we see a struggling second-language writer. Her lack of proficiency in English prevents a teacher from seeing her academic accomplishments. Assessment practices in bilingual classrooms or for two-language children with previous schooling that do not look at student literacy in two languages are, in effect, not looking at children as a whole.

Belcher and Braine (1995) state that academic literacy processes are never "neutral, value-free and nonexlusionary" (p. xiii). Delpit (1988) has further cautioned that the "culture of power," which includes linguistic forms and communicative strategies, reinforces the power differential between participants of linguistically and culturally diverse backgrounds. An extension of this is that assessment practices for Spanish-speaking students currently reflects and reinforces this culture of power. This is seen in the adaptation of English writing rubrics into Spanish with their emphases on linear logic and notions of balance between mechanics and content in writing assessment. Williamson (1993) acknowledges

> Writing assessment currently serves to enforce the norms of a particular dialect of English and equates success with mastery of that dialect and with joining the cultural group for whom the use of that dialect is the norm. Changing the writing assessment to allow for a diversity of usage involves changing the rules for people who have previously enjoyed success. (p. 35)

This, then, is the challenge. For writing assessment to be authentic for Spanish speakers who are developing biliteracy, the rules need to change.

Many states are now using writing rubrics to determine which students have met state writing standards. Some states allow students to write in Spanish as a way of meeting the standard; however, if Spanish writing competence is judged by English writing standards, Spanish speakers are still less likely to meet state writing standards, even if assessed in Spanish. Bilingual programs, as well as their students, are once again assessed as being ineffective even when holistic assessment measures are used.

Montaño-Harmon (1991) and Delpit (1988) suggest that when students write in English they be explicitly taught and encouraged to use English discourse patterns. Further, when they are writing in Spanish, they need to be explicitly taught and encouraged to use the discourse patterns of Spanish. Only in this way can students truly become biliterate.

There is a very promising trend in some school district bilingual programs that emphasizes biliteracy as a program goal. Biliteracy is possible, and it is desirable; however, the assessment of progress toward biliteracy must include the development of authentic assessment practices that include forms, functions, and discourse patterns of each language. Teachers and directors of assessment must question the simplicity of adaptation of English language assessments into Spanish and other languages. Creation of authentic assessment requires looking at how individual languages work and how children develop when they learn to read and write in these languages and in second languages. One size does not fit all.

Writing rubrics can be very useful tools for helping teachers assess student progress, for aligning instruction and assessment, and for having conversations about the language arts curriculum. They can also be powerful tools for assessing emerging biliteracy or to assess students' knowledge of their first language. We encourage teachers and schools to use them and to make them authentic for use in English and Spanish.

Educators must use parallel structures when creating writing rubrics; however, the content of writing rubrics must represent accurately the language being assessed. The rubrics included in this chapter's Appendix are appropriate for both English and Spanish writers because they do not demand English linear sequence. This logical sequence can vary from English to Spanish. Teachers, however, must understand how logical sequence in Spanish may differ from English. Similarly, for primary grades, the rubrics do not judge a student's mastery of writing conventions (spelling, punctuation, etc.), and therefore, Spanish speakers who primarily write using invented (or phonemic) spelling are not penalized.

In the case of the two rubrics in the Appendix, we suggest that the Spanish rubric be revised in the following ways. For intermediate students, schools and teachers should discuss exactly what Spanish conventions students are expected to control to be considered a competent writer. These need to be explicitly stated. Examples include if students are expected to use accent marks in commonly used words (e.g., *mamá, papá*) or in the third person singular in the preterite tense (e.g., *comenzó, hablé*). Other examples include spelling rules such as those for using h, b/v, ll, and y. Knowing exactly which conventions students are expected to control can help to inform instruction for teachers.

Finally, we end this article where we began, with a second look at Lupe. By creating authentic writing samples that look at student development in two languages, we no longer see Lupe as a student who is "struggling in writing," and having "problems putting ideas together." Assessing Lupe in two languages enables us to see her as a developing biliterate who is a competent and thoughtful writer in Spanish and who is using her literacy in Spanish as a bridge to English. Authentic two-language assessment enables us to observe Lupe's strengths and her instructional needs. In short, assessment in two languages helps us understand the whole student, not bits and pieces.

DISCUSSION QUESTIONS

1. How might writing assessment in two languages be used by teachers who are not bilingual teachers or for students who do not receive instruction in two languages?

2. Do students learning to write in Spanish stay in invented spelling stages longer than students learning to write in English? If so, how should writing rubrics be revised to accommodate this difference across languages?

3. In assessing the writing of Spanish speaking and English speaking students in intermediate grades, should mechanics and content be given equal weight? Justify your answer.

4. Primary students are given a fictional prompt (a shy dragon), and intermediate students are asked to write about a real event (a favorite birthday). Would it be better for all students to write about real events? Justify your answer.

5. Discuss how writing assessments that utilize rubrics can be used to improve writing instruction.

REFERENCES

Belcher, D., & Braine, G. (Eds.) (1995). *Academic writing in a second language.* Norwood, NJ: Ablex.

Camp, R. (1993). Changing the model for writing assessment. In M. Williamson & B. Huot. (Eds.), *Validating holistic scoring for writing assessment.* Cresskill, NJ: Hampton Press.

Carlisle, R. (1989). The writing of Anglo and Hispanic elementary school students in bilingual, submersion, and regular programs. *Studies in Second Language Acquisition, 11*(3), 257–281.

Delpit. L. (1988). The silenced dialogue: Power and pedagogy in educating other people's children. *Harvard Educational Review, 58,* 280–298.

Estrella Brillante Writing Assessment. (1996). Brighton, CO: Adams County School District #27J.

Fredericks, A. D., & Rasinski, T. V. (1997). Involving parents in the assessment process. *The Reading Teacher, 44,* 346–349.

Gersten, R., & Jiménez, R. (1998). *Promoting learning for culturally and linguistically diverse students.* Belmont, CA: Wadsworth.

Goldenberg, C. (1998). A balanced approach to early Spanish literacy instruction. In R. Gersten & R. Jiménez (Eds.), *Promoting learning for culturally and linguistically diverse students.* Belmont, CA: Wadsworth.

Hunter, D., Jones, R., & Randhawa, B. (1996). The use of holistic versus analytic scoring for large-scale assessment of writing. *The Canadian Journal of Program Evaluation, 11*(2), 61–65.

Kaplan, R. (1970). Cultural thought patterns in intercultural education. *Language Learning, 16*(11).

Luther, F. (1997). *First nations preservice women teachers' experiences and perceptions regarding technology.* Unpublished doctoral dissertation, University of Saskatchewan.

Montaño-Harmon, M. (1991). Discourse features of written Mexican Spanish: Current research in contrastive rhetoric and its implications. *Hispania, 74*(2), 417–425.

Muñoz-Sandoval, A., Cummins, J., Alvarado, C., & Ruef, M. (1998). *Research in bilingualism: Implications for assessment.* Paper presented at the Annual Meeting of the American Education Research Association (AERA), San Diego, CA.

Rhodes, L., & Shanklin, N. (1993). *Windows into literacy: Assessing learners K–8.* Portsmouth, NH: Heinemann.

Townsend, J., Fu, D., & Lamme, L. (1997). Writing assessment: Multiple perspectives, multiple purposes. *Preventing School Failure, 41*(2), 71–76.

Weld County School District #6 Writing Assessment. (1993). Greeley, CO: Weld County School District #6.

Williamson, M. (1993). An introduction to holisitc scoring. In M. Williamson & B. Huot (Eds.), *Validating holistic scoring for writing assessment.* Cresskill, NJ: Hampton Press.

Models for Evaluating Writing English and Spanish

LEVEL

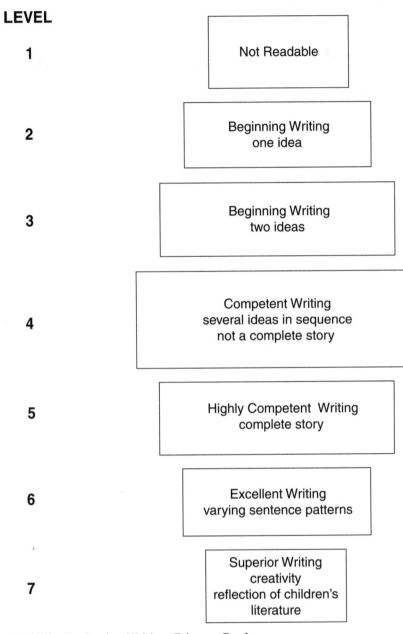

1	Not Readable
2	Beginning Writing one idea
3	Beginning Writing two ideas
4	Competent Writing several ideas in sequence not a complete story
5	Highly Competent Writing complete story
6	Excellent Writing varying sentence patterns
7	Superior Writing creativity reflection of children's literature

Model for Evaluating Writing: Primary Grades

LEVEL

1

Not Readable unsustained writing

2

Beginning Writing significantly deficient in several skill areas

3

Marginally Competent deficient in one or more skill areas

4

Competent Writing basic skills OK spelling, complete sentences, varying sentence patterns, punctuation, and capitalization

5

Highly Competent Writing thinking, complicated sentences, descriptive vocabulary*

6

Excellent Writing one passage of superior writing

7

Sustained Superior Writing literary style

Model for Evaluating Writing: Intermediate Grades

* The student can compose a highly competent paper with characteristics of level 6 or 7 writing. The paper, however, is not competent in one or more basic skills listed above for level 4.

NIVEL

1

> Escritura Pre-inicial
> No se puede leer

2

> Escritura Inicial
> Una idea

3

> Escritura Inicial
> Dos ideas

4

> Escritura Competente
> Varias ideas en un orden logico, pero no
> cuenta un cuento completo

5

> Escritura Muy Competente
> Cuento completo

6

> Escritura Excelente
> Oraciones que tienen diversas
> ideas y formas variadas

7

> Escritura Superior
> Creatividad que
> refleja la literatura
> infantil

Modelo Para Evaluar La Escritura: Grados K, 1, 2

NIVEL

1

> Escritura Pre-Inicial
> Escritura incompleta o
> que no se puede leer.

2

> Escritura Inicial
> Tiene fuerte defectos en
> varias destrezas.

3

> Competente Marginal
> Tiene defectos en una o mas
> destrezas.

4

> Competente
> Destrezas basicas en un nivel aceptable,
> ortografia, oraciones completas, oraciones
> con pensamientos variados, punctuacion, el
> uso de mayusculas. Tal vez sea un cuento
> que no es interesante.

5
(3*)

> Muy Competente
> Demuestra pensamientos con
> oraciones complicadas, vocabulario
> descriptivo, demuestra madurez.

6

> Excelente
> Demuestra una habilidad
> superior en escritura. Un
> trozo de escritura excelente.

7

> Superior
> Demuestra una
> habilidad superior de
> escritura sostenida.
> Usa un estilo literario.

Modelo Para Evaluar Escritura Nivel Intermedio: Grados 3, 4, 5

3* El/la estudiante puede producir un trabajo muy competente con caracteristicas de escritura al nivel 6 o 7. Sin embargo, el trabajo no demuestra competencia en una o mas destrezas basicas necesarias para llegar al nivel 4.

4 Assessment of Reading Comprehension Strategies for Intermediate Bilingual Learners

LORRAINE VALDEZ PIERCE
George Mason University

Ms. Brown

Ms. Brown, a middle school reading specialist, has an English-as-a-second-language (ESL) student, Roberto, who speaks English quite well but has a reading problem. Ms. Brown believes her students need a firm grounding in phonics before advancing to basal readers. Roberto appears to be bored by the phonics worksheets and has shown no interest at all in the basal readers. He seems to be lazy and unconcerned about his lack of progress. Ms. Brown has students work alone at their desks because using group work makes them get disruptive and off task. After all, reading is an individual process, isn't it? Ms. Brown has told the ESL teacher that Roberto would probably learn to read sooner if he were more motivated, or if his parents valued education more, or even if they stopped speaking Spanish at home. That would probably do it. Roberto has done poorly on the reading subtests of the standardized achievement tests required by the state for high school graduation. He also does not do well on the matching and multiple-choice tests Ms. Brown gives for reading comprehension. Ms. Brown suspects Roberto may have a learning disability.

Ms. Green

Ms. Green, Roberto's ESL teacher, has a different picture of his reading abilities. Even though Roberto is not yet a proficient reader, he has shown an interest in action comic books, sports magazines, and books on photography. When Ms. Green brings in news articles on current events, movies, and popular TV shows, Roberto wants to sit with

friends and tell them everything he knows about these subjects. According to her anecdotal records, Roberto has some problems with decoding but is well on his way to
using reading strategies such as activating prior knowledge, predicting, and summarizing to enhance his reading comprehension. Based on his initial reading interest interview and Ms. Green's subsequent observations, Roberto seems full of interests and
a desire to share them.

Roberto, an energetic 13-year-old, likes Ms. Green because she lets her students
talk in class and read fun stuff, not boring stuff like in Ms. Brown's class. Ms. Green
has a whole classroom library of interesting books and magazines that he likes to take
home and from which he studies new words. Ms. Brown seems to think he is slow, but
Ms. Green has shown a real interest in his likes and dislikes. Roberto knows he is not
a good reader, and he would like to get better, but he doesn't think Ms. Brown's class
is going to help him very much.

What the Research Says

In the situation just described, we have been privy to three different perspectives
of a bilingual student's reading progress: his reading teacher's, his ESL teacher's,
and his own. We have also seen how the same student can be perceived differently
depending on each teacher's approach to teaching reading. This perception is
shaped by a teacher's understanding of how reading in a first and subsequent
languages is the same yet different, awareness of recent findings from research
on reading comprehension, and familiarity with innovative approaches to assessment. To understand the most promising approaches for assessment of reading
with second language learners, we begin with a brief overview of research and
emerging trends from the fields of second language acquisition, reading instruction, and authentic assessment.

The research in second language acquisition indicates that the process of reading in first and additional languages is similar except for two important resources
that language learners bring to reading in a second language: shared prior (and
cultural) knowledge and proficiency in the language of the text (Peregoy & Boyle,
1997; Chamot & O'Malley, 1994). Because ESL/bilingual students come from such
a wide variety of backgrounds, their prior knowledge about reading and their experiences with reading vary. In addition, students come with culturally based concepts and principles that may differ from those reflected in English language texts.
Some students may have experience using reading strategies in the native language
but may not be aware of their application in a second language. This is important
because reading strategies, like other learning strategies, do not necessarily transfer
from one language to another automatically (Grabe, 1988). In Roberto's case, the
ESL teacher was clearly taking advantage of Roberto's prior experience and knowledge to motivate him to read and talk about what he reads. Roberto shows some
evidence of using reading strategies but probably needs to consolidate these by
reading challenging English language texts and acquiring new strategies.

Research over the past two decades in the field of reading instruction indicates the benefits of teaching reading comprehension strategies directly. These benefits are especially evident when reading strategies are taught to developing readers. Students who are provided extensive amounts of time for reading in class, opportunities to collaborate with others on reading-related tasks, and encouragement to make personal responses and engage in discussions of reading are more likely to become better readers (Fielding & Pearson, 1994). For students reading in content areas (such as social studies and science), inappropriate background knowledge or schema can limit reading comprehension, as can limited knowledge of text structure and reading strategies (Alvermann & Phelps, 1994; Vacca & Vacca, 1996). Teaching students how to use prereading, during-reading, and postreading strategies can help students make the most of time spent reading in content areas (Peregoy & Boyle, 1997). In the field of second language reading, giving choices for what students read, providing access to high-quality texts, and encouraging free voluntary reading are all widely advocated (Freeman & Freeman, 1992; Kim & Krashen, 1997; Peregoy & Boyle, 1997). In addition, encouraging students to work on carefully structured group tasks provides scaffolding for linguistic and social development for all learners (Kagan, 1994). Ms. Green sets up learning activities so that students have choices in what they read, get to talk about what they read, and engage in tasks that are carefully structured to promote each student's active application of reading comprehension strategies.

In addition to insights provided by the fields of second language acquisition and reading research, recent trends in assessment in general education can help inform assessment approaches for English-language learners. These trends suggest the limitations of standardized achievement tests when used as the sole indicators of student achievement (Herman, Aschbacher, & Winters, 1992). Standardized tests are limited in that they tend to assess lower-order skills. Even advanced placement (AP) tests call for only single-answer responses, not problem solving, generated responses, or direct demonstrations of competence. In the case of English-language learners, language becomes a confounding variable that makes it difficult to determine a student's need for language or for content area instruction. It may also be that students need to learn test-taking skills. To be valid and useful, assessment needs to match what students are learning in classrooms and provide information on learning processes and the products of learning.

An increasing number of researchers and practitioners now support the use of innovative, alternative assessments such as performance-based and authentic assessments with English-language learners (Fradd & Hudelson, 1995; Gardner, 1996; Gottlieb, 1995; Mathias, 1993; McNamara & Deane, 1995; O'Malley & Valdez Pierce, 1996; Pearson & Berhoff, 1996; Smollen, Newman, Wathen, & Lee, 1995). Assessment is authentic when it is embedded in classroom instruction and reflects real-life tasks, involves the learner in his or her own assessment, and has as its purpose to inform instruction. Proponents of alternative and authentic assessment realize that assessment results are useful for more than just assigning student grades or determining whether students are to remain in a bilingual or ESL program. Assessment results can best be used to provide the teacher with feedback on how to change direction in the lesson plan to better meet students' needs. Ms. Green uses authentic assessments such as anecdotal records, reading strategies rating scales, and journals to monitor each student's progress and to modify her instructional plans based on student performance.

Active involvement of students in monitoring their own progress may help increase student motivation, learning, and self-esteem (Herman, et al., 1992; O'Malley & Valdez Pierce, 1996; Paris & Ayers, 1994). Students who can learn to assess their own progress are on their way to becoming independent learners who can take standardized achievement tests of reading with confidence. When students are provided with a purpose for assessment and clear criteria for evaluation of their work (in the form of scoring rubrics, checklists, and benchmark papers), they are better able to set goals for learning and to work toward self-improvement. In addition, when students are asked for their input on how they are to be assessed, and when assessment activities are tied to real-life tasks and personal experiences, student motivation may increase and positively affect learning. Roberto's ESL teacher is enrolled in a graduate class in which she is learning how to lead her students in the process of self-assessment. She plans to help each student monitor his or her own learning over the course of the year.

Implications for Practice

Based on our brief review of the research on second language acquisition, reading instruction, and innovations in assessment, what implications can we see for the assessment of bilingual learners reading in a second language? If prior knowledge plays an important role in learning how to read, then we need to assess a student's activation of that knowledge. This may include knowledge of culture, history, content areas, and text structure. Because teaching reading comprehension strategies directly helps increase reading achievement, then we need to assess the extent to which bilingual students are able to apply these strategies before, during, and after they read. Providing time in class for students to read helps improve reading ability, and we need to assess how students use this time, what choices they make in reading, and how much they understand of what they read. By creating opportunities for students to work together on reading-related tasks and projects, we help improve reading comprehension. We need to assess not only the product of this collaboration but also the process. To what extent did each student participate? More importantly, we need to set up collaborative classrooms that provide regular chunks of time for students to work together on meaningful reading-based activities. In encouraging students to make personal responses to what they read, we help them comprehend more. We need to assess the quality of thinking behind those responses. Finally, if guiding students to monitor their own progress helps them become independent readers, then we also need to assess how students are applying these self-assessment strategies.

Practical Classroom Applications

Approaches to assessment of reading must better capture current research and practice in the teaching of reading and in second language acquisition. In this section, we look at applications of assessment in second language reading with a focus on reading comprehension strategies. These include prereading, during-reading, and postreading strategies. First, we examine opportunities for assessment of prereading strategies with the use of an anticipation guide. Second, we will look at assessment of during-reading strategies through a reciprocal teaching activity. Last, we turn postreading activities such as journals into opportunities for assessment of reading strategies. The activities described here can probably be used with students of all ages, although some are more appropriate for one age group than another. Dialogue journals, for example, can be used with children as young as kindergarteners (Routman, 1994), while reciprocal teaching might be more useful with older students. Anticipation guides can be written at the reading level of beginners or read aloud to them to ensure their participation.

In turning instructional activities for reading into assessment tools, we must keep three things in mind: (1) to document and record what we observe; (2) to compare student performance to a specific standard or criterion (rather than making subjective judgments or comparing students to each other); and (3) to provide clear feedback to students on their progress on a regular and frequent basis. We can document application of reading comprehension strategies through the use of scoring rubrics, checklists, anecdotal records, and other assessment tools. The standards and criteria to which student performance are compared are provided in these documents. By keeping systematic records of student progress, we can provide students (and their parents) with feedback on what they can do well and what they still need to work on. Once learning goals have been set, the teacher can guide students in setting priorities and realistic time frames for increasing reading comprehension.

Assessment of Prereading Strategies

Various types of instructional activities may be used to assess student knowledge and to set a purpose before reading. These include brainstorming, previewing, graphic organizers, guided imagery, student-generated questions (as in know-want to know-learned or K-W-L activities) field trips, videos and films, experiments, book or text study guides, and anticipation guides (Peregoy & Boyle, 1996; Vacca & Vacca, 1996). To demonstrate assessment of prereading strategies, we describe the use of an anticipation guide. The purpose of an anticipation guide is to activate students' prior knowledge, encourage predicting of the reading content, set a purpose for reading, and motivate students to read (Alvermann & Phelps, 1994; Peregoy & Boyle, 1997; Tierney, Readence, & Dishner, 1995). Because an anticipation-guide activity is conducted in small groups, it promotes collaboration between students (supported by the research on reading comprehension) and development of oral language proficiency.

Before reading a text, students using an anticipation guide are asked to react to several statements by expressing an opinion on familiar but controversial subjects or those which appear to have logically or intuitively correct answers. For example, a statement such as, "It is better to be rich than poor," will probably elicit an opinion from just about everyone. After students express their individual opinions on each statement, they can discuss them in small groups and try to reach consensus on each one. Then they predict whether their point of view is supported by the author of the text. The controversial and logical aspect serves to involve students with the text. Students read to determine whether their predictions are correct. When students have a purpose for reading, they are better able to monitor their comprehension than when they do not. During the discussion of student predictions, the teacher must be open to a wide range of answers and be nondirective in responding to them to encourage independent thinking (Vacca & Vacca, 1996). After reading, students compare their positions to those of their peers and of the author. At this point, misconceptions can be discussed and clarified. Anticipation guides are particularly useful for bringing to light strongly held misconceptions on a subject and increasing the acquisition of new concepts, especially in math and science (Alvermann & Phelps, 1994).

For those students who are not yet proficient enough to read the text independently, the teacher can choose from a range of scaffolding approaches to facilitate participation. In construction, scaffolds are structures that provide access and safety to out of reach places. Teachers can provide scaffolding in various ways, for example by previewing vocabulary or building background knowledge. One way to support weaker readers is to pair them with a buddy who can assist either with translation or clarification in the second language. Another way to assist these learners is to allow them to prepare the text in advance so that they are familiar with the topic and vocabulary before working in small groups. A final option is to allow readers to join the group discussion without feeling obligated to read the entire text.

In drafting statements for an anticipation guide, teachers must consider students' prior knowledge and go beyond facts to strongly held opinions that are misconceptions or that can be defended from multiple perspectives (Tierney, et al., 1995). For example, a statement on the number of calories burned during exercise represents a fact, while a statement on the personal value of exercise represents an opinion. For language minority students, teachers must be careful to express statements in such a way as to avoid offending a student's deeply held cultural and/or religious beliefs; however, challenging those beliefs should not be considered the same as condemning them. An example of an anticipation guide appears in Figure 4.1. It has been modified from Tierney, et al. (1995) to allow for group interaction and discussion as well as for reaching consensus on a position. Reaching consensus can be used to teach students that it is sometimes necessary to compromise to move forward as a group. As you review the anticipation guide, think of how you might use it to assess students' application of prereading strategies. Figure 4.1 has been developed for high intermediate English language learners in the upper elementary grades. For

FIGURE 4.1   Anticipation Guide

Directions: For each statement below, put a T in the blank space under "I think" if you agree with each statement. Put an Y in the space if you do not agree with the statement. Mark the position of your group under "My group thinks." Predict what the author thinks. Then read the chapter to determine if the author agrees with your group.

The Blessings of Liberty: What should the government do?

Agree	T
Disagree	Y

I think	My group thinks	Author thinks	
_____	_____	_____	1. The government should check on religions to be sure they are OK.
_____	_____	_____	2. People should be able to say anything without getting in trouble.
_____	_____	_____	3. The government should make sure nothing bad is on TV.
_____	_____	_____	4. The government should stop people from meeting together to plan something dangerous.
_____	_____	_____	5. It is the job of the government to let only good people have guns.
_____	_____	_____	6. The government should never be able to search people's homes.

Source: Adapted from a draft by Peggy McCormick (1997), Grades 5–6 ESL (intermediate level)/Social Studies teacher and George Mason University graduate student.

beginning readers, teachers should modify the language, add visuals, or opt for oral language use only.

After students conclude discussions in their small groups (about 20 minutes), and before they read the text, the teacher can ask for a report from each group to determine how they reached consensus on each statement. They can also discuss the different sides presented in response to each statement. After reading, the teacher can again lead a whole-class discussion on how each group's predictions compared to those of the author. For students who are not yet able to participate orally in whole-class discussions, the teacher can ask for a show of hands in response to questions on the text or have students raise color-coded cards indicating agreement or disagreement.

In planning for assessment of anticipation guides, we need to think of the possible purposes of the assessment. We could observe and record how students express themselves through oral language, how they cooperate with each other, how they find evidence in the text to support their points, or how well they write in response to what they read. Or, we could focus on how students use prereading strategies such as activating prior knowledge and predicting the content of the text. Two approaches that might prove fruitful in recording students' involvement with anticipation guides are anecdotal records and student self-assessment.

To use anecdotal records, the teacher notes student behaviors that indicate progress in the use of prereading strategies. You should focus on a student's ability to formulate an opinion on the reading topic, to make predictions on the content of the text, and to use evidence from the text to support opinions and predictions. To guide your observations, you could use a format such as that in Table 4.1 to record what students do in small groups. By reviewing your notes on how students use prereading strategies, you can identify those that most students need to work on and plan for instruction to increase students' effectiveness in using them.

To encourage students to reflect on how they use prior knowledge and how they modify their understanding after reading, teachers can adapt a self-assessment format similar to the one in Figure 4.2. This example asks students to identify where they reached consensus with their group and which of their predictions were confirmed in the text. They are also asked to rethink their predictions and to clarify why or how they changed their predictions after reading. For students who need extra linguistic support to respond to self-assessment questions, you may want to provide partially completed responses with options from which students can choose. Some students may respond to visual or pictorial cues such as checkmarks (✓) or X's for *agree* or *disagree,* respectively. You may conduct the self-assessment orally; however, the self-assessment may not yet be possible for beginning level students, especially if you have not provided them with regular and frequent opportunities to engage in peer and self-assessment through both oral language and writing.

TABLE 4.1 Anecdotal Record for Anticipation Guide

Student Names	Expresses an Opinion/Prior Knowledge	Predicts Content of Text	Uses Evidence from Text to Support Points
Ahmed	Hesitates in expressing his own views; seems to think there is a "correct" answer; appears to have little prior knowledge on this topic	Predicts but seems to think the author must be "right"	With some assistance
Carmen			
Santo			
Shana			

FIGURE 4.2   Self-Assessment for Anticipation Guide

Directions: Write short answers for the following questions.

1. With which of your ideas did your group agree?

2. With which of your predictions did the author agree?

3. On which predictions did you change your mind after reading?

4. Why did you change your mind after reading?

5. What have you learned from this activity?

Assessment of During-Reading Strategies

In addition to using strategies before reading, good readers apply strategies while they are reading to monitor their comprehension. Instructional activities that can promote during-reading strategies with English-language learners include note-taking, semantic maps, vocabulary study, modeling questioning strategies, learning logs, jigsaw reading, directed reading-thinking activities (DRTA), think-alouds, and reciprocal teaching (Peregoy & Boyle, 1997; Vacca & Vacca, 1996). These activities are particularly effective because they engage the learner in verbalizing the strategies they are using to make sense of print. These activities also involve collaboration, which helps develop thinking skills and oral language. Finally, activities such as notetaking and semantic maps help less proficient learners demonstrate their comprehension using graphic organizers.

In this section, we focus on reciprocal teaching for assessment of during-reading strategies. Reciprocal teaching reflects the research on explicit teaching of reading strategies (Tierney, et al., 1995). This research indicates that students must be provided with a clear definition for each strategy and made aware of its relevance and how to use it. In addition, students must be given feedback on their use of the strategy through guided practice. By giving students opportunities to try out the strategy, teachers show students how to monitor their own use of the strategy through self-assessment. The teacher models the strategies and gradually gives more responsibility to the students to apply them. Finally, students are provided with opportunities to try out the strategies in independent learning tasks.

The purpose of reciprocal teaching is to get intermediate to advanced readers to actively apply reading comprehension strategies while reading (Palincsar & Brown, 1984; Vacca & Vacca, 1996). Like the anticipation guide, a reciprocal teaching activity requires students to work in small groups, thereby increasing opportunities for collaboration and oral language development. In reciprocal teaching, the students take turns being the teacher and demonstrate for each other how to apply reading strategies by thinking aloud. As you read about this activity, think of how you might use it for assessment to gather information on students' application of reading comprehension strategies during reading.

Often while using group activities such as reciprocal teaching, teachers express concern that not all students participate equally. To overcome this limitation, collaborative activities can be structured to include each of the following elements: individual accountability, positive interdependence, and simultaneous interaction (Kagan, 1994). In reciprocal teaching, each student is individually held accountable for verbalizing application of several reading comprehension strategies. The specific reading strategies used in reciprocal teaching are *summarizing, predicting,* and *asking questions for clarification.* These three strategies are among the most difficult for language learners to master because of the complex nature of the language being used. Reciprocal teaching is an activity that can be used once students have become familiar with each of these reading strategies. By modeling this activity a number of times with the whole class and allowing them to apply strategies to unfamiliar texts in small groups, teachers can help students learn to use during-reading strategies independently. The key to reciprocal teaching is teacher modeling using a think-aloud process, describing thinking and reasoning processes that help make sense out of text, especially when students come to words they do not know. Another important element of this activity is adjusting the demand of the task when students experience difficulty. The teacher lowers the demand until students become more skilled at using reading comprehension strategies. Then the teacher gradually withdraws support so that students can apply the strategies independently.

Before starting, activate students' prereading strategies by asking them what they think the title means, what any subtitles might refer to, and what the pictures or illustrations might suggest about the content. Teaching students to tap prior knowledge related to the topic can help increase reading comprehension. To use the reciprocal teaching activity, select a reading passage that challenges but does not frustrate your students. This is your students' instructional reading level. In multilevel classes (those with students exhibiting a wide range of language proficiency), use different readings appropriate to each level, and conduct the demonstration in small, proficiency-level groups. Put between six and eight paragraphs of the text on a transparency, and give each student a copy. Tell students that you are going to demonstrate a three-step process for applying reading strategies to unfamiliar texts. Write these steps on the overhead projector or chalkboard: (1) Summarize, (2) Ask questions for clarification, and (3) Predict.

In the first step, *summarize* the main idea of the first paragraph orally and in writing. Review the essential elements of a summary, or take the time to introduce them here and follow up with many opportunities for summarizing in other activities. In the second step, *demonstrate how to ask questions for clarification* of meaning in the same paragraph. This assumes that you have provided previous practice on various questioning patterns that students can apply to this particular text. In the third step, *show students how to predict* what they think the following paragraph or the rest of the text is about. Guide students in using inferencing skills to make their predictions.

Demonstrate the three steps again, but this time ask the whole class to help you. Guide students in going beyond "What does this word mean?" kinds of questions to "I wonder why she [the author] thinks that . . ." questions. Students need to learn to read beyond words they do not know and to use context (semantic and syntactic cues) to extract meaning from texts. Ask students to generate questions for things that are unclear or that they do not understand. Provide scaffolding by restating students' questions that are incompletely formed or grammatically incorrect. Write each question on the board or overhead projector to further reinforce the sound-symbol connection. Engage students in a dialogue to clarify any misunderstandings using a thinking-reasoning process. Model for students how to use prior knowledge, how to read ahead to check for meaning, and how to guess the meaning of words from the context. If an unknown word appears to hold the key to meaning, encourage students to look it up in the dictionary, but only after all contextual resources have been tapped. For example, you can demonstrate for students the thinking process you go through when you come to an unknown word by using a think-aloud process.

After you have demonstrated the three steps of reciprocal teaching with the second paragraph, guide students in carrying out the three-step process with the next few paragraphs in groups of three or four. Each student gets a turn at being the teacher or leader and thinking aloud the use of each of the three strategies (summarizing, questioning for clarification, and predicting). Each leader engages his or her groupmates in a dialogue to make sense of the paragraph under discussion. Students who are ready to be challenged beyond their instructional level (readers not frustrated by the reading text) can work in groups with stronger readers. Heterogeneous grouping in this case can help both weak and strong students increase language skills (Kagan, 1994). By giving each student a turn at verbalizing strategies used during the reading process, you are holding each student accountable for learning how to use these during-reading strategies. When language learners are supported with in-class activities that promote application of reading strategies, they are much more likely to apply these strategies during independent reading than when they are not. Once students learn how to use a few strategies, you can lead them in making decisions as to when to use different strategies during breakdowns in comprehension. For beginning readers, the three-step reciprocal teaching process may be too much to attempt at once. When this is the case, try modeling only one of the strategies at a time until most students have had an opportunity to apply all three strategies to a reading text.

So, how do we turn a reciprocal teaching activity into assessment? We might use anecdotal records, group records, a checklist, or a rating scale. In this case, we use an analytic rating scale designed especially for language learners. An analytic scale assigns a separate rating to each aspect of performance and provides more diagnostic information than a holistic scale. A total score does not need to be calculated because the purpose of using an analytic scale is to diagnose areas of strength and weakness rather than to obtain an overall score. The sample analytic rating scale in Table 4.2 can be used to record student application of reading strategies, reading comprehension, use of oral language, and level of participation in the small group. For additional information on using anecdotal and group records in reciprocal teaching with second language learners, refer to Valdez Pierce (1998).

TABLE 4.2 Analytic Rating Scale for Reciprocal Teaching Activity

Rating	Reading Strategies	Reading Comprehension	Oral Language Use	Participation
4	Applies all 3 strategies: summarizes, asks questions for clarification, and predicts	Shows comprehension of main ideas through comments and questions	Uses language structures appropriate to each strategy; uses adequate vocabulary to communicate effectively	Takes a full turn at being the leader; provides support to others when needed
3	Applies only 2 of the 3 reading strategies	Shows some misunderstandings or partial comprehension of main ideas	Uses language structures appropriate to each strategy; makes some errors in grammar or syntax; uses adequate vocabulary to communicate effectively	Takes a full turn at being the leader; may not provide support to others when needed
2	Applies only 1 of the 3 reading strategies	Shows many misunderstandings or little comprehension of main ideas	Uses language structures appropriate to only 1 or 2 strategies; makes many errors in grammar and syntax; uses limited vocabulary and communicates partially	Takes a partial turn at being the leader; may not provide support to others when needed
1	Applies none of the 3 reading strategies	Shows little or no comprehension of main ideas	Uses few or no language structures appropriate to each strategy; makes many errors in grammar and syntax; uses limited vocabulary and communicates only minimally	Takes a limited turn at being the leader; does not provide support to others when needed

Assessment of Postreading Strategies

Once readers have finished reading a text, they must organize the information it contains to retain and build on it. Postreading strategies help students accomplish these tasks (Lapp, Flood, & Farnan, 1996; Peregoy & Boyle, 1997; Tierney, et al., 1995; Vacca & Vacca, 1996). One strategy that assists memory retention is writing.

Students can be asked to take and organize notes on what they read, to respond to what they read, and to summarize what they read. Different kinds of writing after reading might include graphic organizers, summaries, and journals. In this section, we show how to use journals for assessment of students' comprehension and retention of reading.

Journals can be of various types and include dialogue journals, double-entry journals, and literature response journals. They can be kept in spiral-bound note-books, three-ring notebooks, or in student-made booklets. Each entry is dated to record progress. In each type of journal, English-language learners are asked to write their questions, reactions, or concerns on something they have read or discussed in class and to share it privately with the teacher or a peer. For English-language learners, journal writing is functional (as in requesting information) and conversational in tone (Peyton & Reed, 1990). Journals invite open-ended responses from students, allow for regular, individual feedback from teachers, and provide insights into what each student is thinking and learning (Peregoy & Boyle, 1997; Peyton & Reed, 1990; Routman, 1994; Tierney, et al., 1995; Vacca & Vacca, 1996). Journals also promote fluency in both reading and writing, encourage risk-taking, and validate personal feelings and experiences (Routman, 1994). An important benefit of journal writing is that it increases communication between students and their teachers and allows them to get to know each other better (Peyton & Reed, 1990). Journals are nonthreatening because they are not typically corrected or graded.

Dialogue journals represent an authentic communicative exchange between the student and teacher on something read or related to reading (although they can also be used for personal communication not related to reading). Through literature response journals, English-language learners come to understand that reading can serve each individual's purpose and that going beyond factual information in a text and making a personal response to that text is strongly encouraged. With double-entry journals, language learners make one entry on the nature of the text and another on its personal meaning for them or on what they feel they have learned. These journals can provide scaffolding for reflecting on what students have read.

In addition to making personal responses to what they read, students can also write something from the perspective of a character they have read about (Vacca & Vacca, 1996). In history, they could take the role of a fictitious or real person living during a certain period of time and make an entry from that person's perspective. In science, students could take the role of an animal or force of nature and describe an event from that entity's perspective. In mathematics, students can write about their responses to lessons in light of previous experiences. This can provide insights to the teacher as to the nature of student attitudes and background in mathematics.

Based on evidence of student needs in their journals, teachers can plan minilessons on writing conventions, including how to put spaces between words, how to use punctuation, how to form paragraphs, and other writing skills. Teachers need to be sure to let parents know the purposes for journal writing unless they want to get complaints that they are not doing their job by not correcting students' journal entries for standard writing conventions (this has happened to teachers I know).

To encourage students to write in their journals, it is important to model the process various times on the overhead projector and to provide regular blocks of time in class for students to write in their journals. Demonstrate for students by brainstorming orally the kinds of questions or topics you might want to write about in response to reading or to something in your personal experience related to the reading. The brainstorming session can serve as an organizing framework or outline for things to write about while also developing oral language proficiency. Write a personal journal entry on the overhead projector in response to something your students have been reading. Do this a number of times before asking students to make their own journal entries. Through your entries, show students that they are to relate their feelings, attitudes, and concerns about something they have read or experienced. In guiding students to write, ask them to choose a topic that is important to them, tell what happened, and tell what they feel about it.

Posing inferential questions for students to consider in their journals and brainstorming these in class can provide scaffolds to writing (Routman, 1994). Questions such as the following can help develop students' critical thinking skills while reading:

> What might the character do if . . . ?
> What do you predict will happen in the next section?
> What surprised you in this chapter? Why?
> What did you learn in this chapter?

By modeling appropriate responses to these and other questions with the class, you can give students the confidence and ability to respond to what they read in their journals.

For beginning readers, you could lead the class or small group in a read-aloud and have them draw or write a response in their journals. Read aloud a few pages of text and follow this up with oral language brainstorming to generate ideas on how students might respond. For example, you could read aloud a story and have students take the role of one of the characters. Or, they could write a different ending to the story. In this way, even emerging readers and writers can begin to respond to what they read through journals.

While not every journal entry needs a response, teachers should read and respond to selected entries in each student's journal at regular intervals, perhaps every two or three weeks. Responses should focus on the message conveyed in the journal rather than on the form. This is particularly important with English-language learners to encourage them to take risks in their new language. It is only by attempting to communicate through writing that students learn to write. In responding, you can support students' observations, clarify misunderstandings, and suggest learning goals for reading or writing rather than make corrections to the student's writing. Your responses should add new and relevant information to expand students' learning while also modeling appropriate writing conventions. Tierney, et al. (1995) suggest teachers keep their comments nonjudgmental and nonprescriptive. Focus your comments on the positive, and encourage students to keep writing.

To assess the use of journals, we need to think about the purpose of having our students write. For what criteria do we want to hold the students accountable? We could consider several dimensions: a required number of journal entries; entries made on a regular rather than a sporadic basis; evidence of personal response or reflection in entries; and going beyond description to evaluation of what one has read. Even though journals may not be graded or may be optional, this does not mean that they cannot be used as part of the evaluation of students' reading comprehension. To evaluate journals, we need a purpose and criteria that reflect that purpose. To assess dialogue journals and literature response journals, we can use scoring rubrics similar to those in Tables 4.3 to 4.5.

Recordkeeping

Teachers are busy people who do not need more paperwork to clutter up their day; however, we do need to keep track of student progress, and we need to do

TABLE 4.3   Journals/Reading Response

Ideas for responses:

- Favorite part or character
- Something the book reminds you of
- Why you liked or didn't like it
- Scary, funny, sad, or happy part and why
- How you feel about it
- Someone else who might like it and why

Today's Date	Book Title	Author	I Read from Page ____ to Page ____	My Response

Source: Adapted from a draft by Maria Baker (1996), grade 3 teacher and George Mason University graduate student.

TABLE 4.4   Dialogue Journal Scoring Rubric

Level 4
Makes regular, twice-weekly entries in journal; may exceed minimum.
Makes clear and appropriate references to materials read.
Consistently relates readings to his or her own life experiences.
Relates and develops personal reactions and thoughts and / or raises relevant questions stimulated
   by readings.

Level 3
Makes regular, twice-weekly entries in journal, but may miss some.
Refers to materials read but occasionally lacks reflection or clarity.
Often relates readings to his or her own life experiences.
Relates personal reactions and thoughts or raises questions stimulated by readings, but at times
   these may be unclear or incompletely developed.

Level 2
Makes irregular entries in journal.
May refer to materials read, but references frequently lack reflection or clarity.
May not relate readings to his or her own life experiences.
Relates personal reactions and thoughts to text in a limited manner.

Level 1
Makes few or no journal entries.
Seldom refers to materials read.
Does not relate reading to his or her own life experiences.
Does not relate personal reactions to and thoughts about text.

Source: Adapted from a draft by Mary Ann Cunningham (1996), George Mason University graduate student. Prepared for post–high school age adult ESL students, intermediate proficiency.

this in a systematic manner. One way to do this would be to keep blank forms of your assessment tools readily available in a binder or file so that they are ready when you are. Another way is to keep an assessment calendar to set dates for when you plan to conduct specific instructional activities and when you plan to assess student performance on learning tasks such as application of reading strategies. You can schedule staggered assessments in which you assess a few students each week. Yet another way to monitor student progress is to teach students how to keep assessment portfolios. Assessment portfolios are selective (as opposed to collections portfolios that include all student work) and include samples of student work that show progress toward learning goals (such as learning how to summarize or how to make a personal response to reading), criteria for evaluation of student work, and student reflection and self-assessment on that work. Teachers would have to take the time needed to teach students how to engage in self-assessment and how to apply criteria to their own work, and while this does take

TABLE 4.5   Literature Response Journal Scoring Rubric

Level 4
Provides a personal response to the literature with examples from the text.
Describes the main ideas and characters accurately.
Organizes main ideas in separate paragraphs.
Makes few errors in spelling and punctuation.

Level 3
Provides a personal response to the literature with some examples from the text.
Describes the main ideas and characters with some misunderstandings.
Puts main ideas in separate paragraphs that could be better organized.
May make repeated errors in spelling and punctuation.

Level 2
Provides a limited personal response.
Describes the main ideas and characters with some misunderstandings.
Puts main ideas in separate paragraphs that could be better organized.
Makes frequent errors in spelling and punctuation.

Level 1
Describes the text but does not provide a personal response.
Describes the main ideas and characters inaccurately.
Writes without paragraphs.
Makes frequent errors in spelling and punctuation.

Source: Adapted from O'Malley & Valdez Pierce (1996) and a draft by Claudia Zarikow (1996), George Mason University graduate student. Prepared for grade 10 English language arts ESL students with intermediate language proficiency.

some time in the beginning, teachers and researchers report that the time becomes less as these portfolios become routine (Herman & Winters, 1994).

Students need to be evaluated periodically, but not everything the student does needs to be evaluated. Using staggered assessment cycles, teachers can assess each student's use of reading comprehension strategies at least once and preferably twice during each grading period (typically a nine-week period). Teachers can inform students of the results of the assessment through reading or portfolio conferences. Students need clear, descriptive feedback to improve their approach to reading. Conferences can be limited to about ten minutes per student and can be conducted during class while other students are working in small groups, before or after school, or during a lunch or study period. To the extent that the teacher uses carefully structured cooperative learning activities and/or learning centers effectively, he or she will be able to make time to assess students while they work in these groups. Assessment that is simultaneous to instruction is authentic and saves time.

Teachers can show parents how their children are doing by sending home a checklist of the reading strategies that their child has been able to demonstrate, a scoring rubric with a level indicated and accompanied by teacher comments or by drafting a brief narrative on the child's overall strengths and weaknesses in reading comprehension.

Summary

By using routine instructional activities for reading to evaluate English-language learners' use of reading comprehension strategies before, during, and after reading, we can help these students actively apply reading strategies and become independent learners. It is not enough, however, to simply engage students in activities such as anticipation guides, reciprocal teaching, and journal writing. We need to keep objective records of our observations as teachers, and we need to do this on a regular, systematic basis. We can keep objective records by specifying the standards and criteria to which English-language learners are to be held accountable on scoring rubrics, checklists, and rating scales. We can do this by building assessment of reading comprehension strategies into our daily and weekly lesson plans. We also must share the results of our assessments with the learners themselves and their parents in as clear a manner as possible to help students set learning goals related to reading.

Conclusion

How might both of Roberto's teachers help him improve his reading comprehension? Having reviewed research and recent trends from the fields of second language acquisition, reading instruction, and assessment, we can see that Roberto's teachers can do several things. First of all, Roberto's teachers could collaborate to identify his priority learning needs in reading and to plan instructional and assessment activities that meet those needs. ESL and bilingual teachers need to collaborate with grade-level (mainstream) teachers to effectively address each learner's priority needs. Second, they can help activate prior knowledge to motivate him to read and to set a purpose for reading. Using an activity such as an anticipation guide can help accomplish this by activating prereading strategies. Third, they can teach reading comprehension strategies directly. They can do this by modeling, demonstrating, and involving Roberto in applying these strategies to what he reads. An activity like reciprocal teaching provides a practical vehicle for application of during-reading strategies. Fourth, they can provide time for reading in class and for Roberto to discuss what he reads in well-structured groups, in which each student is accountable for learning. Fifth, they can create opportunities for Roberto to collaborate on reading-related projects to expand his comprehension levels. Sixth, they can show him how to make personal responses to reading through journals of various types. Making written entries in journals

can help all readers apply postreading strategies that help them retain what they
have read. Finally, Roberto's teachers can use each of these instructional activities
to evaluate his progress in reading and to modify instruction to meet his changing
learning needs. They can monitor his progress using teacher-made tools such as
rubrics, checklists, and rating scales. By documenting Roberto's reading progress
using objective criteria, they will be better able to chronicle his growth and to
help him set learning goals in reading.

DISCUSSION QUESTIONS

1. The research on improving reading comprehension shows the need to teach reading
   strategies directly. In your experience, which reading strategies have you taught
   students? Which reading strategies would you like to be able to teach?

2. What other instructional activities, besides the ones described in this chapter, have
   you used or are you aware of for teaching reading comprehension strategies?

3. Draft an anticipation guide and an assessment tool to accompany it. Get feedback
   from a partner on your work.

4. What reading comprehension strategies would you like to learn more about?
   Discuss with a partner, and make a plan for learning what you need.

5. What have you learned from this chapter that will help you develop tools for
   assessing students' application of reading comprehension strategies?

REFERENCES

Alvermann, D. E., & Phelps, S. F. (1994). *Content reading and literacy: Succeeding in today's diverse classrooms.* Boston: Allyn & Bacon.

Chamot, A. U., & O'Malley, J. M. (1994). *The CALLA handbook.* White Plains, NY: Addison Wesley Longman.

Fielding, L. G., & Pearson, P. D. (1994). Reading comprehension: What works. *Educational Leadership, 51*(5), 62–68.

Fradd, S., & Hudelson, S. (1995). Alternative assessment: A process that promotes collaboration and reflection. *TESOL Journal, 5*(1), 5.

Freeman, D., & Freeman, Y. (1994). *Whole language for second language learners.* Portsmouth, NH: Heinemann.

Gardner, D. (1996). Self-assessment for self-access learners. *TESOL Journal, 5*(3), 18–23.

Gottlieb, M. (1995). Nurturing student learning through portfolios. *TESOL Journal, 5*(1), 12–14.

Grabe, W. (1988). Reassessing the term "interactive". In P. L. Carrell, J. Devine, & D. Eskey, (Eds.), *Interactive approaches to second language reading.* pp. 56–70. Cambridge: Cambridge University Press.

Herman, J. L., Ashbacher, P. R., & Winters, L. (1992). *A practical guide to alternative assessment.* Alexandria, VA: Association for Supervision and Curriculum Development.

Herman, J. L., & Winters, L. (1994). Portfolio research: A slim collection. *Educational Leadership, 52*(2), 48–55.

Kagan, S. (1994). *Cooperative learning.* San Juan Capistrano, CA: Kagan Cooperative Learning.

Kim, H., & Krashen, S. (1997). Why don't language acquirers take advantage of the power of reading? *TESOL Journal, 6*(3), 26–29.

Lapp, D., Flood, J., & Farnan, N. (1996). *Content area reading and learning: Instructional strategies.* Boston: Allyn and Bacon.

Mathias, S. P. (1993). Speaking portfolios in the EFL classroom: Supporting communicative, humanistic instruction. *Portfolio News, 4*(3), 12, 17.

McNamara, M. J., & Deane, D. (1995). Self-assessment activities: Toward autonomy in language learning. *TESOL Journal, 5*(1), 17–21.

O'Malley, J. M., & Valdez Pierce, L. (1996). *Authentic assessment for English language learners: Practical approaches for teachers.* White Plains, NY: Pearson Education.

Palincsar, A. S., & Brown, A. L. (1984). Reciprocal teaching of comprehension-fostering and comprehension-monitoring activities. *Cognition and Instruction, 1*(2), 117–175.

Paris, S. G., & Ayers, L. R. (1994). *Becoming reflective students and teachers with portfolios and authentic assessment.* Washington, DC: American Psychological Association.

Pearson, B., & Berghoff, C. (1996). London Bridge is not falling down: It's supporting alternative assessment. *TESOL Journal, 5*(4), 28–31.

Peregoy, S. F., & Boyle, O. F. (1997). *Reading, writing, & learning in ESL: A resource book for K–12 teachers.* New York: Addison Wesley Longman.

Peyton, J. K., & Reed, L. (1990). *Dialogue journal writing with nonnative English speakers: A handbook for teachers.* Alexandria, VA: Teachers of English to Speakers of Other Languages (TESOL).

Readence, J. E., Bean, T. W., & Baldwin, R. S. (1995). *Content area reading: An integrated approach, 5th Ed.* Dubuque, IA: Kendall/Hunt.

Routman, R. (1994). *Invitations: Changing as teachers and learners K–12.* Portsmouth, NH: Heinemann.

Smollen, L., Newman, C., Wathen, T., & Lee, D. (1995). Developing student self-assessment strategies. *TESOL Journal, 5*(1), 22–27.

Tierney, R. J., Readence, J. E., & Dishner, E. K. (1995). *Reading strategies and practices: A compendium.* Boston: Allyn & Bacon.

Vacca, R. T., & Vacca, J. L. (1996). *Content area reading, 5th ed.* New York: HarperCollins.

Valdez Pierce, L. (1998). Reciprocal teaching: Reading strategies at work. In J. D. Brown (Ed.), *New Ways of Classroom Assessment.* Alexandria, VA: Teachers of English to Speakers of Other Languages (TESOL).

5 Assessment in the Content Areas for Students Acquiring English

SANDRA ROLLINS HURLEY AND SALLY BLAKE

University of Texas at El Paso

Mr. Tran

Mr. Tran teaches middle schoolers literacy in the content areas in a large U.S. southern coastal city. Students in his school district represent more than twenty different languages. Many are first-generation immigrants. Spanish speakers (using various dialects of Spanish) from Latin America and the Caribbean are the largest group. Some from Caribbean nations speak both English and a French Creole (which often varies from island to island). There is also a fairly large number of Asian students who bring with them diverse languages. Many of Mr. Tran's students are bilingual (although English is not always one of their languages). Their previous educational backgrounds are as diverse as the language and ethnic families they represent.

Mr. Tran uses an interdisciplinary approach to science, math, and social studies instruction because he understands that people learn best when they can see connections and construct meaning from the content. Further, this approach makes it possible for Mr. Tran to personalize instruction to meet the diverse needs of his students.

A recent learning project centered on the nature of scientific inquiry. In this project students collected data (e.g., daily high and low temperatures, wind speed and direction, rainfall) using a weather station on the school campus provided by a local television station. The station is one of the school's business partners in education. In math they used the data to answer questions (e.g., What is the average temperature this month?). While working in cooperative groups collecting and analyzing the data, students spontaneously generated a number of other questions. A student in one group noted that the cool, rainy January weather they were experiencing was very different from her tropical Caribbean home where January was the dry season. Lucinda's comment sparked a lively discussion about weather the students had experienced.

Building on student interest, Mr. Tran suggested they search the Internet for sites that provide global weather information. The youngsters found several, including some with satellite maps, forecast information, and warnings of dangerous weather systems.

The students began to systematically collect weather data on a number of international cities (sparked by curiousity about the weather in places they or their families had lived). Once each week they charted and graphed the data looking for similarities and differences. This led to a study of climate and the impact of climate on how people live, what they eat, the houses they build, etc. Students used textbooks, tradebooks, interviews with family and community members, and on-line sources in their inquiry. The learning project culminated with student groups sharing research results with the class. Some groups chose traditional oral presentations using charts, tables, and maps to illustrate findings. One group employed song and dance to describe climate and culture in Guatemala. This group painted a stunning mural that accurately depicted the plants and animals of Central America as a backdrop for their performance. Another group used realia, real-life objects and artifacts, in their presentation. The group that included students from the islands of Jamiaca and Dominica effectively used recipes and tastes of foods they'd prepared to demonstrate how climate, history, and ingenuity combined to create such dishes as Jamaican jerk pork and Dominican provisions—part of the heritage of slave ancestors who escaped sugar cane plantations and subsisted in rain forest jungles.

Mr. Tran used his observations of the students, knowledge of cognitive learning theory, a good understanding of district, state, and national content and performance standards, and his own experiences as an English-language learner to facilitate the youngsters' acquisition of content knowledge and language. He provided the scaffoding (lots of oral language support, modeling, direct instruction, cooperative learning groups, hands-on experiences) to insure student success. As the students read, talked, wrote, listened, learned to navigate the Net, and developed their presentations, Mr. Tran constantly monitored comprehension, collected writing samples, and made notes about developing language proficiency. This ongoing assessment embedded in daily instruction helped Mr. Tran develop curriculum, instruction, and ways to support his students as they read science, mathematics, and sociocultural texts and conducted personally meaningful scientific inquiry. He helped them understand and use the unique and technical vocabulary they discovered in their investigations. Perhaps most importantly he helped the students see themselves as capable of doing serious scientific inquiry and as successful learners.

Mr. Tran understands well the difficulty of acquiring a new language and learning academic content simultaneously. In the late-1970s when he was eight years old, his family arrived in the United States after leaving their home in Vietnam. Although he was a fluent speaker of both Vietnamese and French and knew a number of English words and phrases, his first few years of U.S. schooling were challenging and often frustrating. Therefore, when another teacher in Mr. Tran's sixth grade team gave the students an exam from the textbook and few students did well on the paper-and-pencil test, Mr. Tran was not surprised nor was he disappointed. He knows his students have better understanding than is reflected by the test results. He knows that they, just like he once did, have difficulty articulating in English what they know and can do. For this reason Mr. Tran uses a performance-based approach to assess content knowledge as part of the cycle of instruction and assessment. Mr. Tran uses the information gained from students to inform instruction. Assessment and instruction, therefore, are woven together in an endless cycle. Learning activities and student responses are part of the ongoing assessment that helps Mr. Tran plan additional teaching and learning activities. By watching this exemplary, knowledgeable teacher, who is passionate about student learning, we can learn much about assessment of literacy in the content areas for English-language learners.

Research Background

Demographics

Predictions based on the last national census suggest that there are already 3.3 million children, between 5 and 17 years of age, who have limited English proficiency (Alvermann & Phelps, 1998). Moreover, another six million school-age youngsters speak languages other than English at home (Minami & Ovando, 1995). Without the ability to use reading to engage in a variety of ways of thinking, our students will be incapable of communicating in our society (Conley, 1995), and communication is vital to quality of life issues—academic, economic, and social ones.

Seventeen states require English-language learners (ELLs) to pass one or more content-area tests to receive a standard high school diploma (Rivera & Vincent, 1997). These states approach testing ELLs in several ways: (1) deference of ELL students from the first administration of the test, (2) allowing test accommodations, (3) making the test available in students' native languages, and (4) using alternative assessment procedures. Although these practices offer some benefit in making high school graduation tests more accessible to these students they only accommodate the needs of a limited number of ELLs (Rivera & Vincent, 1997).

English-language learners are diverse in their language and literacy abilities. No single description applies to all students—as is clear by the profile of youngsters in Mr. Tran's classes. Further complications arise when you think about the distinction between second-language acquisition and second-language learning. According to Gee (1996) "acquisition is a process of acquiring something (usually subconsciously) by exposure to models, a process of trial and error, and practice within social groups, without formal teaching" (p. 138). First language development for native English speakers is primarily a matter of acquisition although formal schooling is also involved—it is not unusual for native speakers to study English for twelve or more years. For most of us, using a second language is attained by some mixture of acquisition and schooling (Alvermann & Phelps, 1998), just as most of us develop our first language through a combination of acquisition and schooling. School success depends in large measure on students' ability to read and learn from text, that is, their content literacy.

Content Literacy and English-Language Learners

Content reading gets its name from the first priority of subject matter teachers: to teach content. Every subject (or content area) has its own content or defining set of facts, concepts, and principles that are neither static nor solid (Conley, 1995). Literacy, once associated almost exclusively with written text is now thought of in broader terms. Literacy relates to the ability to construe meaning in any of the forms used in the culture to create and convey meaning (Alvermann & Phelps, 1998). Most researchers agree that the traditional notion of literacy and its association with text has been replaced by the concept of multiple literacies: cultural, civic, computer, scientific, and technological literacies. Content literacy is the ability to use reading and writing to learn subject matter in a given discipline and how a student uses literacy to learn.

The work of Lev Vygotsky, a Russian psychologist, has greatly influenced how we currently view teaching and learning content literacy. A Vygotskian perspective on learning assumes the learner benefits from having someone guide the learner. He believed that mental functioning originates in social, communicative processes and that language is a tool vital to this process. An emphasis on the sociohistorical and cultural aspects of language as a mediator of even the most private forms of thinking has a profound influence on how we view literacy acquisition and development (Alvermann & Phelps, 1998). Language plays a vital role in understanding technical terms and greatly influences the success of students in the content-related fields. Language helps a learner make sense of the world, to understand and be understood. As a result, language and meaning cannot be severed from one another (Vacca & Vacca, 1993). Non-English-speaking students are expected to adapt to two or more languages and still make sense of content reading. Because developmental English speakers have to acquire English language skills and knowledge that students who arrive in school speaking English already possess, supplemental performance and assessment standards should be developed (August, 1994).

Collier (1995) provides evidence that to succeed in school, students must develop the cognitive and academic skills required for learning academic subject matter. To achieve this goal, teachers must integrate language learning with content learning, make use of learners' experiences, and focus on higher-level cognitive skills. Instead of seeing language merely as a means of communication, teachers must see language as a medium of learning. The challenge is to identify effective ways in which instruction and assessment in language and academic content can be successfully combined, so as to introduce children to a new language and a new set of cultural experiences simultaneously. The language of instruction must be adapted without watering down the content, and materials must be used that follow the core curriculum but are adapted or supplemented for students acquiring English (Tinajero & Schifini, 1997). This is a huge challenge complicated by the fact that textbook and technical writing are among the most difficult types of literacy processes.

Nature of Expository Text

Expository text, that is text written to provide an explanation, is generally more difficult for all students to comprehend than narrative text, or text written to tell a story. Primary reasons are the unique structure and the often specialized and technical vocabulary. Expository text is also usually less redundant and less "reader friendly" than narrative.

Likewise, technical writing is more difficult to do well than narrative writing. Technical writing tends to be succinct, linear, and hierarchical. It lacks the discursive redundancies found in most narratives. Clearly written reports, explanations, and directions can be difficult even for professional writers. That difficulty is multiplied for ELLs.

Content Area Text Structure.   In English, narrative has a predictable beginning, middle, and end structure. Expository text, on the other hand, may be structured in any of the following ways:

1. *Topically.* Science texts may have one unit on mammals and another on mass and matter. A government text may move from a chapter on the Constitution to one on the three branches of government. Such an arrangement can make it difficult for students to see connections between content from section to section.
2. *Chronologically.* History texts are usually structured from past to present.
3. *Numerically.* Charts, graphs, tables, and other graphic aids may be arranged using numbers.

Teachers like Mr. Tran have developed methods of simultaneously teaching text structure and assessing whether students understand. Examples are included in the section on practical classroom applications.

Content Area Vocabulary.   Another issue that directly influences the reading comprehension of ELLs is the specialized and often technical terms used in the content areas. Vocabulary in content area classes may not be used outside the classroom (few of us talk about *divisors* and *quotients* or *vertebrates* and *invertebrates* except in math or biology class); therefore, students typically use or practice these terms only when doing school work. Because so many English words have multiple meanings, students can become confused. The commonly used meaning of a word may be quite different from the specialized meaning in a content area. *Infinite* is commonly used to mean unlimited or without end. That somewhat vague meaning differs from the precise definition in mathematics that defines *infinite* as "a set is infinite if it has a proper subset with which it can be put into one-to-one correspondence" (Bennet & Nelson, 1985, p. 56). Opportunities for confusion about vocabulary abound and ongoing assessment of student comprehension must be embedded within instruction (Figure 5.1).

Enhancing Comprehension of Concepts and Vocabulary

Educators have long known that a strong relationship exists between

- vocabulary knowledge and comprehension
- prior knowledge and comprehension
- active engagement with text and comprehension
- metacognitive awareness and comprehension (McNeil, 1992)

Because of these relationships, comprehension is a continuous process; it is not simply a postreading occurrence. Mr. Tran engages his students in activities de-

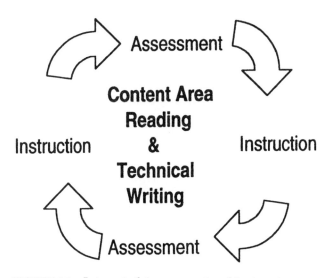

FIGURE 5.1   Integrated Assessment and Instruction.

signed to increase vocabulary knowledge, activate existing schema, and keep them actively engaged and aware in pre-, during, and post-reading phases. These instructional activities have the dual purpose of providing assessment information. Several are described in the section on practical classroom applications.

While content area reading is more difficult for most students simply because of the nature of expository writing, it is even more challenging for ELLs. Because ELLs have historically suffered from disproportionate assignments to lower curriculum tracks on the basis of inappropriate assessment, changes in assessment have much to do with whether or not equity becomes a reality in education.

Implications for the Classroom

A primary classroom implication from the foregoing research background is directly related to the increasing language diversity in U.S. schools. As educators we must work at making our classrooms equitable learning environments for all students. To do that, we need to find ways to assess effectively students' comprehension in content area reading and development of technical writing ability. That knowledge enables us to plan effective instruction.

Equity Issues in Assessment

Considering the large, growing, diverse groups of ELLs entering U.S. schools, almost every teacher and every school district serves or will serve ELLs (LaCelle-

Peterson & Rivera, 1994). All assessment programs in all states should report on the educational progress of ELLs in terms of developing English proficiency and content knowledge. There seem to be four major equity issues that repeatedly appear in the literature influencing learning and assessment.

1. Encouragement of development of native language abilities rather than submersion in English and eradication of language and culture
2. Equal curriculum access for all children rather than tracking and labeling ELLs
3. Equal participation in meaningful interaction with challenging subject matter, peers, and teachers rather than limited participation
4. Real world application and success in learning the challenging content areas rather than useless memorization of facts and watered down curricula

An important question to ask is what information should assessment provide to educators, parents, and students?

Information Needed from Assessment

The information that content area teachers need to know about learners is largely determined by two factors. First, students vary greatly in the extent to which they are prepared to read and write technical material, and second, the nature of content area reading requires applications of reading skills that make direct instructional assistance necessary (Lapp, Flood, & Farnan, 1996). Lapp, Flood, and Farnan identify seven categories of information that content area teachers need to know about their students and that should be considered when planning within the cycle of instruction and assessment.

> (1) students' ability to perform the kinds of integrated reading and writing tasks that make up much of learning in the content areas, (2) students' interest and attitudes, (3) the reading strategies that students employ when they attempt to understand and apply content area reading, (4) students' background knowledge of the subject matter, (5) students' instructional reading levels, (6) the extent to which particular materials are appropriate for student use, and (7) students' skill with study techniques. (p. 388)

Classroom assessment in content areas should be ongoing and flexible (Ryder & Graves, 1994). End of semester or one shot assessment does not give educators a full view of student understanding. Multiple indicators and continuous checking for understanding should be used to assess ELLs' learning and consequently to develop instruction.

Guiding Principles of Assessment

While many approaches to assessment problems have been suggested in recent reform recommendations, six basic principles for classroom assessment may be used to summarize the research. These principles are supportive of ELLs and just good practice for all students. Cooter and Flynt (1996) summarize these principles as follows:

Principle 1. Assessment Activities Should Help Teachers Make Instructional Decisions. Assessment activities should reveal insights into the effectiveness of certain teaching methods, classroom environmental features, materials selected to enhance learning, grouping strategies, and actual learning of the content. For example, Mr. Tran used insight gained from Lucinda's remark about differences in January weather in parts of the world to develop an integrated, interdisciplinary learning project that built on students' own experiences and interests.

Principle 2. Assessment Strategies Should Help Teachers Find Out What Students Know and Can Do . . . Not What They Cannot Do. When teachers understand what students know or how far skills have developed in a target area, appropriate planning can be prepared that extends their knowledge. The performance-based assessment that was a part of the student-group presentations allowed students to demonstrate their strengths while providing Mr. Tran with information on areas that need more work.

Principle 3. The Holistic Context for Learning Should Be Considered and Assessed. The term *holistic context* implies that teachers consider all factors that have an impact on teaching and learning. This includes affective responses toward the subject area, classroom environment, parental and cultural attitudes toward schooling, and physiological needs. This is particularly important for youngsters learning English as a second or other language. These students bring rich cultural background to the classroom simply by virtue of their life experiences. Rather than ignoring the background and prior knowledge of students, life experience can be used by knowledgeable teachers to enhance student achievement. In Mr. Tran's class, students learned about the world (including science, social studies, and math content) from one another. Students and their families were sources of knowledge just as texts, maps, and websites were sources of knowledge.

Principle 4. Assessment Activities Should Grow Out of Authentic Learning Activities. Authentic assessment strategies involve the daily collecting of evidence of student learning as they perform real-world application tasks. Part of the assessment for each student would likely include a qualitative-analytic evaluation of portfolio contents. Mr. Tran's students' portfolios included written reports and narratives; audio recordings of their music; drawings and paintings; student-made maps, charts, graphs, and tables; and videotapes of presentations.

Principle 5. Best Assessments of Student Learning Are Longitudinal. . . . They Take Place over Time. Multiple samples of students' work taken from a variety of situations constitute valid evidence of what students can do. This approach avoids the assessment phenomenon created when teachers use the quick pencil-and-paper approach to assessment. While it is easy to give a pencil-and-paper test as one teacher in the middle school team did, such tests are very limited at providing useful information if students still learning a language cannot read and write English sufficiently to show what they know and are able to do.

Principle 6. Each Assessment Activity Should Have a Specific Objective-Linked Purpose. Quality assessment grows out of careful observations, discussions, and conferences with students. As teachers discover what students can do, natural assessment questions arise concerning the depth of understanding. For teachers of ELLs, it is particularly important to keep principle 6 in mind, for if the objective is to assess the degree to which students can engage in hands-on scientific inquiry or whether they solve an algebraic equation, assessment cannot be language dependent. For example, a student may be able to design and carry out an elegant demonstration to show that mass and weight are not the same. That same student, however, may have difficulty articulating the concept in English. Mr. Tran allows children to include their native language when discussing and writing about their work. Language differences should be more than tolerated; they need to be celebrated and affirmed (Alvermann & Phelps, 1998).

These implications and principles have practical applications for the classroom.

Practical Classoom Applications

Writing, discussing, concept mapping, and reading their own thoughts are vital to the success of content literacy. Middle schoolers must be involved in assessment processes because that can help them become more metacognitively aware as they use language to communicate. A large body of research evidence exists showing that students who are active, engaged, and cognizant of their own thinking processes learn more. Helping students learn how to learn is a major objective of content area teachers.

The following assessment procedures provide a broad view of student understanding to both teacher and student. These types of assessment are also accessible to parents in ways that standardized, norm-referenced test results rarely are. Use of content reading-writing inventories, learning journals, concept-vocabulary maps, and portfolio performance-based events allow ELLs to communicate their understanding of the concepts without being language dependent. Each of these also helps students learn how to learn more effectively.

Content Reading and Study Skills Inventory

The Content Reading and Study Skills Inventory (box) can be used as an individual or small or large group activity. The greatest value is usually obtained from conversations about student responses. The teacher should help students see the importance of engaging with the text pre, during, and postreading and brainstorm ways to for them to do so.

Learning Journals

Journals can be a tremendous learning tool for ELLs in content area classes. Learning journals are more flexible than typical learning logs in which students

Content Reading and Study Skills Inventory

Directions: The purpose of this activity is to help you understand how you read and study your textbooks and to help you think of more effective study reading strategies. There are no correct or incorrect answers. Just place an X under the answer that is most true for you. For some questions, you will need to write a response.

Before Reading

	Never	Sometimes	Always
1. Do you look over the chapter just to see what it's about, perhaps stopping to look at pictures or read captions and titles?			
2. Do you think about what you've already heard or read about the topic?			
3. Do you wonder or ask yourself questions about what the chapter is about?			
4. Do you know what the teacher will expect of you after reading (answer questions, summarize what you read, etc.)?			
5. If you do anything else before reading an assignment, write about it on a separate page if you need more space.			

During Reading

	Never	Sometimes	Always
6. Do you expect (most of the time) to understand what you read?			
7. As you are reading, can you identify which parts of the assignment you can understand and which parts are confusing?			
8. Do you stop to read captions under pictures, look at maps, charts, etc.?			
9. Do you mentally translate words or phrases from English to your first language and think about them in your first language?			
10. When you do not understand, what do you do? Write your answer on a separate page if you need more space.			

After Reading

	Never	Sometimes	Always
11. Do you go back and reread confusing sections?			
12. Do you write questions to ask the teacher or a classmate about things you don't understand?			

Never   Sometimes   Always

13. Do you make notes in your first language or in English to help you remember important information?

14. Do you make drawings to help you remember?

15. Can you explain what you read in your own words?

16. Can you usually predict the questions your teacher will ask about the material?

17. Do you talk with someone (a classmate, family member, teacher, etc.) about what you read?

18. Describe how you study for tests. Write your answers on a separate page if you need more space.

may simply log in pages read, activities completed, and perhaps a comment (often forced) about what was learned. Learning journals may include assigned pages and activities because that helps students learn to organize their work. Journals also provide a place for students to record personal responses to content and vocabulary including questions. Confusing concepts and terms are noted.

Scientists, scholars, and adventurers have maintained learning journals. This time-honored method of recording observations, thoughts, and questions has been used for centuries. Students enjoy looking at copies of journals of Leonardo Da Vinci, Lewis and Clark, Sigmund Freud, Thomas Edison, and their teachers.

Because the major purpose of learning journals is to communicate ideas, problems, observations, and so on, the writing is personal and active. Usually only the individual student and teacher read them unless a student elects to share. Emphasis is placed on content (what the learner writes or illustrates graphically) not on grammar or mechanics (how it is written) (Alvermann & Phelps, 1998). Learning journals provide a longitudinal record of a student's literacy development and understanding of content knowledge. Thought and language can be effectively used together in learning journals. Figures 5.2 and 5.3 are examples of two different types of learning journals. Luis recorded his observations in an unstructured journal. Paulina used a structured journal observation form.

Concept and Vocabulary Maps

Concept maps, advance organizers, outlines, semantic webs, and other types of graphic organizers have long been made by teachers and curriculum developers to illustrate structure and connections between concepts and vocabulary terms. Student-made graphic outlines of content also have powerful potential for ELLs. Student-made concept maps by their very nature require the integration of content with oral and written language. Additionally, they allow for almost seamless integration of instruction and assessment.

Luis

¿Que sabemos de Imanes?

Si ponemos (+) con Se separan.
Si ponemos (+) y (-) se juntan.
Pueden pegarse cuando son
metales.

Vocabulario

Iman dos objetos que se atraen cuand.
Son de metal o hierro
Repelar-Cuando dos Objetos se separan
Norte, Norte o Sur, Sur.
Atraer-Cuando Norte y Sur se juntan

Brujula-Un instrumento que enseña direccion

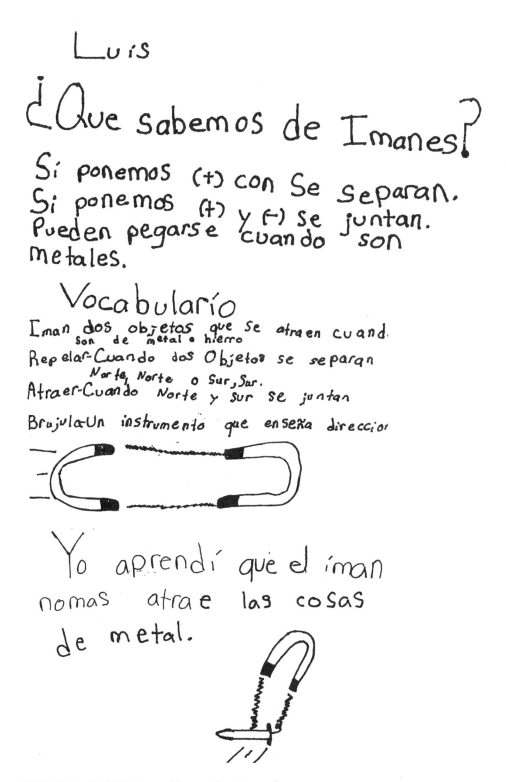

Yo aprendí que el iman
nomas atrae las cosas
de metal.

FIGURE 5.2   Luis' Science Observation Journal.

Name *Paulina* ✦   Date *9/21/99*

Salt Down and Oil Up

Purpose of experiment: to observe and record the interaction of three different substances---oil, water, and salt---having three different densities.

Procedure:

Measure ½ cup water---pour into cup (add food coloring to provide a greater contrast)

Measure ¼ cup canola oil---pour into cup

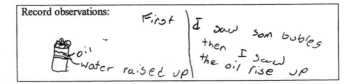

Record observations:

First | I saw som bubles then I saw the oil rise up
oil
water raised up

What will happen if you add salt to water and oil? Write your predictions.

Measure ¼ teaspoon table salt

Sprinkle a few pinches of salt on oil

Predictions:

    I think that the oil is going down when we put the sart in.

Record observations:

    What happened first is that the salt got stuck in the middle and looked like a circle

Discuss observations and different densities of substances.

Water	Oil	Salt
bottom of cup	Middle of cup	bottom of cup

FIGURE 5.3   Paulina's Learning Journal.

Journal observation form developed by Suzane Meyers, a student at The University of Texas at El Paso in Dr. Sally Blake's class.

For example, cooperative learning groups of four or five students each can preview a chapter in their text and work together to outline key ideas by making a concept map. Figure 5.4 is a sample prepared from a chapter in a U.S. history textbook on the Cold War. At the end of the project, students can again make concepts maps (Figure 5.5).

The added detail and connecting information indicate the improved understanding one would expect at the end of a unit of study. So while concepts can be excellent instructional tools to enhance comprehension, they can also be used as meaningful pre- and postassessments.

In science, vocabulary maps (Figure 5.6) typically begin with the core concept to be learned and move outward to encompass key vocabulary.

Portfolios and Performance-Based Assessment

The following examples of performance-based assessment activities designed to be included in portfolios are adapted from National Science Standards (1996) and the Kentucky Education Reform Act (KERA) (1991). They are particularly suited for ELLs because each effectively integrates the use of communication skills while learning and demonstrating knowledge of science content. The activities shown are especially appropriate for introducing students to the nature of scientific activity, building background knowledge about what science is, and actively engaging them in doing science. Assessment criteria used with the activities are included.

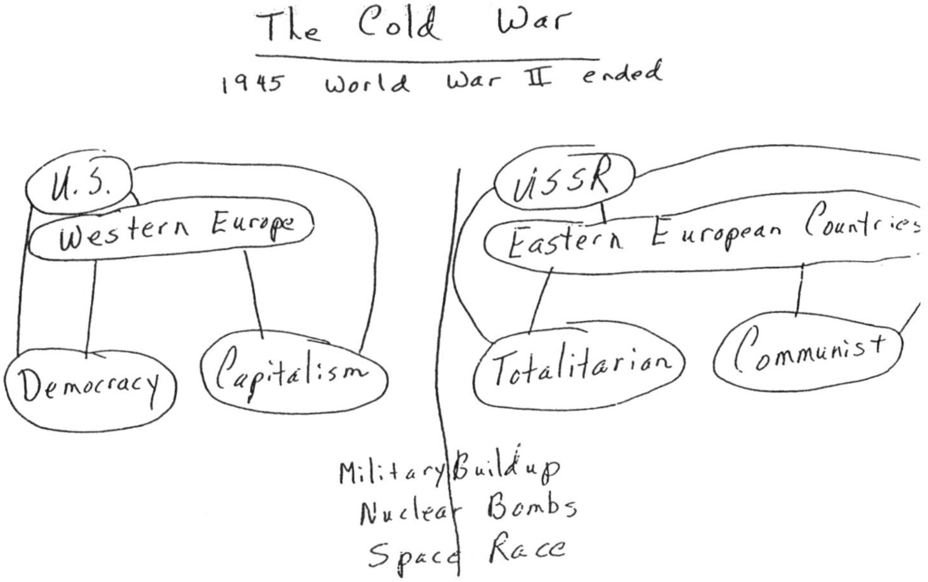

FIGURE 5.4   A sample concept map at beginning of project.

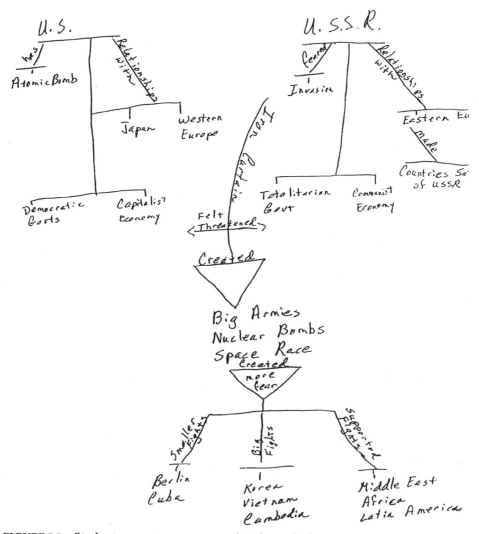

FIGURE 5.5   Student concept map prepared at the end of a project.

This approach to assessment allows Mr. Tran to determine the depth of students' thinking and their ability to apply content knowledge. While use of technical vocabulary is an important element in content reading, it is even more important that teachers of ELLs determine the students' ability to think about and apply concepts. Reading assessment in the content areas must be considered in the context of the total assessment program. Improving assessment in the

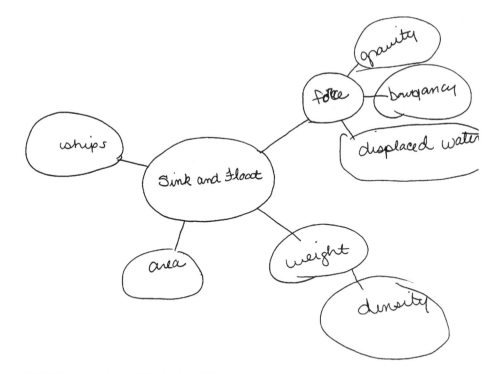

FIGURE 5.6   Science Vocabulary Map.

content areas is dependent on understanding how formal and informal assessment fits together and the role language plays in learning (Lapp, Flood, & Farnan, 1996).

Reflections

As the public school population changes rapidly, more and more classrooms will exhibit the language and cultural diversity seen in Mr. Tran's class. A more complex knowledge-based and diverse society creates new expectations for teaching and learning. To help diverse learners master challenging content, teachers must go far beyond dispensing information, giving a test, and assigning a grade. Teachers must know their subject areas deeply, and how to best facilitate literacy learning, and they must understand how students think as well as what they know to create experiences that produce learning. Moreover, as students with a wider range of learning needs enter and stay in school—a growing number whose first language is not English, many others with learning differences, and still others with learning disabilities—teachers need access to the growing knowledge that exists about how to teach different kinds of learners effectively (National Commission on Teaching and America's Future, 1996). Thus performance based assessment is essential.

Concept: *Nature of Scientific Activity*

Portfolio Task
Students design and conduct an investigation of some aspect of animal behavior and write about the design of the investigation, results, and conclusions. Native language is allowed and diagrams are encouraged.

Event Task
Students are provided a plan for a paper airplane. They construct two to three airplanes with different modifications, test their flight, and identify as many variables as they can that affect the distance of flight. Students then propose characteristics and their best design for a paper airplane, defending their position on the basis of their findings.

Event Task
Students are provided a bag of trash. They infer where the various materials originated and construct a chart showing possible ways the garbage might be discarded. They also infer which of the ways identified is least harmful to the environment.

Performance Criteria
The extent to which students
- accurately identify and control variables
- accurately and consistently collect, record, and interpret data
- make appropriate and accurate conclusions based on data
- accurately measure and estimate during the problem-solving process
- state appropriate hypotheses

Concept: *Patterns*

Event Task
Given a cross section of a tree, students determine the age of the tree and differentiate between wet and dry years.

Event Task
Students write letters to a friend in different states describing the seasonal changes in their area and how they affect their lives.

Portfolio Task
Students design and conduct demonstrations that illustrate the role of energy as a factor in physical changes.

Performance Criteria
The extent to which students
- use patterns to give meaning to phenomena
- use patterns to explain past, present, and future events
- identify and predict patterns

Concept: *Systems and Interactions*

Portfolio Task
Students select materials for an aquarium or terrarium containing both plant and animal life and explain how the organisms are related to each other. Discussions may be taped, or students may write their explanations in a journal.

Event Task
Students design and construct a simple machine from a variety of objects that can be used to elevate a box of books from the floor to the table (without direct lifting). Students produce a sketch and an explanation of how the apparatus works.

Event Task
Students identify the components of an electric circuit and the role each component plays (energy source, conductors, etc.). Students explain the impact on the circuit if components are changed.

Performance Criteria
The extent to which students
- identify components of a system or subsystem and the roles components play in the system
- identify interactions of systems
- identify and explain the concepts and interactions of systems and subsystems

Concept: *Models and Scale*

Portfolio Task
Students invent a nonhuman organism and describe the necessary body organs essential to its life.

Event Task
Students build a working model of a circuit, incorporating a battery, bulb, and wire. They draw a plausible illustration of the circuit.

Portfolio Task
Given a standard area map, students create a topographical map and a corresponding relief map using clay models and plastic boxes filled with water. (A photograph of the model should be placed in the portfolio with the maps.)

General Performance Criteria
The extent to which students
- identify and describe components necessary to the proper functioning of the model
- use models to explain or predict the behavior of objects, materials, and living things in their environment
- construct models to represent real-world objects or phenomena
- demonstrate an understanding of scale and proportion

Concept: *Constancy*

Portfolio or Event Task
Students conduct an experiment to demonstrate how heartbeat rate varies around a stable norm.

Portfolio Task
Students design and conduct an experiment to determine how length and/or mass and initial displacement affects the period of a pendulum.

Portfolio Task
Students draw illustrations of the moon's position and appearance over two months recording with date and time in a chart format.

Performance Criteria
The extent to which students
- identify and/or explain the interacting factors which contribute to constancy
- identify or explain any disruptive factors

Good assessment of students learning English helps form instruction and develops students' language and content learning. The cycle of formative assessment and instruction used by exemplary teachers like Mr. Tran provides optimum support for student achievement. Content area reading is vital to insure that all students have equal opportunity to compete and survive in a technologically changing society, and authentic assessment will give students the understanding and confidence to move into the new century.

DISCUSSION QUESTIONS

1. Why is expository text (content area reading and technical writing) typically more difficult for students than reading and writing narrative text?

2. Can teachers use best practices in assessment and simultaneously meet the unique needs of English-language learners? Why or why not?

3. Why is it important to engage students in pre-, during-, and postreading activities?

4. What is the purpose of graphic organizers?

5. Describe ways in which performance-based assessment can be used with portfolios.

REFERENCES

Alvermann, D. E., & Phelps, S. F. (1998). *Content reading and literacy.* Needham Heights, MA: Allyn and Bacon.

August, D. (1994). *For all students: Limited English proficient students and goals 2000.* Washington, DC: National Association of Bilingual Education.

Bennett, A. B., & Nelson, L. T. (1985). *Mathematics: An informal approach.* Needham Heights, MA: Allyn and Bacon.

Collier, V. P. (1995). Acquiring a second language for school. Directions in language and education. *National Clearinghouse for Bilingual Education, 1*(4), 1–12.

Conley, M. W. (1995). *Content reading instruction.* New York: McGraw-Hill.

Cooter, R. B., Jr., & Flynt, E. S. (1996). *Teaching reading in the content areas.* Englewood Cliffs, NJ: Prentice-Hall.

Gee, J. P. (1996). *Social linguistics and literacies: Ideology in discourses, 2nd ed.* London: Taylor and Francis.

Kentucky Education Reform Act (1991). Kentucky Legislative Act.

LaCelle-Peterson, M. W., & Rivera, C. (1994). Is it real for all kids? A framework for equitable assessment policies for English language learners. *Harvard Educational Review.* 64(1), pp. 55–75.

Lapp, D., Flood, J., & Farnan, N. (1996). *Content area reading and learning.* Needham Heights, MA: Simon & Schuster.

McNeil, J. D. (1992). *Reading comprehension. New directions for classroom practice, (3rd Ed.)* New York: HarperCollins.

Minami, M., & Ovando, C. J. (1995). Language issues in multicultural contexts. In J. A. Banks & C. A. McGee Banks (Eds.), *Handbook of research on multicultural education* (pp. 427–444). New York: Macmillan.

National Commission on Teaching and America's Future (1996). *What matters most: Teaching for America's future.* New York: National Commission on Teaching and America's Future.

National Research Council (1996). *National science education standards.* Washington, DC: National Academy Press.

Rivera, C., & Vincent, C. (1997). High school graduation testing: Policies and practices in the assessment of English language learners. *Education Assessment 4*(4), 335–355.

Ryder, R. J., & Graves, M. F. (1994). *Reading and Learning In Content Areas.* New York: Merrill

Tinajero, J. V., & Schifini, A. (1997). *Into English (teacher's edition).* Carmel, CA: Hampton-Brown Books.

Vacca, R. T., & Vacca, J. A. L. (1993). *Content area reading.* New York: HarperCollins.

6 Assessing Bilingual Students

When Policies and Practices Meet in the Classroom

**DOUGLAS FISHER, DIANE LAPP,
AND JAMES FLOOD**
San Diego State University

LUCY SUAREZ
San Diego Unified School District

This book contains a number of innovative strategies that teachers have developed and used to assess students who are acquiring English. Thus far, the chapters have focused on several assessment issues—young children, writing, comprehension. Each chapter has provided a rationale and a research base for integrating assessment and instruction. Before we delve further into assessment, let's talk with Mrs. Martinez. You met Mrs. Martinez in Chapter 1. As you recall, she is a bilingual teacher. Within her classroom of twenty-five students, two students receive support from the resource specialist and four students with limited English proficiency receive support services from a bilingual educator. This print-rich environment is filled with both Spanish and English words, phrases, books, etc. Spanish and English are not the only languages spoken in this class. Three students, Bevian, James, and Erica, speak Tewa, a Native American language of the region.

Mrs. Martinez teaches in a two-way bilingual program (Baker, 1993). We have had the opportunity to learn a lot from looking inside her classroom. Now let's listen to a conversation between Mrs. Martinez and her new student teacher, Mr. Riley. Mr. Riley hopes to become a bilingual educator and to teach fifth or sixth grade when he finishes his credential work. We have added references to the conversation so that readers know where to find more information on topics that interest them.

MR. RILEY: As I was observing you I wondered how you know when to assess students?

MRS. MARTINEZ: Well, there are two answers to your question. Some assessments, such as the state achievement test or the language proficiency tests, are scheduled by the district. These tests arrive with very specific instructions, and we administer them on the day that has been planned by the district well in advance. On the other hand, assessments that I use to make decisions about instruction and learning occur all the time. You'll remember when I asked the students to write poems. They had read poems, written poems in small groups, and then wrote their own poem. I used their final poem to assess writing style, fluency, and mechanics. It also gave me insights about how they understood the directions and their current interests. I also had the students individually read their poems aloud to me. While listening to their reading, I assessed their English language fluency, word choice, and word attack skills. You see, assessment is both episodic and continuous. It is something that I do all day every day as a teacher. As I observe my students as they perform on various tasks, I assess their growth and needs and based on this, I plan the next steps in their instruction (West, 1998).

MR. RILEY: Now I understand a little more about timing, but how do you know which assessments to use?

MRS. MARTINEZ: This is a more difficult question. For assessments that I use to plan instruction, I like to use real-life settings (Valencia, Hiebert, & Afflerbach, 1994). I prefer these assessments because they reflect the range of tasks the students are required to complete in class, including oral interviews, story retellings, writing samples, observations, checklists that I make, and student self-assessments. I vary the types of assessments that I use at any given time, and experience has taught me to collect lots of information before making decisions about students. I like to see multiple measures of their performance in both English and the languages they use at home (Lapp & Flood, 1992). I think this gives me a more realistic view of them. As you have probably noticed, the students keep their work in portfolios. I call these "showcase portfolios" so that the students know we are looking for examples of our best work. The portfolios in this classroom are divided by thematic unit because that is our organizational system. Other teachers at our school divide portfolio entries by subject area or time of year. I'm sure that there are lots of ways of organizing portfolios. I have organized the portfolios in my class around the standards for fourth grade. All of my students are required to learn specific things, either in English or in their native language. These standards have significantly influenced the organization of the portfolios as well as the ways in which I assess the students (LaCelle-Peterson & Rivera, 1994; Tucker & Codding, 1998).

MR. RILEY: That is very interesting. I was wondering how to assess a student's subject matter knowledge. What might you do?

MRS. MARTINEZ: My, don't you have interesting and hard questions! This is an area that we talk about a lot in the lounge and in staff meetings.

The question is whether you are attempting to assess content knowledge or language fluency. This question is so often asked in regards to students who are English-language learners. However, I think this is a false dichotomy. Every assessment is an assessment of literacy (Barr, Kamil, Mosenthal, & Pearson, 1991). Think about it, everything you are asked to do in an assessment situation involves some combination of reading, writing, speaking, listening, or viewing. As a result, some of my colleagues create native-language versions of subject matter assessments that they administer. They do so because they want to know what the student knows about the topic. This is a difficult task given the range of languages that are represented in our school. We must be careful to keep in mind the difficulty in creating an English-equivalent version. For example, you can imagine the number of regional dialects that must be considered or the vocabulary differences between two languages. At the very least, when assessments are translated into another language, they should be "back translated" by another person to insure the meanings are consistent.

Another strategy is to make sure that subject matter assessments are both comprehensible and conceptually appropriate (Lapp, Flood, & Farnan, 1996). Many of my colleagues have developed and implemented a number of accommodations and modifications (NASBE, 1996). These include extra time, small-group administration, oral versions (items read aloud), use of dictionaries, use of calculators, preferential seating, instructions provided in native languages, frequent breaks during assessment time, an administration of the assessment by persons familiar with the student and his or her primary language (see Table 6.1).

MR. RILEY: You change groups a lot, are you doing assessment during that time as well?

MRS. MARTINEZ: I believe assessment is continuous therefore, I'm always assessing students. In addition to the portfolios that the students maintain, I have my own records. You've probably noticed me writing quick notes on Post-it notes. At the end of the day, all of these little notes get transferred into my records. These records contain my anecdotal notes about each child's content knowledge and literacy development. I like to periodically review these notes and look for evidence of increased fluency in English as well as the languages used in their home. If I think a student isn't progressing, I can plan specific lessons, provide individual instruction and reassess the student during small group activities (Au, 1993; Flippo, 1997).

MR. RILEY: You said that you look for increased fluency. How do you know the language proficiency of students?

MRS. MARTINEZ: Language proficiency is a very important topic for teachers, students, and school systems. There are a number of ways that people assess language proficiency. I'm sure you've learned a lot about this in your reading methods course. Most districts, including ours, use standardized proficiency tests. The common ones are Language Assessment

TABLE 6.1   Assessment Accommodations for English Language Learners

Accommodation	Student is . . .
Flexible Scheduling	
Time extension	Provided with extended time
Duration	Provided periodic breaks
Successive administrations	Administered the assessment in sections over time
Multiple days	Given several days to complete the assessment
Setting	
Individual administration	Administered the assessment in a separate location
Small group administration	Given the assessment in a separate location with a small group of peers
Test Directions	
Rewriting directions	Provided simplified language in directions; provided additional examples; provided cues (e.g., arrows or stop signs) on the answer form
Emphasizing key words in directions	Given directions with highlighted instructions or underlined verbs
Reading directions aloud	Provided oral directions for the assessment; reread directions for each page of questions
Native language	Provided with instructions in language of choice
Use of Aids	
Special equipment	Provided auditory tape of test items; provided with markers to maintain place
Proctor / reader	Reread oral comprehension items; read passages, questions, items, and multiple choice responses; provided cues to maintain on-task behavior
Equipment to record responses	Provided tape recorder for taping responses; provided typewriter or word processor with spell and grammar check
Scribes	Provided adults to record answers on paper
Computational aids	Provided use of calculator, abacus, or arithmetic tables

Scale (LAS), Basic Inventory of Natural Language (BINL), Bilingual Syntax Measure (BSM), and Idea Proficiency Test (IPT). While there are good arguments against standardized tests, there are also some very important reasons that we continue to use them (August & Hakuta, 1998). Most importantly, I think, is that these tests keep us focused on the language capabilities of the student. This allows us all to agree on the definition of each level of proficiency.

However, it is important to remember that these assessments will not tell us if a student answered incorrectly because he or she didn't know the concept, didn't understand the language, or didn't have the cultural vocabulary. These assessments also don't tell us the strategies that the students used to decode and make meaning of the text or the type of assistance they may need to develop their fluency. This is why I believe a combination of measures that can provide a more comprehensive measure of performance are needed for instructional planning (Flippo, 1997; Valencia, Hiebert, & Afflerbach, 1994).

MR. RILEY: A lot of what you have said seems useful for assessing all students. Is there anything specific about assessing students who are English-language learners? How do we know when they are ready to transition to the regular classroom?

MRS. MARTINEZ: You are very insightful. Linking instruction to assessment is good for all students. However, you probably also know that programmatic decisions are based directly on students' performance on language proficiency assessments. Although there is great variability among schools in the way assessments are used, most districts have entrance and exit criteria for English-as-a-second-language and bilingual programs. I know that students are ready to transition to the English-only classroom when (1) they can read successfully in their dominant language. This means they should be reading at the 2.5 grade level if they are in the third grade. In grades four to six, they should not be more than one year below their grade level as measured by a standardized, norm-referenced test administered in their dominant language; and (2) they exhibit oral proficiency in both languages as determined by an oral language proficiency assessment device like the Bilingual Syntax Measure (BSM) I and II (Harcourt Brace). If they are ages four to eight, they should perform at level four on BSM I, and if they are age nine and above, they should perform at level four on BSM II.

We do make exceptions to these two criteria if

a. An older student has immigrated who demonstrates skills at grade level or above in the primary language but a lower oral proficiency score in English. Time is an important factor.
b. Parents or the student are opposed to primary language instruction. Attitudes greatly influence one's motivation.
c. A newly transferred student is already reading, writing, and speaking fluently in both languages.
d. The teacher's judgment, which is based on observation, suggests that the student will succeed without primary language support.

Policies governing transitioning differs among districts. We continue to discuss the when, why, and how of transitioning because we do not want to act too quickly or slowly. Again, decisions are based on the assessment of students' performance (Lapp & Flood, 1992).

MR. RILEY: WOW, I see that I have a lot to learn about assessments. I think I have a better idea of what they are, when to do them, and what I will learn from them. I guess I need some more experience with integrating assessments into my instruction. You seem to do it so easily and you know your students so well!

Lessons Learned

Assessment has always been and probably always will be a major component of schooling. Now more than ever educators are inundated with a multitude of choices as they select assessments that will provide appropriate information about students' strengths and needs so that instruction that insures literacy growth for all students can be designed. This has proved especially challenging for teachers of students who are English-language learners (August, Hakuta, & Pompa, 1994; LaCelle-Peterson & Rivera, 1994; Rivera & Vincent, 1997). Current tools for assessment range from informal teacher-made measures to standardized tests. Teachers often use assessments to monitor literacy development and to understand the day-to-day performance of their students.

In addition to the assessments that are used to plan instruction and monitor literacy development, several "high-stakes" assessments are used to make placement decisions for students in special or categorical programs and to provide information for accountability systems and policy analysis (Cummins, 1981; Tucker & Codding, 1998). Statewide assessment information is often used to assess the success of specific programs, such as bilingual education or Title 1 services.

This conversation between Mrs. Martinez and Mr. Riley identified several issues worth examining. These include

1. The link between assessment and instruction must be fluid, realistic, and continuous. Additional information on how Mrs. Martinez makes this link is provided in Chapter 1.
2. There are many reasons to assess students. Not only do teachers use assessments to guide their instruction, but schools are held accountable for the performance of students on statewide assessment systems.
3. Standards-based reform is having a significant impact on assessment, especially for English-language learners. The alignment of assessments to these standards is an important task for teachers to consider.
4. Assessments impact the educational programs for many students, including access to specialized services. Teachers must understand the criteria and support services that are available to students in their district.

Reasons to Assess Students

The public is paying more attention to whom gets tested, what types of tests are used, and what the data mean. Mrs. Martinez noted that teachers must understand that there are multiple types of assessments, even within one state or district system. Assessments vary on the following characteristics: the subject areas and grade levels tested, the item formats used, and the type of skills required (basic versus higher order thinking). Depending on the purpose of the assessments, results can be reported at several different levels: student, classroom, grade, school, district, state, or nation.

Teachers must also understand that students can be assessed for a wide variety of purposes, including:

- Diagnosing individual performance (e.g., assessing developmental status, monitoring and communicating student progress, certifying competency)
- Improving instruction (e.g., evaluating instruction, modifying instructional strategies, identifying instructional needs)
- Evaluating programs
- Providing accountability information

As Mrs. Martinez also pointed out, assessments are much more likely to be based on rigorous academic standards for all students. Students who are English-language learners are expected to master the same content area knowledge as their peers (LaCelle-Peterson & Rivera, 1994). Regardless of the reason or reporting level, teachers are encouraged to base their assessments on district or state expectations of students. For example, in Mrs. Martinez's fourth grade class, all students are expected to demonstrate the same knowledge in social studies as other students in the district. Their performance in this content area includes:

- Writing a story placed in a former time and placing historical events in the proper place in the story line
- Utilizing maps, globes, and other geographic tools to derive information about the relationships between people, places, and the environment over time
- Analyzing the importance of a multicultural perspective that respects the dignity and worth of all people
- Examining major religions and philosophical traditions to evaluate the ways that different societies have tried to resolve ethical issues

The ways in which students demonstrate their knowledge or skill on these standards or expectations vary (Lee & Fradd, 1998). Some teachers use retelling inventories, others use writing rubrics, some create plays and performances, while still others use essay and multiple-choice tests. Regardless of the method, teachers use the information they gather to determine if students have mastered the standards, if any information needs to be reviewed, and which students need further assistance to demonstrate their knowledge (e.g., West, 1998). In other words, teachers use their assessment information to guide their instructional and curricular decisions and their decisions about transitioning students from bilingual programs (August & Hakuta, 1998; Baker, 1993; Padilla, Fairchild, & Valadez, 1990).

Standards-Based Reform

The national effort to improve the educational achievement of America's school children is grounded in the establishment of rigorous learning standards at every level of elementary and secondary education. In developing a standards-based system, policymakers and educators hope to refocus teaching and learning on a common understanding of what communities expect students to know and be able to do as a result of their public school experience. Once established, the standards provide the foundation for curriculum development and assessment systems (Lee & Fradd, 1998; Tucker & Codding, 1998). Curriculum frameworks are outlines that establish benchmarks for curriculum content at the various grade levels, thus providing the broad context from which districts then develop their specific curricula. In some states these frameworks merely provide voluntary guidance to local districts as they develop their curriculum. In other states, the frameworks provide the foundation for new statewide assessment systems and guidance for textbook approval, curriculum priorities, and instructional strategies.

The Relationship Between Standards and Assessment

The proponents of standards-based systemic reform maintain that if high, rigorous standards are created for all students, and clearly communicated to educators, students, family members, business leaders, policymakers, and the community at large, then a coordinated effort can be mounted that focuses on increased achievement (NASBE, 1996). The intended result is that all students, rich and poor, those with limited English proficiency, and students with disabilities will achieve (National Research Council, 1997). In other words, the expectations for all students are increased, and the entire system is focused on helping students achieve those higher expectations.

Student assessment, then, becomes the process by which these standards are measured; however, many of the current assessment systems are not aligned with district or state standards. In addition, in some places, the only tests used are norm-referenced, multiple-choice tests that are unable to be given to students with limited English proficiency or those who have disabilities. As a result, many students, including those who have limited English proficiency, are excluded. The result is assessment data that is not reflective of the student population and may or may not provide useful information about the attainment of standards.

There is also a need to effectively understand and use authentic assessment, such as portfolios, on a school-wide basis to support the curriculum and content standards (Valencia, Hiebert, & Afflerbach, 1994). Assessments that build on student strengths and provide more complete pictures of students' development are needed. This assessment strategy can be equally "applied" across all students by allowing for individualized measurement of each student's personal growth and development. In Mrs. Martinez's classroom, students complete these assessments in the language of their choice. Using this information, Mrs. Martinez learns more about each students' language development and preparedness for transition.

Assessments and Their Link to Educational Services

For students who are English-language learners, assessments are often used to determine the need for additional services (August & Hakuta, 1998; Padilla, Fairchild, & Valadez, 1990). Federal law requires all school districts to identify students who are English-language learners, and many districts use a screening procedure called the home language survey. This survey asks family members a range of questions about the languages used at home. Most commonly, these include

- Which language does your family speak most frequently at home?
- What language did your child learn first?
- Which language does your child speak most frequently at home?
- Does your child speak any other languages?

This quick survey provides information about the potential needs of students and information on students for whom more information is needed. It does not provide information about how much language a student knows, what the preferred language is, other languages understood, or proficiency in English. Very often, as Mrs. Martinez discussed, standardized tests are used to determine the child's current fluency level. Other chapters in this book provide more detail about these assessments. While these tests have been criticized (e.g., August & Hakuta, 1998), they do allow districts to agree on proficiency levels and the services that are provided for students at various levels.

In addition to the language proficiency level of the student, several additional factors should be considered when making placement decisions. These include the age of the student, previous experience with schooling, maturity, peer language broker availability, and the availability of curriculum accommodations and modifications.

Summary

Assessments for students who are English-language learners are used in a variety of ways (Lapp & Flood, 1992). Teachers, such as Mrs. Martinez, use assessments to inform their instruction and planning. Assessments are also used to identify students' language proficiency. These proficiency levels result in specialized services such as English Language Development and two-way bilingual programs. Assessments can also be adapted and modified for students. One way is to provide the assessment in a variety of languages and encourage students to select the language in which they are most comfortable. This is most commonly done when teachers are assessing content knowledge. Assessment accommodations that are individualized, personalized, and consistent have also been developed. Multiple assessments really are an important part of a teacher's repertoire and should be used to better understand a wide range of student performance. As Mr. Riley said on his last day of student teaching

> Assessments can guide my instruction for all students. I've learned that teachers use assessments all the time. I've also learned that students who are English-language learners can and should be assessed. There are many adaptations and modifications that have been developed to ensure students who are acquiring English are successful, both in school and on assessments.

Mrs. Martinez added

> Yes, assessments are a very important part of the overall literacy program. The only way that I know my students, including those who are English-language learners, are moving along the literacy continuum is to assess their development. It makes me feel so good as a teacher to see the results of the time I spend with children.

DISCUSSION QUESTIONS

1. What is the relationship between standards and assessment?
2. How can teachers support students to participate in assessments?
3. What is the link between assessment and educational services?
4. Why do we assess students?
5. In what ways are assessments beneficial to teachers?

REFERENCES

Au, K. (1993). *Literacy instruction in multicultural settings.* Fort Worth, TX: Harcourt Brace Jovanovich College.

August, D., & Hakuta, K. (Eds.). (1998). *Educating language minority students.* Washington, DC: National Academy.

August, D., Hakuta, K., & Pompa, D. (1994). *For all students: Limited English proficient students and goals 2000.* NCBE Focus: Occasional Papers in Bilingual Education, 10. [http://www.ncbe.gwu.edu/ncbepubs/]

Baker, C. (1993). *Foundations of bilingual education and bilingualism.* Philadelphia, PA: Multilingual matters.

Barr, R., Kamil, M. L., Mosenthal, P., & Pearson, P. D. (Eds.). (1991). *Handbook of reading research.* New York: Longman.

Cummins, J. (1981). The role of primary language development in promoting educational success for language minority students. In California State Department of Education (Ed.), *Schooling and language minority students: A theoretical framework* (pp. 3–49). Los Angeles: California State Department of Education.

Flippo, R. F. (1997). *Reading assessment and instruction: A qualitative approach to diagnosis.* New York: Harcourt Brace.

LaCelle-Peterson, M. W., & Rivera, C. (1994). Is it real for all kids? A framework for equitable assessment policies for English language learners. *Harvard Educational Review, 64,* 55–75.

Lapp, D., & Flood, J. (1992). *Teaching reading to every child, 3rd ed.* New York: Macmillan.

Lapp, D., Flood, J., & Farnan, N. (Eds.). (1996). *Content area reading and learning: Instructional strategies, 2nd ed.* Boston: Allyn & Bacon.

Lee, O., & Fradd, S. H. (1998). Science for all, including students from non-English backgrounds. *Educational Researcher, 27,* 12–21.

National Research Council. (1997). *Educating one and all: Students with disabilities and standards-based reform.* Washington, DC: National Academy.

NASBE (National Association of State Boards of Education). (1996). *What will it take? Standards based reform for all students.* Alexandria, VA: Author.

Padilla, A. M., Fairchild, H. H., & Valadez, C. M. (Eds.). (1990). *Bilingual education: Issues and strategies.* Newbury Park, CA: Sage.

Rivera, C., & Vincent, C. (1997). High school graduation testing: Policies and practices in the assessment of English language learners. *Educational Assessment, 4,* 335–355.

Tucker, M., & Codding, J. (1998). *Standards for our schools: How to set them, measure them, and reach them.* San Francisco: Jossey-Bass.

Valencia, S. W., Hiebert, E. H., & Afflerbach, P. P. (Eds.). (1994). *Authentic reading assessment: Practices and possibilities.* Newark, DE: IRA.

West, K. (1998). Noticing and responding to learners: Literacy evaluation and instruction in the primary grades. *The Reading Teacher, 51,* 550–561.

7 Assessment and Intervention with Culturally and Linguistically Diverse Learners

JIM CUMMINS
University of Toronto

Ms. Sampson

Ms. Sampson (not real name), an English-as-a-second-language (ESL) teacher in a large multiethnic Toronto high school, was concerned that Phan Nguyen (not real name), a student of Vietnamese origin in one of her classes, was experiencing speech and possibly auditory discrimination difficulties that were impeding his learning of English and, as a consequence, other academic subjects. This student's difficulties were much greater than those of other students from the same background. Ms. Sampson contacted the student services department of the school system to explore the possibility of arranging a speech and hearing assessment for the student. She was referred to one of the speech and language pathologists in the department who listened sympathetically to the description of the student's difficulties but who declined to become involved on the grounds that she had "no expertise in assessing ESL students." When pressed as to whether the department's policy excluded ESL students, the speech and language pathologist replied that "We have no instruments that would be valid for such students." When further pressed as to why intervention to assist the student's obvious articulation problems could not be undertaken, the speech and language pathologist reiterated that "There were just too many variables involved" to make intervention feasible. In the absence of any specialized assistance from the student services department, the ESL teacher whose philology training in Europe had included development of expertise in the phonetic alphabet, used this strategy with some success to help Phan acquire strategies to deal with his articulation difficulties in English.

The Problem

This vignette recounts an actual case that illustrates an unresolved dilemma that confronts teachers, policy-makers, and assessment specialists on a daily basis in large urban centers throughout North America: How can we distinguish between language and learning difficulties that are a reflection of the normal process of learning English as a second language from those that may be reflective of intrinsic or "genuine" learning or language disorders that require special education intervention? Despite a considerable body of research on these issues (e.g., Damico, Oller, & Storey, 1983; González, Brusca-Vega, & Yawkey, 1997), until recently the problems of bilingual and multicultural assessment have not been addressed in a sustained way within the mainstream disciplines of school psychology and speech and language pathology.

Within the mainstream interpretive perspective there are currently four main options for assessment of bilingual students' cognitive and academic abilities. None of these adequately resolves the problem of distinguishing "genuine" language or learning disorders from the "normal" developmental patterns of academic learning in a second language. These four options are

1. *Administer the usual diagnostic battery but take account of students' bilingual background in interpreting the test profile.* This first option is still the most frequent. It involves assessing students with verbal and nonverbal measures of ability (such as the Wechsler Intelligence Scale for Children [WISC] 3), while attempting to take account of the student's bilingual background in interpreting the results. The dangers of this approach are evident in the documented overrepresentation of culturally diverse students in various special education categories. For example, in the early 1970s, Jane Mercer (1973) showed that there were between three and four times as many African American and Latino students in classes for the educable mentally retarded as would be expected based on their proportion in the school population. In Texas, Ortiz and Yates (1983) similarly found a threefold overrepresentation of Latino students in the "learning disability" category. More recent documentation indicates that the problem persists (e.g., Jitendra & Rohena-Diaz, 1996; McNamara, 1998; Oller, 1997). Johnson and Supik (1999), for example, reported that the number of limited English-proficient students assigned to special education classes in Texas rose by 11.7 percent between the 1996 and 1997 and 1998 and 1999 school years.

Oller (1997) describes as *monoglottosis* the tendency of monolinguals to ignore or underestimate the influence of language proficiency on individuals' performance of a variety of academic and real life tasks. The history of psychological assessment of bilingual students illustrates this condition, and it is not at all clear that monolingual professionals, whose training has often paid at best lip-service to these issues, are in a position to interpret the meaning of bilingual students' performance on diagnostic measures. The very evident cultural and linguistic biases in commonly used psychological assessment tools together with a lack of awareness of typical patterns of bilingual development among monolingual assessment specialists does not augur well for the validity of interpretations that might be derived from administration of these measures to culturally and linguistically diverse students.

2. *Delay assessment in the hope that the student's poor academic performance is the result of "normal" second language development.* This second option involves adopting a "wait-and-see" attitude and delaying formal testing of students perceived to be "at risk" for several years in the hope that the student's difficulties resolve themselves without intervention. The reasoning here is that because no psychoeducational or psycholinguistic tests are available to assess students who are in the process of learning English (henceforth English-language learning [ELL] students), then neither assessment nor intervention is possible regardless of the seriousness of the student's difficulties.

Clearly, a significant number of students who may require, and have the legal right to, special education intervention are denied access as a result of this orientation. The fact that overrepresentation of culturally and linguistically diverse students in special education categories as a result of biased assessment and inadequate instruction has been characteristic of North American school systems in the past is no excuse to abandon assessment and intervention for these students altogether. The current reality is that both overrepresentation and underrepresentation of culturally and linguistically diverse students represent major unresolved problems.

3. *Administer only nonverbal measures.* A third strategy is to administer only the nonverbal sections of cognitive ability tests. This strategy, like the previous one, does reduce the risks of overrepresentation because, in general, nonverbal measures are less culturally loaded or biased than verbal measures (Cummins, 1984), although by no means free of linguistic influence (Oller, 1997). This strategy, however, fails to take account of the fact that more than 70 percent of students identified as "learning disabled" experience problems in the verbal academic aspects of achievement rather than in the nonverbal aspects. Thus, assessment only of students' nonverbal abilities fails to identify many students who may have genuine learning problems in verbal academics that require special education intervention.

4. *Administer first language assessment.* A fourth strategy is to assess students in their first language (L_1) in addition to English to obtain a fuller picture of the student's intellectual and linguistic development. This strategy, while admirable in intent, is also no panacea. In the first place, this option is usually available only to Spanish L_1 students, and even in this case the supply of bilingual psychologists and speech and language pathologists represents only a fraction of the need. Also, L_1 assessment is often problematic with respect to the appropriateness of interpretive norms that may be derived from monolingual Spanish speakers who have grown up in a societal situation in which Spanish is reinforced both in the school and wider society. By contrast, bilingual students whose L_1 is used minimally or not at all in the school do not have the opportunity to develop high levels of literacy and verbal and academic proficiencies in that language. Frequently, their oral skills in the language also atrophy because of the strong social and educational pressures to give up their home language in favor of English. In addition, the varieties of Spanish that many students speak as their L_1 diverge from the standard Spanish of formal tests. These tests may also discriminate against Spanish L_1 students giving the false impression that students are weak in both their languages.

Thus, a complex array of variables must be taken into account in interpreting the results of L_1 assessment: for example, whether the norms are from the student's country of origin or from a U.S. sample, how long the student has been intensively exposed to English, the degree of support for L_1 conceptual development in both the home and school contexts, the social and peer pressure to replace L_1 with language two (L_2), etc.

Even when the student's L_1 is his or her "dominant" language, interpretation of the test results is not unproblematic. The L_1 and L_2 conceptual repertoire of a bilingual student typically develops according to domains of language use. Thus, domains such as the home and church / mosque / temple may be better developed in the L_1 while domains such as the school, television, and peer interaction may be in the process of becoming more developed in English. As a consequence, separate monolingual testing in either L_1 or L_2, or both L_1 and L_2, underestimates the student's total conceptual repertoire. Testing in either language "misses out" some of the domains that are better developed in the other language. In short, for several years after initial exposure to English, bilingual students are likely to perform lower than monolingual students in both L_1 and L_2 in the areas of verbal and academic abilities. This pattern is not because their abilities in either language are deficient in any sense but because of the developmental patterns that tend to characterize the gradual shift from one dominant language to another.

In short, the teacher would inappropriately conclude on the basis of this pattern that the student has some kind of language or learning problem. The problem is with the test assumptions rather than with the bilingual student. To assess bilingual students as though they had two separate monolingual competencies in their heads and to compare these competencies to monolingual norms ignores the reality of bilingual development (Grosjean, 1989). Not only do the bilingual's two languages develop according to domains of use, bilinguals often codeswitch between their two languages and develop a "contact variety" in which expressions and structures of each language influence the other. To apply monolingual prescriptive norms to these varieties is inappropriate and potentially discriminatory.

An L_1 assessment by itself, therefore, is most useful in the early stages of the student's learning of English. When an immigrant or refugee student arrives in the school, L_1 assessment can provide important information on the student's previous learning and this can be interpreted (cautiously) as an index of academic potential. For most languages, however, L_1 assessment is, of necessity, informal because standardized tests and norms are simply not available. In the context of bilingual programs that aim to promote L_1 literacy, L_1 assessment can play an important diagnostic role as an index of L_1 conceptual and literacy development. In the United States, however, this situation applies primarily to students in Spanish-English bilingual programs.

The need for alternative assessment approaches becomes even more evident in the context of research findings related to the length of time ELL students require to catch up academically in English.

Research Findings on the Length of Time English-Language Learners Require to Catch Up Academically

A number of large-scale studies have reported that, on the average, at least five years is required for ELL students to attain grade norms on academic aspects of English proficiency (Collier, 1987, 1992; Cummins, 1981; Klesmer, 1994; Ramírez, 1992). Collier's data are particularly interesting in that most students were from relatively affluent backgrounds attending a district (Fairfax County, Virginia) that was regarded as having an exemplary ESL program (and no bilingual education). She reports that children who arrived in the United States between ages eight and twelve, with several years of L_1 schooling, required five to seven years to reach national norms in reading, social studies, and science. Those who arrived before age eight required seven to ten years to attain national norms, while those who arrived after age twelve often ran out of time before they could catch up academically in language-based areas of the curriculum. A considerably shorter period of time was usually required to catch up in math.

Cummins (1981) also reported that five to seven years were required for immigrant students from non-English-speaking backgrounds to catch up academically in English proficiency. Students who had been in Canada for three years were approximately one standard deviation (the equivalent of 15 IQ points) behind grade norms despite the fact that after three years most would have become relatively fluent in English

Klesmer's (1994) study involved a representative sample of almost three hundred twelve-year-old ELL students in a metropolitan Toronto school district. Detailed assessments of English proficiency, background data, and teacher ratings were obtained. Klesmer reported that teachers considered most ELL students as average for their age in speaking, listening and reading after twenty-four to thirty-five months in Canada. In the area of writing, teachers considered ELL students to have almost reached the mean for Canadian-born students after five or six years. The test data, however, showed significant gaps between the ELL students and a control group of English-as-a-first-language students (N=43) in all areas, except nonverbal ability, even after six years length of residence. The control group performed at the level of test norms while the ELL students were considerably below test norms on verbal academic measures. Klesmer (1994) concluded that

> there is strong evidence to suggest that the academic/linguistic development of ESL students follows a distinct pattern. It requires at least six years for ESL students to approach native English speakers' norms in a variety of areas; and it appears that, even after six years, full comparability may not be achieved. (p. 11)

Other research suggests that a much shorter period of time (less than two years) is usually required for immigrant students to attain peer-appropriate levels of proficiency in conversational aspects of their second language (e.g., González, 1986; Snow & Hoefnagel-Hohle, 1978).

There are two reasons why such major differences are found in the length of time required to attain peer-appropriate levels of conversational and academic skills. First, as outlined above, considerably less knowledge of language per se is usually required to function appropriately in interpersonal communicative situations than is required in academic situations. The social expectations of the learner and sensitivity to paralinguistic and contextual cues greatly facilitate communication of meaning. These cues are largely absent in academic situations such as reading a text on social studies. In other words, mastery of the academic register of language to native speaker levels takes longer because this register encompasses specific lexical, syntactic, and discoursal features that are not generally available in everyday conversational linguistic interactions. They are available primarily in classrooms and in written texts and, therefore, the quality of students' school experiences is likely to play a significant role in the rapidity with which ELL students get access to these functions of language.

The second reason is that native English-speakers are not standing still waiting for ELL students to catch up. A major goal of schooling for all children is to expand their ability to manipulate language in increasingly abstract or decontextualized situations, and every year native English-speaking students gain more sophisticated vocabulary and grammatical knowledge and increase their literacy skills. ELL students, therefore, must catch up with a moving target. It is not surprising that this formidable task is seldom complete in one or two years. By contrast, in the area of conversational skills, most native speakers have reached a plateau relatively early in schooling in the sense that a typical six-year-old can express herself as adequately as an older child on most topics she is likely to speak and understand most of what is likely to be addressed to her. While some increase in sophistication can be expected with increasing age, the differences are not particularly salient in comparison to differences in literacy-related skills.

Implications of the Research for Assessment and Intervention

The research data on the length of time typically required for ELL students to catch up in English verbal academic performance have implications both for assessment and intervention. For assessment, these data reinforce the problematic nature of the assessment options previously considered. English verbal academic assessment ignores what bilingual students know in their L_1 and underestimates their potential until they have been learning English for at least five years. Delaying assessment and adopting a "wait-and-see" attitude risks denying intervention for up to five years to students who may need it. An L_1 assessment may be useful in the early stages (in cases in which assessment instruments exist) but interpretation becomes increasingly challenging as students' length of residence increases and concepts in domains associated with school and literacy are increasingly developed in English rather than in L_1.

One strategy that addresses these assessment concerns involves using an innovative assessment procedure (the Bilingual Verbal Abilities Tests [BVATs]) to estimate the combined L_1 and L_2 verbal conceptual repertoire of bilingual students. Assessing the combined L_1 and L_2 knowledge of bilingual students acknowledges the dynamic nature of bilingual development and the fact that students' knowledge is distributed unevenly across different domains in both languages. The BVATs, therefore, potentially can help answer the question of whether a particular student's academic difficulty is caused by some form of "intrinsic" learning disability or simply reflective of the normal process of catching up academically in English.

In the upcoming sections, the BVAT is first described and then an intervention project is described that used the BVAT as a tool for assessing the impact of bilingual family literacy activities.

Assessment: The Bilingual Verbal Abilities Tests

The BVAT (Muñoz-Sandoval, Cummins, Alvarado, & Ruef, 1998) was developed specifically to address the assessment concerns previously outlined. Three verbal tests derived from the Woodcock Johnson–Revised battery (picture vocabulary, oral vocabulary, and verbal analogies) constitute the BVAT together with translations of these tests into fifteen additional languages (Arabic, Chinese, French, German, Korean, Haitian Creole, Hindi, Italian, Japanese, Polish, Portuguese, Russian, Spanish, Turkish, Vietnamese). The goal of the procedure is to take account of the realities of the bilingual student's language development by estimating the student's total conceptual and language repertoire regardless of the specific linguistic source. In other words, the BVAT combines verbal-cognitive L_1 and L_2 assessment in the same instrument. Items that the student fails in English are subsequently assessed in the student's L_1 to ascertain whether the student has that knowledge or ability developed in L_1 despite the fact that it is not yet developed in English. The English score is combined with the increment from L_1 testing of items missed in English and the total score ($L_2 + L_1$) is interpreted in relation to test norms.

As documented by Muñoz-Sandoval, et al. (1998), bilingual students in the early stages of learning English are likely to gain considerably from the L_1 incremental scores, while those who have been learning English for more than five years or who are in situations in which rapid language shift is occurring gain much less from L_1 testing. The construct of bilingual verbal ability represents an estimate of the underlying proficiency that is common to the bilingual's L_1 and L_2 (Cummins, 1984, 1996) together with the unique verbal concepts in L_1 and L_2 that are distributed across different domains in the bilingual student's L_1 and L_2 and are not yet common to both languages.

Although considerably more research and practical experience are required to assess the usefulness of the BVAT, there are some potential uses for both clinical and classroom-based assessment. The following uses have been identified by the authors (Muñoz-Sandoval, et al., 1998) of the instrument.

Clinical Assessment

- The BVAT enables more equitable assessment of bilingual students' verbal academic ability to be carried out earlier than would be the case with English-only assessment, which underestimates bilingual students' verbal ability for at least five years after they start learning English. It can be used, therefore, in conjunction with a nonverbal ability test and academic achievement measures to provide a comprehensive assessment of bilingual children's academic ability and performance.

- The BVAT provides important additional information relevant to identification of learning disabilities among bilingual children. Because children's knowledge in their L_1 is taken into account in the assessment, clinicians can place greater confidence in their judgment regarding the nature of children's educational needs and in their recommendations regarding placement. The BVAT reduces the risk of overrepresentation of bilingual students in special education. Also, bilingual children who may need special education assistance can be identified much sooner and more reliably than previously.

- Identification of gifted and talented bilingual students is facilitated through use of the BVAT. Conventional identification procedures for gifted and talented programs underestimate children's verbal abilities for at least five years, very much reducing the possibility that gifted bilingual children will be identified. English-only identification procedures penalize children for their bilingualism. By contrast, the BVAT *rewards* children for their bilingualism by taking account of what they know in both their languages.

Classroom and Preclinical Assessment

- The BVAT can provide teachers in bilingual or English-only programs with information on children's verbal academic ability that supplements assessments of children's English academic achievement. It can also be used to monitor growth in academic development over time.
- For children who are transitioning from bilingual to English-only mainstream classrooms, the BVAT can provide teachers with (a) a measure of children's English cognitive academic language proficiency and (b) a measure of children's overall verbal academic ability that includes both English and L_1 conceptual knowledge. This is likely to be a more accurate estimate of children's academic potential than what is provided either by English-only assessments or from observation of children's English academic performance.
- For children who are receiving remedial support before formal special education referral, the BVAT can supplement the direct observation of classroom and support teachers with a more formal assessment of the child's verbal academic abilities. This form of assessment can provide important information as to whether referral for full psychological assessment is warranted.

In summary, the BVAT goes some way to overcoming the problems diagnosticians typically encounter in attempting to assess bilingual students' academic potential. By combining L_2 and L_1 assessment, the BVAT potentially provides a more complete picture of the bilingual student's verbal academic abilities. I emphasize, however, that assessment does not stand alone. It assumes meaning only when it is explicitly linked to intervention. The relationship between assessment and intervention is a two-way process: assessment should clearly inform intervention, but the results of prior intervention should also inform assessment and placement decisions. Intervention does not have to wait until assessment is concluded.

Intervention: The Centrality of Reading for Academic Language Development

Clearly, a variety of intervention strategies have been articulated in the literature on bilingual students' academic development (see, for example, Tinajero & Ada, 1993; Cummins, 1996). Here, however, I focus only on one central aspect of any intervention strategy: the crucial role of both L_1 and L_2 reading in accelerating students' academic development.

The difference in length of time typically required for students to attain peer-appropriate levels in conversational versus academic verbal skills suggests that both ESL and regular classroom instruction should focus not only on developing students' conversational fluency in English but also on their academic proficiency in the language. Students must gain access to the language of literature, science, math, and other content areas. As previously mentioned, this academic language entails vocabulary that is much less frequent than that typically found in interpersonal conversation, grammatical constructions that are unique to text and considerably more complex than those found in conversation, and significant cognitive processing demands that derive from the fact that meanings expressed paralinguistically in conversation (e.g., gestures, facial expressions, intonation, etc.) must be expressed linguistically in text.

Where do students find access to this complex textual language? Simply expressed, the language of text is found primarily in books and in classroom instruction. Students' knowledge of academic language and their ability to use it in their own writing, therefore, is crucially dependent on what they read. In other words, if ELL students are not reading extensively in a variety of genres, they are not getting access to the language of academic success.

The importance of reading for ELL students who are experiencing academic difficulties is dramatically illustrated in a two-year project carried out in six schools in an inner-city area of London, England that showed major improvements in children's reading skills simply as a result of sending books home on a regular basis with the children for them to read to their parents, many of whom spoke little English and were illiterate in both English and their L1 (predominantly Bengali and Greek) (Tizard, Schofield, & Hewison, 1982). The children attending the two schools that implemented the "shared literacy" program made significantly greater progress in reading than a comparison group in two different schools who received additional small-group reading instruction from a highly competent reading specialist. Both groups made greater progress than a control group in two schools who received no special treatment. Teachers involved in the home collaboration reported that children showed an increased interest in school learning and were better behaved.

Of particular importance is the fact that the differences in favor of the shared literacy program were most apparent among children who were initially having difficulty in learning to read. By contrast additional small-group reading instruction was least effective for these students who were experiencing reading difficulties. This finding suggests that involving culturally diverse parents in a family literacy project can be a highly effective and cost-effective strategy for intervention to assist students who are at risk of reading failure. The impact of this project in motivating students to read can be seen from the fact that the students in the two "shared reading" schools exhausted the supply of books in the school libraries that were appropriate for early elementary grades simply because they read so much.

Several reasons can be suggested for the success of this project. First, it changed fundamentally the relationship between the schools and community. Partnerships were established that enabled parents to play an important role in helping their children succeed academically. Second, the project motivated students to read more, and the more students read, the stronger their reading skills become (Krashen, 1993; Fielding & Pearson, 1994). Third, many students likely would have translated or paraphrased the story for their parents in their L_1 because the parents would have had limited knowledge of English. This constitutes a cognitively demanding activity that may have increased students' overall ability to analyze the semantic and syntactic aspects of text. Whatever the underlying reasons for the dramatic impact of this program, the role of parents is a largely untapped resource in accelerating students' academic development. Clearly, books can be sent home in students' L_1 as an alternative to or in addition to books in English. The crucial aspect of this type of family literacy project is that students become motivated to read for pleasure outside of school because only in books do they find the academic language they need to succeed in school.

The following section considers a practical application of the Tizard, et al. (1982) findings in an intervention involving Portuguese-background bilingual students in Toronto, Canada.

A Practical Application of the Shared Reading Program and BVAT Assessment

To assess the extent to which initiation of family literacy activities in L_1 would increase grade one and two students' verbal academic performance, a project was undertaken in an inner-city Toronto school with a high proportion of Portuguese background students. The students received thirty minutes of Portuguese instruction daily through the provincially funded International Languages Program; however, the bulk of their schooling since prekindergarten (age four) had been in English.

As part of the project funding, sixty Portuguese books suitable for early primary students were purchased for the school library and over the course of a seven-month period these were sent home with the students on a regular basis for reading with their parents. When students returned one book they were eligible to take home another. Students were also encouraged to take home books in English if they so desired. The BVAT was used on a pre- and post-test basis to assess gains in verbal academic performance in comparison to a similar group of Portuguese background students from a nearby school who did not participate in a family literacy project. Twenty-three grade one and twenty-three grade two students participated in the family literacy project, and the comparison group consisted of sixteen grade one and fifteen grade two students.

For most students in the study, language shift from Portuguese to English was already well underway as a result of the power of English and the relative lack of reinforcement of the L_1 in the social environment. A previous study in the same schools (Cummins, 1991) had shown that only a small percentage of students maintained strong fluency in Portuguese past the grade-one year, but those who did maintain Portuguese were performing better academically in English reading. Therefore, it is not surprising that for most grade-one and two students (N=77) tested in both Fall (November) and late Spring (June), little increment was observed on the BVAT when items missed in English were retested in Portuguese. This contrasts with the significant increments observed for many Hispanic students in Texas (Muñoz-Sandoval, et al., 1998).

Despite the overall minimal increment attained as a result of L_1 assessment, for some students the increment would have made a considerable difference in diagnostic interpretation of the test results. One grade-two student, for example, whose parents had immigrated from Brazil at the start of the student's schooling (three years previously) would have obtained a grade equivalent of K.7 (W score = 463) on the oral vocabulary subtest and a grade equivalent of K.6 (W score=471) on verbal analogies had the English score (Fall administration) been interpreted by itself. The increment derived from assessing the student's Portuguese knowledge resulted in grade equivalents of 1.5 (W=472) and 1.7 (W=480). If the English score in the Fall had been taken at face value, this student might have been viewed as a candidate for special education intervention because her score was one-and-a-half years behind grade level. The inappropriateness of this interpretation is clear from the fact that this student was performing at grade level by the end of the grade-two school year when combined English and L_1 scores were taken into account.

Although the intervention period was short (seven months), a significant difference was observed between treatment and comparison groups on the picture vocabulary measure when November scores were used as a covariate and June scores as dependent variable. The group that engaged in the family literacy project showed significantly better ($p<.001$) performance by the end of the school year. This finding was consistent for both grade-one and grade-two groups when analyzed separately (grade one, $p=.01$; grade two, $p=.05$). No significant differences were observed on the other two subtests. The total number of books students reported reading was significantly related to June picture vocabulary ($p<.05$) and approached significance for November picture vocabulary ($p=.05$). Correlations with the other measures did not attain significance.

Although this is a small scale study, it provides some limited support for the usefulness of involving parents and students in family literacy activities in the early grades in either or both L_1 and L_2. It also suggests that the BVAT is potentially sensitive to changes in vocabulary knowledge that might be brought about by such family literacy activities. Furthermore, although L_1 assessment of items missed in English made little difference for the majority of the sample because of the advanced stage of language shift that three to four years of schooling had effected, for some students the increment made a very significant difference that would be diagnostically significant in a special educational testing situation.

Conclusion

Assessment of culturally and linguistically diverse students has, up to now, relied on inadequate conceptualizations of the nature of both language proficiency in general and bilingual students' language development in particular. English proficiency has often been viewed implicitly as a unitary construct, and the very different developmental patterns of L_2 conversational and academic language have not been taken into account in the assessment process. The result has been widespread overrepresentation of bilingual students in special education.

Partly in reaction to this historical pattern of overrepresentation, many assessment specialists currently tend to err on the side of caution and postpone assessment of bilingual students for several years or administer only nonverbal cognitive measures. As outlined previously, these strategies risk denying intervention services to students who may urgently require such services.

When L_1 assessment has been implemented, the implicit assumption has frequently been that bilinguals can be assessed as though there were two separate monolingual proficiencies in their heads. This strategy fails to take account of the research on the close developmental relationship between L_1 and L_2 when both are promoted either through home interaction or instruction in school (Cummins, 1996). L_1 assessment has also failed to take account of the fact that languages develop according to domains of use, with the result that separate L_1 and L_2 assessment likely underestimates the totality of a bilingual's conceptual repertoire. I have suggested that diagnostic assessment of bilingual students should attempt to take account of the totality of the bilingual's combined knowledge in L_1 and L_2. The BVAT represents an initial attempt to provide such an instrument.

In addition, however, diagnosticians and educators should not wait for formal assessment results before initiating intervention. The time periods required for bilingual students to catch up academically suggest that active steps should be taken from the beginning to maximize students' opportunities and incentives to engage in reading and writing activities. The research project previously outlined and other research (Tizard, et al., 1982) suggest that involving parents in this process can pay significant dividends even when the parents may not have had opportunities themselves to become literate and may speak little or no English. There are obviously many other strategies for increasing students' opportunities and incentives to engage in literacy in the early grades (e.g., establishing reading buddies with older students, language experience approaches). Extreme caution should be exercised in categorizing bilingual students as disabled or handicapped in any way unless we can document that they have had maximum opportunity and incentive through their instruction to participate in literacy activities.

In other words, the traditional special education paradigm has viewed intervention as following the assessment process; the perspective articulated here suggests that assessment is likely to be appropriate and valid only when it follows an effective classroom or school-based intervention process. The role definition of the assessment specialist, therefore, must change from simply being an administrator of tests (as the speech and language pathologist in our vignette viewed herself) to becoming an advocate for students who are experiencing academic or language difficulties and working directly with classroom teachers to intervene and resolve these difficulties.

DISCUSSION QUESTIONS

1. What are the causes of overrepresentation of bilingual students in special education programs? What weight would you assign to assessment compared to instructional factors?

2. To what extent is any testing of cognitive ability or IQ justified in schools? Work with a partner (or in two groups) to make the case for an against IQ testing in schools. One partner or group should make the case for IQ testing and the other should argue against it.

3. The concept of a "learning disability" usually entails a distinction between the student's "ability" and "achievement," which cannot be attributed to cultural, linguistic, or other socialization factors. In light of this definition, what do you think are the best ways to determine whether or not a student from a culturally and linguistically diverse group has a "genuine" learning disability? How important do you think teachers' classroom observations should be in this process compared to formal psychoeducational assessment?

4. In view of the positive outcomes from sending books home for children and parents to read together reported in the chapter, do you think it would be more beneficial to send books home in English or in students' home language?

5. The current funding of special education provision in the United States requires that eligible students be identified by formal assessment instruments and placed in the appropriate program on the basis of this assessment. As a result of limited funds in many districts, this process can take a considerable period of time (e.g., up to six months). What kinds of intervention should educators attempt to undertake with underachieving students while they are on the waiting list for psychoeducational assessment, and how do you think they may be able to find the resources to carry out this intervention?

REFERENCES

Collier, V. P. (1987). Age and rate of acquisition of second language for academic purposes. *TESOL Quarterly, 21,* 617–641.

Collier, V. (1992). A synthesis of studies examining long-term language-minority student data on academic achievement. *Bilingual Research Journal, 16*(1,2), 187–212.

Cummins, J. (1981). Age on arrival and immigrant second language learning in Canada: A reassessment. *Applied Linguistics, 2,* 132–149.

Cummins J. (1984). *Bilingualism and special education: Issues in assessment and pedagogy.* Clevedon, England: Multilingual Matters.

Cummins, J. (1991). The development of bilingual proficiency from home to school: A longitudinal study of Portuguese-speaking children. *Journal of Education, 173,* 85–98.

Cummins, J. (1996). *Negotiating identities: Education for empowerment in a diverse society.* Los Angeles: California Association for Bilingual Education.

Damico, J. S., Oller, J. W. Jr., & Storey, M. E. (1983). The diagnosis of language disorders in bilingual children: Surface-oriented and pragmatic criteria. *Journal of Speech and Hearing Disorders, 48,* 385–394.

Fielding, L. G., & Pearson, P. D. (1994). Reading comprehension: What works. *Educational Leadership, 51*(5), 62–68.

González, L. A. (1986). The effects of first language education on the second language and academic achievement of Mexican immigrant elementary school children in the United States. Unpublished paper, College of Education, University of Illinois at Urbana-Champaign.

González, V., Brusca-Vega, R., & Yawkey, T. (1997). *Assessment and instruction of culturally and linguistically diverse students with or at-risk of learning problems.* Boston: Allyn and Bacon.

Grosjean, F. (1989). Neurolinguists beware! The bilingual is not two monolinguals in one person. *Brain and Language, 36,* 3–15.

Jitendra, A. K., & Rohena-Diaz, E. (1996). Language assessment of students who are linguistically diverse: Why a discrete approach is not the answer. *School Psychology Review, 25,* 40–56.

Johnson, R., & Supik (1999, September). More students served in bilingual and ESL programs but more LEP students assigned to special education. *IDRA Newsletter.* (http://www.idra.org/Newslttr/1999/Sep/Roy.htm)

Klesmer, H. (1994). Assessment and teacher perceptions of ESL student achievement. *English Quarterly, 26*(3), 8–11.

Krashen, S. (1993). *The power of reading.* Englewood, CO: Libraries Unlimited.

McNamara, B. E. (1998). *Learning disabilities: Appropriate practices for a diverse population.* Albany: State University of New York Press.

Muñoz-Sandoval, A., Cummins, J., Alvarado, C. G., & Ruef, M. (1998). *The bilingual verbal abilities tests.* Itasca, IL: Riverside Publishing.

Mercer, J. (1973). *Labelling the mentally retarded.* Los Angeles: University of California.

Oller, J. W. Jr. (1997). Monoglottosis: What's wrong with the idea of the IQ meritocracy and its racy cousins? *Applied Linguistics, 18*(4), 467–507.

Ortiz, A. A., & Yates, J. R. (1983). Incidence of exceptionality among Hispanics: Implications for manpower planning. *NABE Journal, 7,* 41–54.

Ramírez, J. D. (1992). Executive summary. *Bilingual Research Journal, 16,* 1–62.

Snow, D. E., & Hoefnagel-Hohle, M. (1978). The critical period for language acquisition: Evidence from second language learning. *Child Development, 49,* 1114–1128.

Tinajero, J. V., & Ada, A. F. (Eds.). (1993). *The power of two languages: Literacy and biliteracy for Spanish-speaking students.* New York: Macmillan/McGraw-Hill.

Tizard, J., Schofield, W. N., & Hewison, J. (1982). Collaboration between teachers and parents in assisting children's reading. *British Journal of Educational Psychology, 52,* 1–15.

8

Needed: A Framework for Integrating Standardized and Informal Assessment for Students Developing Academic Language Proficiency in English

SANDRA H. FRADD AND OKHEE LEE
University of Miami

The teacher pondered what to do to ensure that his students performed well on the upcoming statewide writing assessment, while keeping them motivated to learn academic content he realized was also important. As he thought about how to meet the demands of assessment-driven instruction while using informal assessment to promote learning, he turned to the class and said:

T: OK, now we need to get really good at writing our five-paragraph responses. Here's a new prompt I would like for you to try today.

JOSÉ: Oh, no, not again. Do we have to? We have already written paragraphs three times this week! Can't we do something else today?

MARÍA: Yeah, can't we do science? We haven't done it all week.

JORGE: Yeah, all we do is practice for tests. When can we do things we like to learn?

T: OK. You win. Let's rewrite the paragraphs you did yesterday, and then we'll do science. I have this really great activity I know you'll love. We're gonna make biospheres.

CLASS: Yeeeeeeaaah!!!! (accentuated with lots of clapping)

The authors recognize the support from the National Science Foundation under Grant No. REC-9552556. Any opinions, findings, and conclusions or recommendations expressed in this publication are those of the authors and do not necessarily reflect the position, policy, or endorsement of the funding agency.

One of the greatest challenges schools face is enabling students from diverse language backgrounds to acquire the academic discourse required to comprehend textbooks and participate in content area instruction (Gardner, 1990; Heath, 1983). Literacy learning can be challenging for many young learners. For students acquiring English language literacy as they gain content area knowledge, the challenge can be particularly great. This chapter considers ways the challenge can effectively be met so that all students have access to the learning opportunities required for academic success. For purposes of this chapter, the students who are the focus of this discussion are referred to as English Language Learners (ELLs).

Like the one described above, most classrooms are filled with sounds and images of students interacting and learning. Meaningful communication grows from a desire to convey ideas, share interests, relate to others, and achieve results. A wealth of student information is potentially available by listening, observing, and analyzing students' meaningful communication. Insights into students' progress in developing academic language is available through such informal assessments, producing information about students' academic progress based on regular observations and collection of student products.

During the past decade efforts to promote alternatives to the narrow instructional focus imposed by standardized, one-size-fits-all assessment have had an impact on the way assessment information is collected, interpreted, and used for instruction (O'Connor, 1992). Although the limitations of standardized assessment are well known, recent research indicates the dichotomy between informal, classroom and large-scale, whole-district assessment continues. In fact, the use of large-scale assessment data remains the preferred source of information about students achievement (Stake, 1999). Not until teachers' decisions about student achievement based on informal classroom procedures are accepted as being valid as the results of standardized tests will teachers be accepted as professional educators (Mabry, 1999). More importantly, not until teachers are able to effectively use informal assessment procedures will students with limited educational opportunities and developing English proficiency have access to the kinds of quality instructional experiences that can enable them to achieve.

Although standardized procedures often discount ELLs' abilities and understandings just as such tests discount their progress in acquiring new knowledge, informal assessment provides potentially powerful alternatives for promoting academic achievement. Difficulties in using informal assessment occur when teachers are unable to link insights gained from interacting with their students in classroom contexts with the information gained from standardized tests.

A framework is needed for integrating standardized and informal assessment information in promoting academic achievement. Such a framework would have utility for enhancing teachers' professional competence and for promoting the practices and policies required to insure students' access to appropriate instruction. Given the reality that most teachers (83%) report that they are unprepared to assess and instruct ELLs (National Center for Education Statistics [NCES], 1999), such a framework could have utility at the national, state, and local levels. At a professional level, this report of teachers' self-evaluation underscores their recognition of a need for in-depth preparation in second language acquisition and assessment to integrate language, literacy, and content instruction using standardized and informal procedures.

In this chapter the assessment of social and academic language is considered in the context of standardized and informal assessment. Because the development of academic and social language plays an important role in students' achievement, we begin with a discussion of these constructs. Next, we examine academic language development in the context of fourth-grade science and literacy instruction involving whole-class and single-student performance on multiple tasks. The chapter concludes with considerations for integrating informal and standardized assessment procedures to promote academic achievement.

Conceptualizing Academic Language

Teachers have long noted differences in students' oral and written communication (Bernstein, 1972; Donaldson 1978). Such notable differences in the language of students learning English led Cummins (1979, 1984) to identify and distinguish between social and academic language. *Academic* language has been characterized as linguistically complex and cognitively demanding, often containing multiple embedded clauses and subtle lexical differences—the language of classroom instruction (Cummins, 1979). Comparable *social* language has been characterized as interpersonal, context-embedded, and dependent on information within the environment in which the communication occurs (Donaldson, 1978).

Students' movement toward the acquisition of academic discourse in classroom contexts has received limited attention in terms of test construction and use (Bartolomé, 1998). In contrast, ELLs' progress, measured by standardized tests, and the comparison of their achievement with English-proficient (EP) students' progress often reveals significant gaps (NCES, 1992). Although efforts at reducing achievement gaps are clearly needed, overreliance on standardized measures can be misleading in measuring students' actual learning gains. In addition, an emphasis on standardized tests can result in a large portion of instructional time being devoted to enhancing test-taking skills, rather than meaningful instruction. Such a focus can also limit teachers' perceptions of the academic language required to perform well on large-scale tests and real-world contexts (Edelsky, 1996). In the following section, we discuss the relationship of standardized and informal assessment in the context of fourth-grade science learning setting.

Measuring Fourth-Grade Students' Academic Language Development

The information discussed here is part of a larger study of ELLs' development of language proficiency, literacy, and science knowledge.[1] Here, we focus on data from fourth-grade Hispanic students in two Hispanic-dominant schools (over 95% Hispanic) in a large urban district in Florida. Because Florida is an English-only state, the focus of this chapter is on instruction in English although some instructional support was provided in students' home languages—Spanish and Haitian Creole.

The Context of Instruction

Although many of the fourth-grade students in our study had transitioned out of English to Speakers of Other Languages (ESOL) programs, more than 20 percent received ESOL instruction in the two schools discussed here. For purposes of this discussion, most of the students would be considered ELLs because they had not yet developed oral or written proficiency at the level of grade peers in other parts of the state or nation (Waggoner, 1993). Even though most of the fourth-grade teachers had state endorsement in ESOL, the ESOL students received additional language arts instruction in special programs.

The two schools served a transient population where enrollment fluctuated between 32 and 35 students per classroom, for a total of approximately 425 students. Both schools used an inclusion model for meeting the instructional needs of exceptional students. As a result, the students presented a normal population, including students with mild learning disabilities, communication disorders, typical, and gifted and talented students. The majority of teachers (12 of 13) were Hispanic. All were highly committed to students' academic achievement.

The Content of Instruction and Assessment

Understanding the instructional components and the context of instruction is essential in promoting effective assessment practices, interpreting standardized assessment results, and integrating information from multiple sources in meeting students' learning needs. In this section, we discuss the components, including the materials and instruction, teacher preparation, and the content of classroom assessment.

The Materials and Instruction.   Information on the curriculum is provided to indicate the important relationship between the content of instruction and the assessment practices used to determine students' academic progress. Because appropriate instructional materials were not available for making science relevant to fourth-grade ELLs, the project developed two units, including student books and materials for hands-on activities, teachers' guides, and pre- and postunit tests. The first unit, the water cycle, presented content on melting, freezing, evaporation, condensation, and precipitation. Instruction in the second unit, weather, built on the first unit in a progression from more concrete to more abstract content. All lessons focused on predicting and measuring changes. Most lessons required two instructional periods, one for hands-on activities and the other for sense-making in analyzing and reporting outcomes. Mathematics instruction became essential in enabling students to record and report the changes they observed during hands-on activities. All content was keyed to the National Science Education Standards (National Research Council, 1996), the Florida Sunshine State Standards for Mathematics and Science (Florida Department of Education [FDE], 1996a, 1996b), and the Teachers of English to Speakers of Other Languages [TESOL] Standards (TESOL, 1997).

In addition to science and mathematics, literacy instruction occurred throughout the lessons. An initiating activity in each lesson required that students use a variety of language functions or specific ways of communicating, such as reporting, comparing and contrasting, and reasoning (Tough, 1986). Meaningful language use was supported through hands-on interactions and follow-up oral and written tasks. Activities requiring observations of changes and measurement of weight, time, temperature, and height were designed to create opportunities to discuss and report findings. Although the activities encouraged explicit, precise language, ELLs participated in the context-embedded activities without difficulty using single words and short responses. In addition, students communicated understandings through tables, graphs, and drawings. The context of instruction, manipulating materials, making observations, and interacting with others in discussing and interpreting changes, provided rich learning opportunities for literacy development. In this context, literacy refers to the representation of information and understandings in multiple formats, including oral and written discourse and tables, charts, graphs, and drawings. These participatory contexts provided teachers with opportunities to observe students' interactions, note their literacy development, and gain insights about students' learning needs.

The Teacher Preparation.   Professional development was central to the project. In the second year (YII), six "focus teachers" participated in workshops and classroom observations. All six were first-generation, Hispanic immigrants who shared both the language and cultural knowledge of their students. Limiting YII participation to these teachers provided in-depth understanding of the instructional process. Insights were used to refine the materials and expand teacher preparation for YIII. During YIII, all fourth-grade teachers in the two schools received the instructional units, supporting materials, and professional development workshops. Focus teachers assisted nonfocus teachers in using the materials. At the conclusion of YIII, all teachers participated in formal interviews concerning the materials, instruction, and the assessment process.

The Assessment.   Several assessment instruments were used with students in science, reading, and writing over the course of instruction. First, during YII and YIII, all fourth-grade students participated in pre- and postinstruction assessment based on the science content from the two instructional units.[2] All students were included in the assessment process for both years because fourth graders are expected to learn the content specified in the Sunshine State Standards for Science at fourth grade (FDE, 1996a, 1996b). The Standards are Florida's guide to content area instruction and the source of content for unit development.

Second, in addition to the assessment of all fourth-grade students, randomly selected "focus students" participated in pre- and post-instruction elicitations to determine their understanding of science content and discourse. Each year fifty students participated in the two elicitations lasting approximately forty-five minutes. A trained bilingual adult, fluent in English and Spanish, interacted with mixed-gender dyads (a boy and a girl) to do hands-on activities from the science units. Activities were conducted in Spanish and English. All elicitations were audio and videotaped and transcribed. Trained bilingual graduate assistants using rubrics designed for the research scored responses from transcripts. To insure consistency in scoring, interrater agreement was established at 90 percent and all discrepancies were reconciled.

Third, in Florida, all public school students participate in Florida Writes! writing assessment in grades four, eight, and ten (FDE, 1998a) using 0 to 6 scoring criteria (6 being the highest). A similar rubric, Science Reporting Rubric[3] (SRR), was developed to promote teachers' recognition of students' progress in acquiring oral and written academic language of science (Table 8.1). The theoretical framework for the SRR derived from second language acquisition research (Fradd & Larrinaga McGee, 1994) in combination with our study of fourth-grade written and oral language samples collected over two years. Because the "reporting" function of "telling about an activity" (Tough, 1986) predominated in these fourth-grade students' oral and written science discourse, it was the focus of rubric development. The use of language to report provides a transition from the narrative of social language, for example, "what I saw and did" to more complex expository academic language, including ordering and sequencing, providing explanations, and making predictions. To facilitate application, the 0 to 6 scoring criteria parallel Florida Writes! indicators (0 to 6); however, the SRR differs from Florida Writes! in ways central to ELLs' acquisition of academic language. Most importantly the rubric differentiates "form" (accuracy in grammar, phonology, spelling, and general mechanics of language use) from "content" (specific knowledge and understandings of science). The half-point increments for the first two levels include early-stage language development, a stage through which monolingual students have already passed.

Finally, during YIII, statewide assessment expanded to include all fourth-grade public school students on the Florida Comprehensive Assessment Test (FCAT), a criterion-referenced assessment test designed to measure reading and mathematics skills (FDE, 1998b, 1998c). Content for the FCAT is keyed to the Sunshine State Standards (FDE, 1996a, 1996b). The FCAT requires single-word, short-answer, and paragraph-length responses. More than 60 percent of FCAT content is from science and social studies (FDE, 1998b, 1998c). The FCAT has begun to refocus attention on the importance of content instruction and academic language development.

Integrating Standardized and Informal Assessment

Quantifying students' performance provides a means for observing growth over time and for comparing individual students with the group. In this section, we

TABLE 8.1   Science Reporting Rubric

Level 0; *Descriptor: None*

No attempt to write

No oral information about activity or concept

Level 0.5

Form	Content
Single words or simple phrases	Little information about science
Little attention to grammar or punctuation	
Difficult to be understood by persons not present	

Level 1; *Descriptor: Little*

Form	Content
Simple phrases or sentences about activity or concept	Little use of science vocabulary
Little attention to grammar or punctuation	Basic information with little attention to main ideas and details
Difficult to be understood by persons not present	

Level 1.5; *Descriptor: Little*

Form	Content
Multiple sentences about activity or concept	Tangential use of vocabulary
Attempts at sequencing information include markers such as "and, . . . then . . ."	Attempts at description of content or activities
	Emerging notions of the main idea
	Emerging expression of similarities and differences
	Reliance on personal experiences for explanations

Level 2; *Descriptor: Emerging*

Form	Content
Written Reports Emerging awareness of grammar and punctuation	Emerging, yet inaccurate, use of science vocabulary
Written and Oral Reports Brief information, focusing on who, what, and where	Emerging description of activity or content without clear relationship to topic
Emerging use of past and future tense	Emerging awareness of the importance of observations in providing descriptions
Emerging use of positions and linking words showing relationships, such as, "so," "because," "due to," and "as a result of"	Main topic with undeveloped or inaccurate details
	Emerging use of comparisons and contrasts and analogies
	Emerging ability to sequence events and activities with recognition of chronological importance

Communication in phrases and sentences with emerging development of paragraphs

Emerging awareness of listener perspective

Comprehensible to sympathetic persons not present

Level 3; *Descriptor: Expanding*

Form	Content
Written Reports Expanding organization of sentences into paragraphs	Expanding use of science vocabulary
Approaching 80% accuracy in spelling, punctuation	Expanding descriptions based on observation and supporting evidence
Approaching 80% accuracy in present and past tense, including subject/verb and noun/article agreement	Expanding use of comparisons and contrasts and analogies
Written and Oral Reports Information clearly topic focused with main ideas and details, in terms of who, what, and where	Main topics with reasonably developed, accurate details
Expanding awareness of listener perspective	Emerging use of explanations or predictions, including: ■ cause/effect ■ classification ■ sequential order ■ relationships of chronological events

Level 4; *Descriptor: Movement toward Adequate*

Form	Content
Written Reports More than 80% accuracy in spelling and punctuation	Adequate use of science vocabulary
	Adequate, clear, relevant descriptions
More than 80% accuracy in present and past tense grammar, including subject/verb and noun/article agreement	Expanding evidence of explanations or predictions, including: ■ cause/effect ■ comparisons and contrasts ■ classification ■ sequential order
Written and Oral Reports Emerging introductions and conclusions not necessarily appropriate or related	Expanding use of relevant analogies
Organization of ideas in multiple paragraphs, although some inconsistencies and unrelated information still apparent	Emerging use of evidence to support statements, including: ■ understanding of system and relationships among subsystems ■ generalizations
Continuing development of language for listener perspective	
Usually understood by persons not present	

(continued)

137

TABLE 8.1   Continued

Level 5; *Descriptor: Movement toward Accurate*

Form	Content
Written Reports Conforms to major aspects of form, including organization of information, grammar, and punctuation *Written and Oral Reports* Clear, appropriate introduction Clear organization in topic related paragraphs with main ideas and supporting details Conclusions not necessarily accurate but show relationships to overall presentation Understood by persons not present	Accurate use of science vocabulary Accurate, complete descriptions Adequate explanations or predictions, including: ■ cause/effect ■ comparisons and contrasts ■ classification ■ sequential order Adequate use of relevant analogies Expanding use of evidence to support statements, including: ■ systems and relationships among subsystems ■ generalizations

Level 6; *Descriptor: Effective*

Form	Content
Written Reports All aspects of form, including organization of information, grammar, and punctuation *Written and Oral Reports* Introductions and conclusions clearly stated and appropriate Ideas convincingly and clearly presented Correct use of elements of scientific reporting with nativelike proficiency	Effective use of science vocabulary Accurate explanations or predictions, including: ■ cause/effect ■ comparisons and contrasts ■ classification ■ sequential order Effective use of evidence to support statements, including: ■ systems and relationships among subsystems ■ generalizations Effective use of complex analogies

discuss the results of unit assessments and their relationship with students' performance on standardized tests.

Student Performance in Science, Reading, and Writing

Science achievement scores by unit (matter and weather) and teacher group (focus and nonfocus) during YII and YIII are presented in Table 8.2. In YII, when only focus teachers used the instructional units, an aggregate achievement difference of twenty points on the two units occurred between the students in the focus (M=47.65) and nonfocus (M=27.71) classrooms. This difference is not surprising because, although all of the teachers were expected to teach the standards-based science content, only the focus teachers used materials directly related to the unit tests. During YIII, when all the teachers used the same materials, achievement scores of the focus (M=60.00) and nonfocus classrooms (M=57.28) were comparable—a significant improvement for all students. Both groups exceeded the performance of the students in focus teachers' classrooms in YII. The YII outcomes suggest that engaging content area materials, when combined teacher preparation and a focus on academic language development, provide ELLs with important learning opportunities. The YIII outcomes indicate all students can achieve when provided with effective instruction. However important, such whole group information does not tell the entire achievement story. More in-depth assessment information is needed to gain insights on the impact of formal and informal procedures on students' learning.

Examples of the Assessment Process

Although educators are in agreement about the need to promote achievement, difficulties arise in determining the most effective means for determining achievement outcomes. When well-conceptualized and implemented, standardized assessment procedures linked to state or national standards can provide important benchmarks for identifying and defining achievement. Emphasis on preparing students to perform well on standardized tests, however, can have negative consequences for many students, particularly ELLs, when test instruction replaces authentic learning opportunities. When the focus of instruction is increased high-stakes test performance, students may appear to achieve without gaining generalizable knowledge or meaningful understanding of content area material. The time devoted to teaching test-taking skills disadvantages students with limited experience using English or little exposure to content information. In comparison, students already literate in English usually have a greater command of the academic language of tests and access to subject knowledge through a variety of sources beyond the classroom. By definition, ELLs are more dependent on both school-based instruction for language development and for content area learning. As a result, they are particularly vulnerable to the consequences of test-focused instruction when it supplants meaningful learning opportunities.

TABLE 8.2 Hispanic Student Achievement Differences on Two Science Units in Classes of Focus and Nonfocus Hispanic Teachers

Year	Group	n	Pretest		Posttest		t	p
			M	SD	M	SD		
YII	**Focus**							
	Matter	165	10.45	7.20	26.61	8.65	24.07	.000**
	Weather	153	9.61	4.43	21.10	4.68	23.75	.000**
	Matter/ weather	140	20.16	8.89	47.65	12.38	27.33	.000**
	Nonfocus							
	Matter	102	12.77	6.64	14.35	6.73	2.67	.009*
	Weather	106	11.26	6.17	12.89	5.39	3.21	.002*
	Matter/ weather	96	24.48	11.13	27.71	10.06	3.55	.001*
YIII	**Focus**							
	Matter	147	11.35	6.75	32.24	10.67	26.03	.000**
	Weather	129	11.98	5.84	26.28	7.75	23.80	.000**
	Matter/ weather	120	24.04	10.59	60.00	15.50	28.83	.000**
	Nonfocus							
	Matter	197	13.07	7.48	30.33	9.77	27.49	.000**
	Weather	190	11.59	6.75	26.39	7.84	21.99	.000**
	Matter/ weather	174	24.90	12.20	57.28	14.73	31.09	.000**

*$p < .01$
**$p < .001$
Maximum score for the matter unit: 69
Maximum score for the weather unit: 63
Maximum combined score (for matter and weather): 132

Because standardized measures of academic achievement can, in reality, become measures of students' acquisition of language patterns and communication formats, increased achievement scores may offer a false image of students' academic attainment (Edelsky, 1996). For example, to score well on the Florida Writes!, students must write a five-paragraph essay with an introductory paragraph stating three ideas related to a specified topic. These three ideas become the subjects of three subordinated paragraphs followed by a concluding paragraph linked to the introduction. Responses are scored high if (a) the introduction is clear, (b) the subordinating paragraphs contain creative ideas and elaborate descriptions, and (c) the concluding paragraph restates the components as a whole. In contrast, authentic academic language requires knowledge of content areas and the use of a variety of expository genre. For example, students engaging in science inquiry must understand how to ask and answer questions, provide evidence of reasoning, and draw conclusions. They must be able to state their claims in sociolinguistically appropriate ways related to audiences' knowledge and interests. Example of a fourth grader's written and oral discourse illustrate differences between writing for a standardized task and communicating academic meaning and content.

Insights from Jorge's Assessment

Jorge had been in the United States for a little over two years when he entered fourth grade. In interpersonal conversations, his English, although spoken with an accent, was clearly understandable. He was attentive to the teacher and worked well with other students. Although shy, his interest in school was evident in his ready smile and eyes that communicated enthusiasm for learning. Jorge's performance on the standardized and informal assessments described next is representative of many other students.

Practicing for the Large-Scale Writing Assessment. At the beginning of YIII, fourth-grade teachers were given the Florida Writes! rubric and encouraged to have students write each week using the five-paragraph format of the state assessment. Each week students' writing samples were scored using the Florida Writes! rubric. Students were also taught to use the rubric in reviewing their own writing. The following is a sample of Jorge's writing in October, in response to the prompt "Most people have someone that they admire. Tell about him/her so that your reader will know as much about this person as you do, and why you admire this person."

> Probably why I would admire my parents is because they love me. My parents are so important to me because they guide me. There important to me because they like to hug me. For example, once I was running fast and I fell down and hurt myself She put a bandage on my right knee.
>
> I admire my parents because they gave me an incredible life. In my incredible, I have talents In my incredible life I have two talents, one is the piano and last is karate.
>
> I also admire because they gave me a nice little sister. I admire my parent because she is sweet and beautiful. She is fun to play with.
>
> My person that I admire is my parents. I like them because they love me, they gave me an incredible and they gave me a little nice sister.

Using the "form" component of the SRR (see Table 8.1), the sample was scored a level 3 because the discourse was organized into paragraphs with evidence of past and future tense indicative of a movement toward level 4. Because this sample used a preestablished format, the SRR could overrate for development. Because the topic was personal opinion, not science, the SRR "content" component was not applicable. Jorge's teacher rated the sample a 3.5 on the Florida Writes! rubric.

Writing instruction throughout the first six months of YIII consisted primarily of improving students' responses in the five-paragraph format. Like most students, as the year progressed, Jorge's writing became more elaborate and complex, as it grew in conformity to the expectations of Florida Writes! In February, Jorge responded to the prompt "We all have important decisions to make in life. Think of a time in your life when you had an important decision to make. Write to explain to your reader why you are sorry about your choice" with this sample.

> We all have important decisions to make in life. My important decision that I made in my life was to become a pianist. I think it was a good decision because kids could love how I play, I can play in big concerts, and for the money.
>
> Probably, why my decision was good to be a pianist was because kids would love how I play. Because I would play a funny folksong. For example, once I played a song name 'Chopsticks' to a bunch of kids and then I play and they all started to giggle.
>
> Also, why my decision was good to be a pianist was because I can play in concerts. So I go and play beautiful songs. For example once I went to a concert and I played classic, Chopin, the song was called Polonaise. Once I played and finish everyone started to clap at me. When I was going to my seat my teacher and her husband, plus the audience congratulated me. Finally, why my decision was good to be a pianist was because for the money. Because if I play for no money my parents and my little sister wouldn't have a home.
>
> My important decision that I made in my life was to become a pianist. I think it was a good decision because kids could love how I play, I can play in big concerts, and for the money.

In writing about a "good" decision instead of one he was "sorry about," Jorge indicated he had misread the prompt. Nevertheless, his teacher was enthusiastic about the response and scored it a 5. Using the form component of the SRR, the sample was a 4. In spite of errors and a lack of grammatical accuracy, Jorge provided a comprehensive sample using present, past, and future tense with cohesive idea organization. Discussion of personal beliefs, rather than science content, precluded a SRR content rating.

On the standardized statewide Florida Writes! assessment in March, Jorge scored 4.2. The state average was 3.0, and the average for both Jorge's school and his class was 3.3. For an inner-city school where the majority of the students were ELLs, it was apparent that substantial progress had been made in acquiring the language measured by the Florida Writes!

Oral Assessment in Science.   On the preinstruction elicitation, Jorge's demeanor was quiet and watchful. He frequently mumbled or spoke in single words and short phrases. In response to the question "What will happen if we heat the water?" Jorge produced his longest intelligible utterance (18 words): "The steam will go up and the water level will go down. The water cycle will be starting." The response indicates Jorge had an initial understanding of the water cycle. Using the SRR, the sample was 1 to 1.5 in form and 1.5 in content.

In contrast, on the postelicitation, Jorge spoke in clear and animated sentences and paragraphs without mumbling. When asked to explain the terms *evaporation* and *condensation* he used in the previous turn, Jorge responded:

> Evaporation is when, the when water, when the sun, the sun is like heating on water. Then, when the sun is beating a lot to the water, like it's boiling, like this (pointing to a picture of the sun above the ocean). The water evaporates to the clouds and condensation is when it hits a cool place, like a top, a cool place, and then it starts getting, turning into liquid. (61 words, 55 not counting false starts)

At the conclusion of the postelicitation, when asked what he did to perform well in school, Jorge stated, "When I don't know something, I mumble and talk soft, and when I do know, then I like to talk out loud. Sometimes I get excited, and I don't say it right." Although Jorge's postinstruction discourse showed substantial development in overall language production, the content of his discourse was still under development. Increased length provided an indication of growth, yet length did not equal development, as the false starts and mazing in the initial segment illustrated: "Evaporation is when, the when water, when the sun, the sun is like heating on water." However, the full transcript showed emerging control of grammar at a level 2 in form using the SRR, an important gain.

As important as the development and control of grammar is, academic language development also requires specific content area knowledge. In content, Jorge's use of key vocabulary terms and his attempt to exemplify them provided an indication of his awareness of two salient features of academic language, definition and exemplification. In spite of this awareness, the sample was rated a 2 because of the lack of clarity in using the terms. Jorge may or may not have known that oceans do not boil when the sun shines. Jorge appeared to be attempting to make an analogy between increasing evaporation by heating a pot of water and the evaporation that occurs when the sun heats the ocean surface. Not only do these samples reveal Jorge's level of discourse, but they also provide starting points for instruction to enhance his knowledge of science and his ability to communicate understanding accurately and effectively.

In addition to illustrating Jorge's growth in academic language development, the pre- and postelicitations also indicate language shift from Spanish to English. In the preinstruction elicitation, Jorge willingly communicated in Spanish, using fully formed, easily understood sentences. In the postelicitation (with the same native Spanish speaker), Jorge declined to use Spanish and indicated a strong preference for English.

Informal Writing in Science.   The last sample provided an additional indication of Jorge's ability to express his understanding of science in writing. To promote science learning beyond the two units, Jorge's teacher divided the class into small groups and provided them with large ten gallon containers in which to construct biospheres, plant seeds, and grow plants. Each group was given different environmental growing conditions for the seeds. As a culminating writing activity for this three-week unit that occurred shortly after the Florida Writes! exam, students were asked to (a) describe the growing conditions of their biosphere and (b) make predictions about what would happen to the plants. Before beginning to write, groups interacted to discuss the growing conditions and make predictions. In small groups, the students shared their ideas, observed the biospheres, and discussed changes that had occurred to the plants during the past weeks. To facilitate the discussion and writing, the teacher and class summarized the growing conditions in the biospheres as the teacher noted the students' ideas on the chalk board. As he wrote, he emphasized the descriptive words the students could use in writing about their biospheres. To ensure everyone understood the assignment, the teacher also wrote the topics on the chalkboard: "describe the growing conditions of your biosphere" and "make predictions about what will happen to the plants."

In spite of the preliminary scaffolding, many students had difficulty with the assignment. One student broke into tears, crying that she did not know where to put the middle three paragraphs. Nine others declared they could not write. Despite encouragement from the teacher and an assistant, some students simply put their heads down and wrote nothing. Jorge wrote:

> What happened in group 3 & 2 was it had the top off and the heat hit and the water evaporated and it's soil got dry. What I think that will happen next is that all the plant are going to dye. Because it's very dry.

Jorge's sample illustrates the difficulty he had in using academic discourse, even when it was made explicit through classroom interactions and teacher scaffolding. On the SRR, his form was rated a 2 and content a 1.5. In spite of his enthusiasm in orally discussing the biosphere, Jorge's writing offers little insight into his understanding of the activity. Because the task required an organizational format different from the highly practiced Florida Writes! Jorge appeared to be unable to respond beyond the most basic level. He, like many of the students, had learned the Florida Writes! format so well that they surpassed the state average, yet they were unable to apply their understanding of the writing process to this science context.

The emphasis on a five-paragraph composition had limited instruction in other important areas of the curriculum. As a result, the students did not acquire the discourse functions of describing or predicting beyond a rudimentary level. Because most of the writing instruction had been specific to the Florida Writes! format, it lacked application for communicating science. As a result, Jorge and the other students suffered the limitations of test-focused instruction, even as they achieved the distinction of being declared "effective writers" and they enjoyed learning science.

Discussion and Conclusions

In spite of the growing recognition of the importance of academic language in school achievement, little research has been conducted to define or describe academic language in classroom contexts (Fradd & Larrinaga McGee, 1994; Bartolomé, 1998; TESOL, 1996).[4] The construct has been operationalized primarily through standardized tests, rather than classroom performance (Edelsky, 1996). As this chapter indicates, such interpretations can provide false pictures of students' progress and instructional needs.

Dependence on standardized assessment to determine performance is particularly troubling in classrooms where ELLs spend a great deal of instructional time developing test-taking skills. This is not to argue against preparing students for taking tests, rather, it is to affirm the importance of instruction to promote meaningful literacy-based learning relevant to real-world contexts. Because teachers require in-depth knowledge of academic language acquisition, from initial stages to full participation (NCES, 1999), a framework is needed to make instruction across subject areas relevant to students' overall language-learning needs.

A working definition of the process of academic language acquisition as developmental and ongoing is needed. Such a definition would include (a) the acquisition of language form, (b) the use of specific discourse functions, such as reporting, describing, and explaining, for communicating in academic and social contexts, and (c) academic content knowledge. Such a definition could be used to integrate the performance indicators and achievement information from different assessment procedures to provide a holistic view of students' language development. The rubric presented here provides a beginning for observing students' growth in these components. Through the use of specifically designed rubrics paralleling those used with monolingual students, teachers of ELLs can assess and promote development of the discourse their students require to communicate effectively.

The notion of a specifically designed rubric for observing grammatical development and content knowledge as two separate, interrelated areas of language acquisition may be a useful heuristic for both assessment and instruction. The use of such a framework could also promote teachers' capacity to integrate standardized and informal assessment information. Although not all states support bilingual instruction by utilizing students' home languages as well as English, the assessment process could inform teachers of students' development of the form, functions, and content required for meaningful communication across languages. Thus, such a framework could enhance teachers' understanding of students' language development and content-area knowledge and insure that meaningful learning opportunities are not delayed because students' lack proficiency in English (Bartolomé, 1998; Edelsky, 1996).

The language samples of Jorge underscore the need to promote integrated language instruction that includes both form and content. As his essays reflect, Jorge sought opportunities to acquire the academic language at school not only for his own personal benefit but also to assist his family and to participate in the larger world. According to his score on the state writing assessment, Jorge's written language was above average; however, as he reached the end of fourth grade, because he did not know how to organize and present his ideas, Jorge had difficulty writing on a science topic he and his classmates had studied for three weeks. Although Jorge and the other students had participated in many context-embedded language-learning activities designed to promote acquisition of specific science content, they lacked an understanding of how to present their knowledge in multiple formats. In exemplifying the strengths and limitations of test-focused instruction, these samples illustrate the need to explicitly link instruction and language development with real world activities that generalize beyond the context in which instruction occurs (Bartolomé, 1998). The examples also underscore the importance of preparing teachers to move students beyond achievement on high-stakes assessments.

Although Florida is an English-only state, there is growing awareness of the importance of biliteracy in the educational process (Fradd, 1996). The need for a multilingual global work force has increased the importance of literacy in more than one language in Florida and across the nation (Fradd & Lee, 1998). A framework for academic language development could be used for student instruction and assessment as well as teacher preparation to achieve higher literacy levels in English and other languages. First, it could provide teachers with insight into the overall language-learning process across written and oral formats in multiple languages. Writing instruction could be integrated throughout the curriculum, such that knowledge gained in improving writing for specific purposes could be made applicable to other tasks and contexts. Therefore, in addition to specific test-taking skills, students would learn a variety of formats for organizing and communicating their understandings. Second, oral and written language instruction could be integrated so that development in one would support effective communication in the other. Third, content instruction, in areas such as science, would be recognized as providing opportunities to expand language development through both hands-on interpersonal activities and formal contexts in which students must use a variety of language functions. Fourth, vocabulary instruction would be used not only to ensure students acquire content-specific terminology but also to promote thinking and framing "big" ideas in which to apply content knowledge. As this chapter suggests, with relevant instructional materials and professional preparation, teachers can foster ELLs' language acquisition and science learning. What is needed is a framework for organizing and integrating such learning opportunities.

This chapter presents the beginnings of a framework with applications in classrooms where teachers provide instruction for accountability and content learning. The example used here illustrates the utility and need for extending the framework across assessment procedures and contexts, grade levels, subject areas, and languages. Informal assessment can provide insights into students' learning strengths and needs not available through standardized assessment. At the same time standardized assessments establish benchmarks toward which all teachers and students must strive. Through the integration of information from both types of assessment, teachers and students can benefit from improved practices that promote achievement for all students.

DISCUSSION QUESTIONS

1. List the components of the assessment framework presented in this chapter, and tell why these are important.

2. What are the three components of language development discussed in informal assessment?

3. Compare and contrast the first three levels of the *Science Reporting Rubric,* and then explain what the authors mean by "developmental" language learning.

4. In this chapter, students exceeded state norms for effective writing yet were unable to write a simple composition about a science activity. How is it possible for students to exceed writing norms and still lack the ability to communicate content from state grade-level standards in writing?

5. This chapter provided multiple examples of Jorge's oral and written communication. Summarize this development, and state what you would do as his teacher to meet his instructional needs in literacy and science learning.

REFERENCES

American Association for the Advancement of Science. (1989). *Science for all Americans.* New York: Oxford University Press.

Bartolomé, L. I. (1998). *The misteaching of academic discourses: The politics of language in the classroom.* Boulder, CO: Westview Press.

Bernstein, B. (1972). *Class, codes, and control: Towards a theory of educational transmission, 2nd ed.* Boston: Routledge and Kegan Paul.

Cummins, J. (1979). Linguistic interdependence and the educational development of bilingual children. *Review of Educational Research, 49,* 222–251.

Cummins, J. (1984). *Bilingualism and special education: Issues in assessment and pedagogy.* Boston: College Hill Press.

Donaldson, M. (1978). *Children's minds.* New York: W. W. Norton.

Edelsky, C. (1996). *With literacy and justice for all: Rethinking the social in language and education 2nd ed.* Briston, PA: Taylor and Francis.

Florida Department of Education [FDE]. (1996a). *Florida curriculum framework: Mathematics — preK–12 sunshine state standards and instructional practices.* Tallahassee, FL: Author.

Florida Department of Education [FDE]. (1996b). *Florida curriculum framework: Science — preK–12 sunshine state standards and instructional practices.* Tallahassee, FL: Author.

Florida Department of Education [FDE]. (1998a). *Florida Writing Assessment Program.* Tallahassee, FL: Author.

Florida Department of Education [FDE]. (1998b). *A handbook of instructional activities for the FCAT in reading: FCAT — Florida Comprehensive Assessment Test.* Tallahassee, FL: Author.

Florida Department of Education [FDE]. (1998c). *A handbook of instructional activities for the FCAT in mathematics: FCAT — Florida Comprehensive Assessment Test.* Tallahassee, FL: Author.

Fradd, S. H. (1996). *The economic impact of Spanish-language proficiency in Metropolitan Miami.* Miami, FL (a white paper funded by the Greater Miami Chamber of Commerce and the Cuban American National Council).

Fradd, S. H., & Larrinaga McGee, P. (1994). *Instructional assessment: An integrative approach to evaluating student performance.* White Plains, NY: Addison-Wesley.

Fradd, S. H., & Lee, O. (Eds.). (1998). *Creating Florida's multilingual global work force.* Miami, FL: Florida Department of Education.

Gardner, H. (1991). *The unschooled mind: How children think and how schools should teach.* New York: Basic Books.

Heath, S. B. (1983). *Ways with words: Language, life, and work in communities and classrooms.* New York: Cambridge University Press.

Mabry, L. (1999). Writing to the rubric: Lingering effects of traditional standardized testing on direct writing assessment. *Phi Delta Kappan, 80,* 673–679.

National Center for Education Statistics [NCES]. (1992). *Language characteristics and academic achievement: A look at Asian and Hispanic eighth graders in NELS: 1988.* Washington, DC: U.S. Department of Education.

National Center for Education Statistics [NCES]. (1999). *Teacher quality: A report on the preparation and qualifications of public school teachers.* Washington, DC: U.S. Department of Education.

National Research Council. (1996). *National science education standards.* Washington, DC: National Academy Press.

National Science Foundation. (1994). *Women, minorities, and persons with disabilities in science and engineering: 1994.* Arlington, VA (NSF-94-333).

O'Connor, M. C. (1992). Rethinking aptitude, achievement and instruction: Cognitive science research and the framing of assessment policy. In B. R. Gifford, & M. C. O'Connor. (Eds.). *Changing assessments: Alternative views of aptitude, achievement and instruction* (pp. 9–35). Norwell, MA: Kluwer.

Stake, R. (1999). The goods on American education. *Phi Delta Kappan, 80,* 668–672.

Teachers of English to Speakers of Other Languages [TESOL]. (1996). *ESL standards for pre-K–12 students.* Alexandria, VA: Author.

Tough, J. (1986). *Talk two: Children using English as a second language in primary schools.* Portsmouth, NH: Heinemann.

Waggoner, D. (1993). The growth of multilingualism and the need for bilingual education: What do we know so far? *The Bilingual Research Journal, 17,* 1–12.

NOTES

1. In 1988 prominent scientists and science educators announced commitment to make science available for all students (American Association for the Advancement of Science, 1989). The dismal achievement of Hispanic students in general and lower socioeconomic level students in particular made this commitment more of a promise than a reality for many ELLs (NCES, 1992; National Science Foundation, 1994). This "promise" became the inspiration for the Promise Project, the study discussed here. Reference for this study is Fradd, S. H., Lee, O., & Sutman, F. (1995–1998). *Promoting science literacy for all Americans, including culturally and linguistically diverse students, keeping the promise* [*The Promise Project*]. National Science Foundation, Research on Teaching and Learning Program. #RED 9552556, Coral Gables, FL: University of Miami.

2. The pre- and postassessment instruments had a high level of consistency, as indicated by Cronbach coefficient Alpha, the internal consistency for matter pretest was 0.83 and matter posttest 0.87. The internal consistency for weather pretest was 0.73 and weather posttest 0.78.

3. Science Reporting Rubric (Fradd, S. H., Lee, O., & Larrinaga McGee, P. [1998]. *Developmental science reporting rubric. An instrument developed for "Promoting Science Literacy for All Americans, Including Culturally and Linguistically Diverse Students: Keeping the Promise."* National Science Foundation, RED 9552556. Coral Gables, FL: University of Miami. This draft version is still under revision.)

4. The TESOL standards are designed to promote language development in classroom contexts (Teachers of English to Speakers of Other Languages. [1997]. *ESL standards for pre-K–12 students.* Alexandria, VA: Author).

9 Effective Instructional Practices and Assessment for Literacy and Biliteracy Development

JILL KERPER MORA

San Diego State University

Rosa Sandoval

Stepping inside the door of Rosa Sandoval's bilingual classroom is like entering a colorful world of storybook adventures. The walls are covered with students' compositions and art work, including the beginnings of a bulletin board for this month's theme: holiday traditions. A large piece of butcher block paper with clusters of words related to holiday celebrations forms the backdrop. Pictures of holiday scenes drawn by the children are hung on clothesline wire, segmenting off the different learning centers and the reading corner, where comfortable pillows and a rocking chair provide the perfect spot for curling up with a book.

The class has been preparing the final publication of their books about María and her family's Christmas celebration based on Gary Soto's delightful story, *Too Many Tamales* (1993). Copies of the book in both English and Spanish are scattered around the room. The book is about how María put on her mother's ring while kneading the *masa* and then thought she had lost the ring in the dough they were preparing for the traditional tamales. In her attempt to stay out of trouble, María has her cousins help her eat as many tamales as they can to find the ring, only to learn that her mother had retrieved it before the children's unfortunate feast.

Carlos and Sonia, two new students who recently arrived from Guatemala, are stretched out in the reading corner doing paired reading of the Spanish version. Later they will generate a list of words in English and Spanish to add to the word wall. In this dual language classroom one word wall has only Spanish words and across the room another wall has English words.

Ms. Sandoval sits behind a half-moon-shaped table with five eager students, notebooks open and pencils poised sitting in front of her. Behind her is a pocket chart with words and sentence strips in English, each describing an event in the Christmas celebration of María and her family. As Ms. Sandoval talks the story through with the students, guiding the conversation with a series of questions, the students rearrange the sentence strips to represent the sequence of events in the story. They read the sentences chorally, then individually, until each student seems confident reading aloud. Then they begin to write a personal response to the story in their dialogue journals. Rosa Sandoval's bilingual second grade class is typical of classrooms in her linguistically and culturally diverse school and community that has a large Latino population. Ms. Sandoval's students all share Spanish as their native language and are learning English as a second language. Most of Ms. Sandoval's twenty-six students were born in the United States but speak Spanish at home. Others are recent arrivals from Mexico and Central America. The community's population also includes a number of Korean immigrants and a few students from other nations who have recently arrived to participate in the growing Pacific Rim trade concentrated in this region.

Emilio and Berta are two students from Mexico who came from a rural environment where they attended school only sporadically. These students will spend time developing their oral language skills and being exposed to dual language print through language experience stories and reading along in the book with tapes of familiar stories in the listening center. At the same time students are receiving formal instruction in Spanish before they listen to the taped versions. She discontinued this activity as the children began to fully comprehend the predictable stories, poems, and fables they read orally. In Ms. Sandoval's classroom, these English-language learners have access to a wide range of challenging books in both languages to continue to develop their emerging reading skills.

Ms. Sandoval also provides direct instruction for students based on the miscue analysis she conducts in individual reading conferences. With the information gained, she personalizes instruction to meet individual student needs. Ms. Sandoval is an example of a teacher who is knowledgeable in biliteracy acquisition and development.

Development of Biliteracy in Bilingual Programs

One of the most challenging and complex tasks facing teachers today is helping second-language learners acquire literacy. Many teachers are developing literacy skills of language-minority students in two languages within the context of bilingual education programs. Because of the critical shortage of bilingual teachers qualified to provide reading and writing instruction in students' primary languages, however, many language-minority children find themselves in classrooms where their first experiences with reading are in their second language. According to a recent study by the National Research Council (August & Hakuta, 1997), 15 percent of all public school teachers in the United States has at least one English-language learner in the classroom. Of these, 66 percent were mainstream classroom teachers serving some English-language learners, while 18 percent served predominantly students from linguistically and culturally diverse backgrounds. The remaining 18 percent were teachers in bilingual classrooms where literacy and academic content are taught in the students, first language and in English. (Percentages have been rounded to the nearest whole number so the total may not equal 100%). Seventy-three percent of the 3.3 million public school students who are learning English as their second language are native speakers of Spanish (August & Hakuta, 1997).

Added to this challenge are factors involving the levels of literacy language-minority students' may or may not have achieved in their primary language through formal or informal instruction. Levels of reading competency attained through bilingual instruction affect students' ability to transfer skills in reading from the first language (L_1) to the second language (L_2) (Koda, 1997; Odlin, 1989; Williams & Snipper, 1990).

There is consensus among literacy educators and researchers that when children learn to read and write initially in the language they bring from home, their chances of successful progress in school reading tasks is enhanced. The National Academy of Science's Committee on the Prevention of Reading Difficulties in Young Children (National Research Council [NRC], 1998) recommended that initial literacy instruction be provided in the child's native language whenever possible. According to the NRC committee, initiating reading instruction in the native language of children reduces the risks of reading problems found among students who, in addition to the ordinary difficulties of literacy development, face the additional challenge of learning to read in a second language. The NRC concluded that the accumulated wisdom of research in the field of bilingual education and literacy tends to converge on the conclusion that initial literacy learning in a second language carries with it a higher risk of reading problems and of lower ultimate literacy attainment. These risks can be reduced through initial literacy instruction in a first language. Au (1998) concluded that the literacy achievement gap between speakers of standard American English in the home and the achievement of language minority children may be the result of the exclusion or limited use of instruction in their home language in many school programs. Decreased opportunities for children to build a foundation for learning to read and write by using their existing language skills accounts for their lower levels of academic achievement. The lack of a literacy foundation in their primary language handicaps many language minority students, especially as they progress through the grades and their literacy skills do not match the demands placed on them by increasingly complex and abstract reading and writing tasks.

Many local school districts have implemented programs that utilize children's first language as a medium of instruction to develop biliteracy. These programs are often a reflection of the linguistic and cultural composition of the communities served by the public schools and the value they place on bilingualism and multicultural diversity. School districts may implement a variety of programs that utilize two languages of instruction to develop biliteracy such as a transitional model or the dual immersion model (Thomas & Collier, 1999). A key factor in effective programs for English-language learners (ELLs) is that literacy in the students' native language is valued in and of itself and that biliteracy is developed (Au, 1998).

In Rosa Sandoval's school and community there is a high value placed on the ability to function effectively in a multicultural society and in an international context. Consequently, even after students make the transition into English reading and writing, they maintain and refine their L1 reading and writing skills throughout their schooling. This is accomplished through academic courses in Spanish that focus on advanced composition and Spanish and Latin American literature so that students benefit from their academic competencies in two languages. Other teachers in Ms. Sandoval's school teach language and literacy to children whose families are new to the United States using English as a "lingua franca" in their classrooms. Rosa's colleagues share many of her challenges in developing students' second-language literacy. The advantage they share is that they work in a coherent and theoretically sound program in which students' progress in language acquisition and literacy development are continually assessed and monitored. The ongoing assessment of students' progress insures that students are capitalizing on their prior knowledge of their native language and consistently transfer the knowledge and skills they acquire in a variety of contexts to enhance reading and writing achievement. Through application of this model of instruction in two languages, students become biliterate through parallel language and literacy experiences (Wiley, 1996).

Bilingual teachers are continually involved in assessment of the degree of transfer of literacy skills and concepts from L1 to L2 as oral language proficiency in English develops. The comprehensive observation survey for Spanish reading skills based on the work of Marie Clay with Reading Recovery is useful for assessing bilingual students' progress in reading in their primary language (Escamilla, Andrade, Basurto & Ruíz, 1996). This assessment includes running records of text reading, letter identification, and tests of word recognition, writing vocabulary and concepts about print. The advantages of the observation instrument in a biliteracy setting is that it allows the teacher to determine the reading strategies utilized by the emergent reader in their dominant language. This information is helpful in determining how the reader is applying reading skills that are specific to Spanish when reading English text. In this way, the teacher knows what skills the second language reader may need to develop that involve such processes as using context clues to figure out the meaning of unfamiliar vocabulary words. When used as a composite picture of the emergent reader's progress, these authentic measures can ensure that early difficulties can be addressed through appropriate instruction.

Approaches to Biliteracy Instruction

While certain aspects of literacy instruction cut across all learning contexts, teachers need access to a large repertoire of teaching strategies to meet the needs of students with varying levels of oral language and literacy proficiency. Teachers often utilize approaches to reading instruction with little modification for students learning English as a second language, in spite of the differences between reading a first and a second language (Chamot & O'Malley, 1994; Hornberger, 1994; Milk, Mercado, & Sapiens, 1992; Miramontes, Nadeau, & Commins, 1997; Reyes, 1992). Over the past three decades, there has been an evolution of theory regarding second-language reading from various disciplines and schools of thought. Theories and models of reading have been studied in light of a growing knowledge base in linguistics and second-language acquisition research. Specific studies have examined how linguistic and prior knowledge factors translate into reading strategies that second-language readers apply based on their competence in their L_1 and their levels of proficiency in their L_2.

A Model of Cross-Linguistic Interaction in L_2 Reading

Historical Overview

In examining the reading process of linguistic factors, an analytic structure was suggested by a model of second-language reading developed by Coady (1979). His model of second-language reading identified and labeled three components or levels in the psycholinguistic process of reading: the decoding level, the semantic-syntactic level, and the meaning or discourse level. The *levels* could be construed to equate to a developmental hierarchy or a top-down process. There is ample research evidence, however, to suggest that meaningful reading is achieved through the effective interaction of various cueing systems rather than a linear progression.

Bernhardt (1991) described the various factors that impinge on the rate of fluency and errors in reading a second language, including the phonographemic features of text, word recognition, and syntax. She noted that syntax as a cueing system behaves differently from other text-based features, in that the number of syntactic errors made by a second-language reader seem to increase as a function of greater exposure and growth in the second language and then decline as the reader develops greater proficiency.

Freeman and Freeman (1997) proposed a "sociopsycholinguistic theory of reading" based on research from miscue analysis. *Miscue* is a term used by Goodman (1965) to describe an oral reading deviation from the text. Miscue analysis is based on the assumption that miscues are not random errors. It is a formal examination of the miscues to determining the strengths and weaknesses of a particular reader (Harris & Hodges, 1995). The sociopsycholinguistic theory of reading holds that meaning is constructed and reconstructed in the process of reading and writing through the use of information from the writing and sound systems (graphophonic), the wording and grammar (syntactic) systems, and the meaning (semantic-pragmatic) systems of their languages. The integration of sociological and psycholinguistic theories of literacy stress the interaction and interdependence between the three cueing systems available to the reader in a process that is based on their background knowledge and experiences. The theory applies to reading in any language, not only second-language reading based on the observation that the strategies of bilingual readers are similar regardless of the language of the text.

Pennington (1994) concluded that phonological discrimination and production skills of L_2 learners of English who speakers of different native languages operate on parameters based on an underlying linguistic model that appear to be language specific. These "phonological parameters" exert a powerful influence on a speaker's production of L_2 sound segments. Swan and Smith (1987) compiled a comprehensive analysis of the patterns of errors that appear in the English interlanguage of speakers of twenty different native languages. These researchers reject the theory that learners of a given native language tend to follow the same route through difficulties in hearing and articulating English sounds regardless of their first language. Instead, they assert that interlanguage features of native speakers of other languages are specific and distinct with evidence of strong mother-tongue influence accounting for many of the characteristic problems learners encounter in English. Consequently, teachers of language-minority students from diverse linguistic backgrounds can increase their effectiveness in instruction by becoming informed about the characteristics of phonology, syntax, and grammar of the languages spoken by their students.

The important points of cross-linguistic interaction in the cueing systems of reading and instructional interventions for second-language readers are summarized in Figure 9.1. The components of the framework are an analysis of three elements: The bullets on the left side of the figure represent the points of cross-linguistic interaction that occur as a reader develops oral language skills and syntactic-grammatical competence in the second language. This component focuses on points of linguistic influence and transfer that come into play in the development of biliteracy. The center of the figure represents the interaction between the cueing systems involved in the reading process. The right side of the figure summarizes the points of instructional intervention necessary to overcome possible difficulties encountered by second-language readers and to support and enhance the development of strong literacy skills.

The three levels or cueing systems are defined as processes in this framework to identify areas of interaction between the reading process and the linguistic competencies of the bilingual reader. Some authors (e.g., Goodman, 1965) discuss four cueing systems. In those descriptions, the semantic and syntactic systems are usually separated. These levels are defined according to the particular areas of challenge each presents in cross-linguistic transfer of strategies and knowledge of the reading process. The teacher must assess these three cueing systems to have a comprehensive picture of a students' strengths and weaknesses in application of reading processes based on their levels of knowledge in the L_1 and L_2.

1. *The graphophonemic cueing system.* In using this cueing system, grapheme-phoneme-morpheme relationships are established and confusion or linguis-

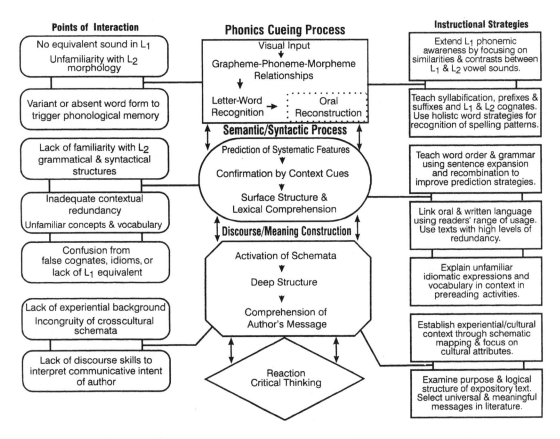

FIGURE 9.1   Linguistic Interaction in L₂ Reading

tic interference may occur because of phonological and spelling pattern differences between the reader's first and second languages.

2. *The semantic and syntactic system.* In the process of recognizing and attaching meaning to words and phrases, equivalent auditory forms or referents for unfamiliar vocabulary words may be variant or absent; or, figurative or idiomatic expressions may be confusing. The reader's lack of familiarity with English syntax and grammar may reduce the ability to use contextual cues in reading and to predict words and meaning for smooth and rapid processing in reading.

3. *The discourse and meaning construction (sometimes referred to as the pragmatic system).* Meaning construction depends on the activation of schema and comprehension of the meaning underlying grammatical forms and on the ability to follow logical structure of the text and understand the communi-

cative intent of the author. There are factors of cultural understanding that affect the ability to grasp the author's underlying message to the reader.

Guiding Principles for Biliteracy Instruction and Assessment

The following is a discussion of how each of the three orientations to reading instruction can be effectively adapted to the learning needs of students. Use of the Checklist of Biliteracy Development (Figure 9.2) help identify points of difficulty that can be addressed through individualized instruction and intervention.

1. *Extend phonemic awareness in the primary language and in English.*

In the Checklist of Biliteracy Development, the categories for the assessment of phonemic awareness is used to determine the reader's use of spelling patterns in combination with discrimination of phonemic differences in words. Bilingual readers who have well developed phonemic awareness and word recognition skills in L_1 are likely to apply these to L_2 reading (Durgunoglu, Nagy, & Hancin, 1993; Jiménez, García, & Pearson, 1996). For those students who have not developed phonemic awareness and an understanding of the alphabetic principle (that is that particular letters and letter combinations represent particular sounds), Rosa provides a variety of activities drawn from emergent literacy practice with her second graders (e.g., letter and sound games, read-alouds from predictable patterned language tradebooks, writing).

2. *Teach syllabification and word derivations such as prefixes and suffixes. Teach cognates in the first and second language. Reinforce attention to spelling patterns through holistic word recognition and analysis strategies.*

In Rosa's bilingual second grade classroom, students are encouraged to conduct word analysis to discover similarities and differences between Spanish and English spelling and meaning. As Marcos and Sonia read the *Too Many Tamales* story first in Spanish and then in English, they discover that many cognates look similar and have the same meaning, such as *interrupt* and *interrumpir*. Ms. Sandoval and the children can then brainstorm a number of other examples that focus on the spelling differences and similarities in meaning, increasing the children's vocabulary in both languages. These activities can help increase students' metacognitive awareness. That awareness can help students see relationships between their two languages rather than viewing them as two separate and unrelated systems.

The Checklist of Biliteracy Development (see Figure 9.2) includes an analysis of the bilingual reader's use of syllabification strategies. A second-language reader may tend to overuse syllabification to the extent that it affects the fluency of their reading (Escamilla, et al., 1996); however, the teacher can

FIGURE 9.2A Checklist of Biliteracy Development. A portfolio and anecdotal records should also be used as supplemental evidence to gauge individual students' level of biliteracy acquisition and development.

L₁ Reading Knowledges and Skills

I. Phonemic Awareness

	Mastered	Attempted

1. Identifies same or different phonemes when presented minimal pairs with different initial vowel sounds.
2. Identifies differences in vowels following same initial consonant.
3. Identifies same or different when presented minimal pairs with different initial consonant sounds.
4. Names words that begin with initial consonant sounds b, d, f, k, l, m, n, p, r, s, t.
5. Creates rhyming words by substituting initial consonants or initial blends bl, cl, fl, gl, pl, br, cr, fr, gr, pr, tr.
6. Identifies the number of syllables in words by tapping out the syllables as they are pronounced.

II. Word Recognition

	Mastered	Attempted

1. Recognizes one- and two-syllable rhyming words based on patterns in a poem or story.
2. Has a sight word vocabulary for names, colors, numbers, days of the week, months of the year, and high frequency words.
3. Uses letter-sound associations together with meaning and context clues to figure out unfamiliar words.
4. Uses syllabication when encountering new words, with subsequent recognition of the word in context.
5. Has fluent oral reading, making meaningful substitutions and omissions.

III. Comprehension

	Mastered	Attempted

1. Reads following punctuation, using appropriate voice inflection and expression when reading orally.
2. Recalls main facts of a story.
3. Recalls the sequence of events in a story.
4. Predicts the outcome of a story or makes logical inferences about the story.
5. Retells a story in his/her own words, stating the main idea and giving some relevant detail.
6. Distinguishes between fact and nonfact or fantasy in a story.

(continued)

FIGURE 9.2   Continued

IV. Composition

	Mastered	Attempted

1. Writes his/her own story and reads it orally with teacher's assistance, expressing his/her ideas clearly.
2. Attempts other forms of written communication such as letters, notes, etc. for a variety of purposes and audiences.
3. Attempts to use various conventions of writing (grammar, punctuation, spelling, etc.)
4. Uses the writing process of gathering ideas, drafting, and revision, etc.

V. Overall L₁ Reading Skills and Practices

	Mastered	Attempted

1. Is an independent reader as determined by an informal reading inventory and/or completion of basal reader at or above grade level.
2. Reads regularly to gain knowledge and for enjoyment.
3. Talks about what he/she has read and otherwise shows reflection on the content and meaning of text.
4. Is at ease during reading activities.

Notes from Anecdotal Records/Portfolio Evaluation:
L₂ (English) Language Skills

I.   Language Usage

	Mastered	Attempted

1. Asks and answers simple questions in English to acquire information.
2. Follows simple directions in English.
3. Initiates conversations with his/her classmates and adults in English.
4. Tells a story or relates an event in English using intelligible vocabulary and grammar.

II. Phonemic Awareness

	Mastered	Attempted

1. Identifies differences in minimal pairs of English words with short vowel sound of *a* as in *bat; i* as in *bit; u* as in *but,* and *u* as in *full.*
2. Names rhyming words with English long vowel sounds.
3. Names English words beginning with initial consonants that are the same in L₁ and English: b, d, f, k, l, m, n, p, r, s, t.
4. Names English words beginning with consonant blends: bl, cl, fl, gl, pl, br, cr, fr, gr, pr, tr.
5. Produces rhyming words by changing initial consonants and blends.

III. Vocabulary and Grammar

	Mastered	Attempted

1. Knows the English labels for concepts from English reading readiness, such as numbers, colors, shapes, and position words.
2. Understands and uses common idiomatic and formulaic expressions for greetings, daily routines, and basic needs.
3. Understands the concepts of synonym, antonym, and multiple meanings of common words (i.e., car, automobile; up-down)
4. Understands and uses orally the vocabulary and idiomatic expressions encountered in basal readers or other texts at instructional reading level.
5. Understands the terminology used by the teacher in English reading instruction to give directions or assign tasks.

IV. English Reading Potential

	Posttest	Pretest

1. Can comprehend a passage from a graded text or informal reading inventory at grade level (usually third grade equivalent) read orally at a normal pace with comprehension.
2. Scores a fluency level on the required language assessment instrument (BVAT, LAS, BSM, IDEA, or other standardized test) or teacher judgment indicates the equivalent of intermediate English.

    BVAT = Bilingual Verbal Abilities
    LAS = Language Assessment
    BSM = Bilingual Syntax Measure
    IDEA = Idea Oral Language Proficiency Test

Anecdotal Records/Portfolio Evaluation:

L₁ and L₂ Language Instruction History:

To what extent has this student received primary language instruction in previous grades in reading and writing? In the content areas?

To what extent has this student received English language development instruction (English as a second language) in previous grades? What methods or strategies were used for this instruction?

observe whether or not syllabification is combined with other strategies, such as the use of context clues as a means of figuring out an unfamiliar word the first time it is encountered in the text. Syllabification is also useful in identifying words that have prefixes, suffixes, and derivations such as the past tense in English.

3. *Teach sentence structure and word order patterns to increase predictability of words in context. Provide opportunities for students to practice rapid recognition of high-frequency words.*

Even when readers can ostensibly "decode" and correctly call out words with standard pronunciation and a high degree of fluency, they may have difficulty understanding what they have read. Children's oral language patterns may differ considerably from the syntactic patterns encountered in texts. Readers are aided by the repetition of patterns and contextual cues. Students should be explicitly taught to exploit this redundancy in written language by demonstrating how information in the text may be supplied in a number of ways.

Successful readers use multiple and integrated strategies for word identification. Rosa teaches her students to chunk letters and words into meaningful groups, to predict and read to confirm their predictions, and use their prior knowledge and background experiences to make sense of text. Her students do paired reading, echo reading, and listen often to read-along books and tapes. The children delight in practicing oral reading to make their own read-along books and tapes to add to the classroom listening library.

4. *Link oral and written language by determining the relationship between oral language proficiency and the biliteracy development. Use texts with high levels of redundancy.*

Stylized syntax, specialized words, and words out of context present the greatest obstacles to comprehension for bilingual readers, while stories with a high levels of redundancy in syntactic patterns were much easier to read and understand. Readers quickly reach the frustration level in attempting to decode and comprehend material that is significantly more complex than their level of oral language. Consequently, teachers of bilingual readers should evaluate the linguistic characteristics of reading texts to address particular difficulties that may occur because of complexity of language, vocabulary and concept load, and idiomatic expressions.

An effective means of addressing the link between oral language proficiency levels of English learners and written text is through the use of the language experience approach (Chamot & O'Malley, 1994: Rueda & García, 1996; Williams & Snipper, 1990). The language experience approach (LEA) is a way to enhance comprehension by linking familiar oral language patterns with written forms. Such a "talk/write" approach recognizes developing oral language skills of students and provides immediate assessment feedback to the teacher.

Ms. Sandoval's students discover the meaning of unfamiliar terms and link their oral proficiency with the written text through several activities. First of all, the children in her class hear and discuss the stories they read before being expected to decipher the written text. Whenever possible, Rosa selects literature that has a parallel version in the students' primary language to build familiarity with the story line and vocabulary. She does this to insure that students do not struggle with unfamiliar meanings in their early encounters with English print. Second, the teacher capitalizes on the linguistic base of the students and their natural tendency to use translation as a reading strategy by encouraging word searches. Third, she selects stories that contain repetitive patterns, predictable language, illustrations that support the text, and frequent use of familiar vocabulary.

The Checklist of Biliteracy Development includes a measure of English reading potential. This informal measure provides an assessment of how much of a graded passage the L_2 reading can comprehend. In other words, this assessment indicates to what degree the reader can use linguistic cueing systems in an orchestrated manner.

5. *Explain unfamiliar idiomatic expressions and vocabulary in context in prereading activities so that these will not impede fluent reading and comprehension.*

The linguist Chomsky (1957) proposed the notion of "surface structure" and "deep structure" of language to explain how syntactic patterns signal differences in meaning. The distinction between surface and deep structure is helpful in understanding the role of syntax in second-language reading. A reader who translates word for word cannot comprehend authentic unedited text, because the meaning is frequently conveyed by groups of words, such as idiomatic expressions. These expressions have a certain meaning in combination with each other that the words when standing alone do not convey. An example is the expression "to run out of gas" in which the words may in fact have a completely different meaning if used in isolation, while as a phrase they convey a specific idea. These expressions could be confused with phrases that use the same words, but to convey different meanings, such as in the contrast between "to run out of gas" as opposed to the meaning of "to run out of the building."

Ms. Sandoval works with the meaning and structure of sentences frequently in teaching. Her sequential order activity, for example, helps students focus on the grammatical structure of sentences with adverbial clauses indicating time and progression. Her second-language readers build their awareness of words that signal important meaning and sort these out from among the function words that serve as linguistic connectors. By having students read chorally and individually, she helps them build fluidity and confidence in their ability to recognize words quickly and easily.

The use of an informal reading inventory such as that of Burns and Roe (1993) or an inventory based on a graded series of readers provides valuable insights into the interaction between linguistic competence and vocabulary comprehension. For example, in the Burns and Roe inventory (p. 77), the story of Crandall Cricket describes how he played his fife and fiddle instead of preparing for the upcoming winter. Second-language readers are unlikely to be familiar with the word *fife* or the verb *fiddling*. Also, expressions like "day in and day out" are not common expressions used in conversation. Drawing on lessons learned from Reading Recovery, an early intervention program for struggling readers, teachers like Rosa often maintain running records of student's oral reading from leveled tradebooks for similar purposes. In oral reading, the teacher can discern hesitation or repetition that might indicate a lack of familiarity with such idiomatic expressions. This could lead to explicit instruction on such forms in prereading activities.

6. *Establish an experiential and cultural context through schematic mapping. Focus on the specific cultural attributes of the text.*
   Using thematic units for literacy instruction is highly conducive to the transfer of concepts and skills between students' L_1 and L_2. Organization of literacy activities around themes provides many opportunities for students to utilize new vocabulary and concepts in different contexts, thus reinforcing new learning. Thematic units also integrate listening, speaking, reading, and writing skills in such a way that students can participate and succeed at whatever level of linguistic competence they have achieved. They learn the different functions and forms reading and writing can take as they engage in critical thinking and reading for enjoyment as well.
   Mapping and clustering are methods of organizing information in a graphic form (examples of each are included in Chapter 5) so that the learner can see the relationship between the major points and elements of exposition. Students should be taught to understand how new information is presented and related to central ideas and elaboration of detail. Teachers can use charting, outlining, and graphic organizers to reduce the linguistic demands of academic text and enhance students' abilities to glean information from more abstract and complex writing (Peregoy & Boyle, 1997).
   Ms. Sandoval utilizes thematic instruction to the advantage of her students. The emerging and fluent readers and writers are encouraged to experiment with literary creations in either language as their interests and skills develop. Students gradually and naturally start to use their L_2 as proficiency and familiarity with the conventions of print develop, adding to the knowledge and skills already developed in their primary language. By providing a print rich environment, Rosa supports and encourages exploration of cross-linguistic characteristics that help her students become sensitive to language and to develop effective second-language reading and writing strategies (Hudelson & Serna, 1994).

7. *Guide students in examining the purpose and logical structure of expository and narrative text. Select universal and meaningful messages in literature.*
   Bilingual readers are helped to achieve higher levels of comprehension by explicit instruction in the organizational patterns and structure of expository

text in English (Dewbury, 1994; Schifini, 1994). Teachers should teach students how signal words are used to indicate logical patterns in the text, such as comparison and contrast or cause and effect. Words and phrases such as *because, therefore, however,* and *in the event that* indicate relationships between ideas or details in the text. Such structural features as a sequence of events can be pointed out to students to increase comprehension in reading and structuring in composition.

A very important aspect of literacy instruction is the selection of meaningful and appropriate multicultural literature (Crawford, 1993). Students who have recently immigrated and are in the process of adjusting to a new language and culture, and those who enjoy the expanded experiences of living in bicultural environments, need to read and appreciate stories with which they can identify. Ms. Sandoval has selected a theme that is universal, because families in all cultures have traditional celebrations and family recipes for special holiday dishes. Soto's *Too Many Tamales* is the story of a Hispanic family in the United States celebrating Christmas. The children can identify with the bicultural elements of the holiday traditions of this family, as they combine the ceremonial preparation of the tamales wrapped in corn husks with scenes of gifts under a Christmas tree decorated with candy canes and tinsel. The story of a daughter's bonding with her mother underlies the universal message of cultural heritage and family tradition. Ms. Sandoval's students benefit from her careful assessment of their strengths and weaknesses and her targeted instruction that takes into account the complex interaction between the two languages in the development of literacy. Her use of authentic literature that conveys universal messages and values build a love of books and a joy in literacy that transcends languages and cultures.

Conclusion

As we leave Rosa Sandoval's classroom, we can reflect on the multifaceted strategies she implements in her classroom to address the diverse linguistic characteristics and learning needs of her students. We must remain cognizant of the fact that decisions regarding instructional approaches and techniques are most effectively made within the framework of a coherent philosophy of literacy instruction and well-designed literacy programs. The most productive instructional program for second-language learners is one that builds on their strengths in their native language and expands and enhances their proficiency and literacy in English. The seven guiding principles and the assessment tools presented here are based on theories of second-language reading that take into account the interaction between different systems for constructing meaning from text. These principles also respect the significance of social and cultural dimensions of learning in the context of diversity. When teachers are knowledgeable about the particular challenges posed by second-language acquisition and linguistic factors in literacy development of bilingual students, they can increase the likelihood of success for themselves as teachers and for their diverse learners.

DISCUSSION QUESTIONS

1. Students enrolled in different types of programs for second-language learners face different challenges and risks. What factors should teachers take into consideration in regard to their classroom management and instructional planning when weighing the risks and benefits of dual language literacy against second-language literacy in English?

2. The paradigm of the three cueing systems involved in the reading process is proposed as a guide to instruction and assessment for second-language readers. What are the advantages to viewing reading processes from this perspective? What factors that impact literacy learning are left out of this model? How can these missing or neglected elements be addressed in instruction and assessment?

3. The need for a consistent and coherent literacy program for L_2 learners is emphasized in this chapter. What factors support design and implementation of effective literacy programs for language minority students? Which of these factors are within the control of classroom teachers? To what extent do teachers' level of expertise and preparation for teaching L_2 learners contribute to program coherence and effectiveness?

4. Thematic instruction is recommended for classrooms where L_2 learners are developing second-language literacy and biliteracy. Yet, planning and teaching based on themes is often difficult, given the time constraints and curriculum structures under which many teachers work. What principles of thematic instruction should be considered "nonnegotiable" for effective L_2 literacy programs? To what extent are these principles applied in other types of curriculum planning models?

5. Oftentimes, teachers with less experience with L_2 learners may have unrealistic expectations for students who are learning to read and write in their second language. How can a well-designed assessment plan assist teachers in sound decision making regarding remedial instruction and support services, grade-level retention and promotion, and other aspects of students' overall academic progress? Is a second-language literacy assessment plan compatible with state and/or school district mandated testing programs using norm-referenced standardized tests?

REFERENCES

Au, K. H. (1998). Social constructivism and the school literacy learning of students of diverse backgrounds. *Journal of Literacy Research 30*(2), 297–319.
August, D., & Hakuta, K. (Eds.). (1997). *Improving schooling for language-minority children: A research agenda.* Washington, DC: National Academy Press.
Bernhardt, E. B. (1991). *Reading development in a second language.* Norwood, NJ: Ablex Publishing.
Burns, P. C., & Roe, B. D. (1993). *Burns/Roe informal reading inventory.* Boston: Houghton Mifflin.

Chamot, A. U., & O'Malley, M. (1994). Instructional approaches and teaching procedures. In K. Spangenber-Urbschat & R. Pritchard (Eds.), *Kids come in all languages: Reading instruction for ESL students* (pp. 82–107). Newark, DE: International Reading Association.

Chomsky, N. (1957). *Syntactic structures.* The Hague: Mourton & Company.

Coady, J. (1979). A psycholinguistic model of the ESL reader. In R. Mackay, B. Barkman, & R. Jordan (Eds.), *Reading in a second language.* Rowley, MA: Newbury House Publishers.

Crawford, L. W. (1993). *Language and literacy learning in multicultural classrooms.* Boston: Allyn & Bacon.

Dewbury, A. (1994). *First steps: Writing resource book of the Education Department of Western Australia.* Portsmouth, NH: Heinemann.

Durgunoglu, A. Y., Nagy, R., & Hancin, M. (1993). Cross-language transfer of phonemic awareness. *Journal of Educational Psychology 85*(3), 452–465.

Escamilla, K., Andrade, A. M., Basurto, A. G., & Ruíz, O. A. (1996). *Instrumento de observación de los logros de la lecto-escritura inicial.* Portsmouth, NH: Heinemann.

Freeman, Y. S., & Freeman, D. E. (1997). *Teaching reading and writing in Spanish in the bilingual classroom.* Portsmouth, NH: Heinemann.

Goodman, K. S. (1965). A linguistic study of cues and miscues, in reading. *Elementary English, 42,* 639–643.

Harris, T. L., & Hodges, R. E. (Eds.). (1995). *The literacy dictionary.* Newark, DE: International Reading Association.

Hornberger, N. H. (1994). Continua of biliteracy. In B. M. Ferdman, R. Weber, & A. G. Ramírez (Eds.), *Literacy across languages and cultures* (pp. 103–139). Albany, NY: State University of New York Press.

Hudelson, S., & Serna, I. A. (1994). Beginning literacy in a whole language bilingual program. In A. S. Flurkey, & R. J. Meyer. *Under the whole language umbrella* (pp. 278–294). Urbana, IL: National Council of Teachers of English.

Jiménez, R. T., García, G. E., & Pearson, P. D. (1996). The reading strategies of bilingual Latina/o students who are successful English readers: Opportunities and obstacles. *Reading Research Quarterly, 33*(1), 90–112.

Koda, K. (1997). Orthographic knowledge in L2 lexical processing: A cross-linguistic perspective. In J. Coady & T. Huckin (Eds.), *Second language vocabulary acquisition* (pp. 35–52). New York: Cambridge University Press.

Milk, R., Mercado, C., & Sapiens, A. (1992). Re-thinking the education of teachers of language minority children: Developing reflective teachers for changing schools. In *NCBE Focus: Occasional papers in bilingual education, 6.* Washington, DC: National Clearinghouse for Bilingual Education.

Miramontes, O. F., Nadeau, A., & Commins, N. L. (1997). *Restructuring schools for linguistic diversity.* New York: Teachers College Press.

National Research Council (1998). *Preventing reading difficulties in young children.* Washington, DC: National Academy Press.

Nilsen, D. L., & Nilsen, A. P. (1973). *Pronunciation contrasts in English.* New York: Regents Publishing.

Odlin, T. (1989). *Language transfer: Cross-linguistic influence in language learning.* New York: Cambridge University Press.

Pennington, M. C. (1994). Recent research in L2 phonology: Implications for practice. In J. Morley (Ed.), *Pronunciation pedagogy and theory: New views, new directions.* Alexandria, VA: Teachers of English to Speakers of Other Languages.

Peregoy, S. F., & Boyle, O. F. (1997). *Reading, writing and learning in ESL.* New York: Longman.

Reyes, M. L. (1992). Challenging venerable assumptions: Literacy instruction for linguistically different students. *Harvard Educational Review, 62,* 427–446.

Rueda, R., & García, E. (1996). Teachers perspectives on literacy assessment and instruction with language-minority students: A comparative study. *Elementary School Journal, 96*(3), 311–332.

Schifini, A. (1994). Language, literacy and content instruction: Strategies for teachers. In K. Spangenber-Urbschat & R. Pritchard (Eds.), *Kids come in all languages: Reading instruction for ESL students*. Newark, DE: International Reading Association.

Soto, G. (1993). *Too many tamales*. New York: G.P. Putman's Sons.

Swan, M., & Smith, B. (1987). *Learner English*. Cambridge, England: Cambridge University Press.

Thomas, W. P., & Collier, V. P. (1999). Accelerated schooling for English language learners. *Educational Leadership 56*(7), 46–49.

Wiley, T. C. (1996). *Literacy and language diversity in the United States*. McHenry, IL: Center for Applied Linguistics.

Williams, J. D., & Snipper, G. C. (1990). *Literacy and bilingualism*. White Plains, NY: Longman.

10 Assessing Our Work with Parents on Behalf of Children's Literacy

ALMA FLOR ADA
University of San Francisco

F. ISABEL CAMPOY
Transformative Educational Services

ROSA ZUBIZARRETA

To the living memory of Paulo Freire:
your love and wisdom continue
to transform the world

In the course of our work with parents, we have had the opportunity to listen to many of the difficulties faced by parents of language-minority children. The following anecdotes highlight some of the issues that we will be addressing in this chapter.

As educators, we need to ask ourselves some difficult questions. What is our responsibility here? In what ways have we been contributing to this problem? What can we do to make a positive difference for language-minority parents and their children?

Assessing Our Work with Parents

When it comes to assessment, our culture's predominant tendency is to focus on assessing others, instead of assessing our own work. Of course, assessing a child's learning can help us learn more about the effectiveness of our own practice, when conducted with that clear intention in mind. Yet too often, the question of "How effective are my teaching practices, and how might I improve them?" gets lost in our focus on assigning grades to students.

When examining our collaboration with parents, it is equally important that we keep the focus on assessing and improving our own efforts. After all, any limiting beliefs or negative judgments we might hold about the parents of our

Parents' Concerns

After listening to a presentation in which parents have been encouraged to communicate with their children, tell stories, and share life experiences as a way to support their children's learning, a mother approaches the presenter. The mother's concern is greater than her obvious shyness. "I have a problem," she says. "How can I follow your recommendations, if I don't speak English? Everyone says that if I speak Spanish to my child, he'll never learn English. Isn't it better for me to just let him watch TV in English, instead of speaking to him in Spanish?"

After another presentation, a parent approaches, pleading for help. "My son is failing high school," she confides. "They want to send him to an alternative school, but he just wants to drop out. I want to help him, to talk with him, encourage him . . . but he doesn't understand me. He doesn't understand my language when I speak to him. . . . I don't know when he forgot his Spanish. When his older sister lived at home, she always spoke to him in English. Now I realize that she was translating everything I said to him. But now she has moved away. She did well in school, she is doing fine with her life. But I am losing my son . . . he is my son, and I can't even talk with him!"

students are likely to lead to reduced communication and cooperation. A sincere and in-depth examination of our own efforts and approaches, however, can allow us to make necessary changes in the area over which we have the most control.

One of the main points of this chapter is that, in addition to assessing our work in the areas of parent education and parent engagement, we need to assess our everyday classroom curriculum with regard to the inclusion of parents, family, and community. If we are not making an effort to include parents' knowledge, wisdom, and history in our curriculum, we are missing powerful opportunities for motivating and supporting students' literacy development. We are also contributing, by default, to a painful gap between the worlds of home and school.

Too often, language-minority children end up alienated, feeling that they do not belong at school. Alternatively, they may come to feel that their home is deficient and that the price of success is to distance themselves from their own roots. Parents, in turn, often believe they have little to offer their children's formal learning, because they do not speak English or have lacked opportunities for formal education.

As educators, we can consciously choose to send a different message to students and their families. By thoughtfully assessing and modifying our curriculum, we can take significant steps towards helping children integrate the worlds of home and school. As we help parents build on their strengths by encouraging them to use their home language, their life experiences, and their human wisdom to engage with their children in beneficial ways, this can also help create more powerful learning environments for children in the classroom.

Brief Background on Research

Erroneous beliefs about minority parents are unfortunately still prevalent among educators. Minority parents are often regarded as not caring or not being willing to be involved in their children's education. As stated by Kerbow and Bernhart (1993), many policy initiatives designed to increase minority parental engagement operate on the false assumption that "levels of parental involvement for these parents are inadequate or at least below expected levels" (p. 115).

Research, however, does not support these beliefs, confirming instead that minority parents have high educational expectations for their children and are willing to invest whatever economic resources are at their disposal on their children's education (Muller & Kerbow, 1993). Research also confirms that minority parents are highly interested in collaborating with schools to help their children succeed academically (Moles, 1993). Looking at the available evidence, Kerbow and Bernhart (1993) conclude: "To claim that these parents are inadequate in their attention to their children's education is straightforwardly mistaken" (p. 134).

While language-minority parents may care deeply about their children's education and hold high hopes for their children, they may not communicate their hopes in similar ways to mainstream parents (see, e.g., Delgado-Gaitan, 1990). In addition to cultural differences, parents may have accepted prevailing beliefs that those with scant formal education have little to contribute to their children's educational development. Often, they may feel that sending their children to school is the best they can offer—only to have their behavior interpreted as "not caring about their children's education." Of course, language barriers, work schedules, and lack of adequate child care can all limit the ways in which parents are able to express their concerns.

Searching for workable alternatives, progressive educators have called for other approaches to working with minority parents. These educators have argued that traditional ways of understanding parent involvement, such as attendance at Parent-Teacher Association (PTA) meetings, overlook the many ways in which minority parents can be powerful supports at home for their children's academic success (Nieto, 1992; Simich-Dudgeon, 1993). Research has confirmed the significance of alternative forms of parent involvement. For example, one of the most important correlations of student achievement is parent-student discussions about school activities and programs (Muller, 1993). Encouraging parents to engage in dialogue with their children results in positive effects on students' academic achievement, even when parents themselves have very little formal education and low levels of literacy (Hewison & Tizard, 1980; Simich-Dudgeon, 1986). These findings have lent support to "home learning activities" as a promising avenue for helping parents increase student achievement (Rich, 1987, 1993; Ramirez & Douglas, 1989; Simich-Dudgeon, 1993).

Despite the promise of home learning activities, too little is said about the language in which these activities might be most effective. Indeed, with few exceptions (Auerbach, 1989; Simich-Dudgeon, 1993) the issue of home language use is rarely mentioned in the literature on parent involvement. Yet research worldwide shows repeatedly that strong home language use in the home correlates with higher student achievement in the language of the school (Cummins, 1981; Dolson, 1985.) Regardless of our position on bilingual education, abundant evidence points to the academic value of promoting home language use at home. Additionally, a shared home language facilitates greater communication between parents and children, allowing parents to offer continued support and guidance to their children.

The above considerations lead us to pose three initial questions. First, to what extent do we regard all parents as concerned about and having high hopes for their children's education, even if they may not be expressing their concerns and hopes in a way that we can understand? Secondly, to what degree do we promote communication at home in the home language, so that parents are able to contribute their strengths towards their children's academic success? Thirdly, to what extent does our curriculum include the use of home learning activities that promote communication between parents and children?

This third question can lead us to consider what other kinds of modifications to our curriculum we might make to encourage greater communication at home between parents and children. When discussing the finding that minority parents appear to have a lower incidence of communication about school-related activities with their children, Muller and Kerbow present the following hypothesis:

> . . . discussion of current aspects of the educational experience may be more likely to come about in families in which parents are able to in some sense "put themselves in the context of the school," figuratively speaking, so that the student and parent have enough commonalty of understanding to be able to talk about what happens to the student. (1993, p. 18)

In other words, one of the likely effects of the disparity between the respective cultures of school and home is reduced communication between parents and children about school matters. This reduced communication, in turn, can affect children's academic achievement.

Yet there is no reason to take the "context of the school" as a given. In our experience, teacher practice can significantly influence the degree to which the classroom culture reflects children's families and communities. Ada (1993), Huerta-Macías and Quintero (1993), and McCaleb (1994) all explore what teachers can do in the classroom to promote parent-child conversations that build on parents' life experiences, family histories, and cultural knowledge. By accessing and incorporating parents' "funds of knowledge" into classroom curriculum and practice, the "context of the school" becomes more reflective of children's families and communities (Moll, 1990). This, in turn, promotes further parent-child communication. Our fourth question, then, becomes: "To what extent does our classroom curriculum and practice, by being culturally relevant and family-friendly, promote parent-child communication?"

By including and honoring parents, families, and community in the curriculum, we increase possibilities for communication between parents and children about school-related activities, which in turn correlates with higher academic achievement. Yet, there are many school factors that correlate with achievement and influence the acquisition of literacy at least as significantly as home factors (Urzua, 1986). Including family and community in the curriculum also influences school factors that affect literacy by creating a stimulating and engaging classroom environment.

The benefits of closer home-school collaboration are not only academic: encouraging children to feel proud of their families and communities helps foster strong family ties. Conversely, when the school's curriculum and practices do not respect children's families, home languages, and communities, the school is contributing to the breakdown of community and family ties, regardless of its good intentions. Using terminology introduced by James Coleman (1991), we can say that schools either *strengthen* or *undermine* the social capital of the families and communities they are supposed to serve.

Children are sensitive to the "hidden curriculum" of the school. The image they hold of their parents—already threatened in a culture whose primary value is economic success—suffers further whenever schools maintain a silent disregard. As children encounter greater and greater difficulty in sustaining their original respect for their parents, they are more likely to look for alternative role models and alternative sources of pride and self-respect. While a few might choose to assimilate and identify with the majority culture, for too many the solution lies in the direction of gang membership. When children lose the ability to speak their home language, *the language their parents speak best,* parents have great difficulty guiding and supporting their children as they enter adolescence and face major choices, challenges, and risks.

The difficulties created for children when the schools do not include parents has been stated eloquently by Comer (1988), "When we ask low-income, minority-group children to achieve well in school—an instrument of mainstream society—we are often asking them to be different than their parents. With parents involved there is no conflict" (p. 219). By encouraging communication between parents and children; by including parents' knowledge, experience, and wisdom in the curriculum; and by honoring the languages that parents speak, we further reduce children's sense of conflict.

Table 10.1 summarizes the four principal questions for self-assessment we have considered in our discussion of the research.

Implications for Practice

The discussion in the previous section points to the need to reexamine and expand previous typologies of parent engagement efforts. Typologies can serve to help sort and organize the various kinds of efforts included in the field of "parent involvement"; however, they also need to be revised and expanded as our knowledge base expands. Epstein's (1987) categories of "parental involvement" include the following areas:

TABLE 10.1   Building Collaborative Relationships with Parents

1. To what extent do we regard all parents as having high hopes for their children's education, even when they may not express their concerns and hopes in a way we understand?
2. To what extent are we promoting home language use at home as a way for parents to support children's learning and development?
3. To what extent does our curriculum include home learning activities as a way to promote conversations in the home language?
4. To what extent are we creating a culturally relevant, family-friendly curriculum that promotes greater parent-child communication?

1. Parent education and family support services
2. Increased communication between home and school
3. Parent-family participation at school in school activities and programs
4. Parent-family participation in advocacy and decision-making
5. Parent-family participation in home learning activities initiated by the school

Considering the discussion on "the context of the school" I add a sixth category: the inclusion of parents, family, and community in classroom curriculum and practice.

As mentioned earlier, the result of including and honoring children's parents, families, communities, and home languages within the school and classroom community affects both home *and* school factors that influence student achievement. It makes communication between parents and children about school-related activities more likely, helps create a supportive school environment, and strengthens relationships between parents and children.

In addition to including this crucial sixth category, we also need a way to assess the quality of our work in each of these six areas. To do so, we need a clear sense of best practice. In turn, our definition of *best practice* is informed by our fundamental philosophy about human beings and how we learn.

In working with children, we are aware of the distinction between a facilitative, constructivist approach that honors children's intelligence and builds on their prior knowledge, contrasted to a "blank-slate" approach that assumes children are empty vessels waiting to be filled (Cummins, 1989). Likewise, teachers must be cognizant of the underlying assumptions and philosophical beliefs that inform our work with parents (Freire, 1984; Auerbach, 1989; Montecel, et al., 1993).

Within each of the six categories of parent engagement, we can position our work at some point along the continuum between a deficit or empty-vessel, perspective, which focuses primarily on what parents lack and an additive or building-on-strengths approach. By doing so, we add a qualitative dimension to each category, turning the typology into a matrix. In this way, we can examine how our beliefs and attitudes shape the work that we do within each of these different areas, limiting or enhancing our effectiveness.

Before proceeding further, we must acknowledge that we all carry within us the seeds of the deficit perspective. As members of this society, we have all been conditioned to compete with one another, to evaluate and rank each other in hierarchical systems based on any number of factors from the amount of money we make to the number of degrees we hold. Even when regarding others from this limited perspective, we often act out of helpful intentions. For example, we may sincerely attempt to help others "climb the economic ladder" by obtaining more educational opportunities. Yet our ability to truly help someone is limited by the degree to which our focus on their deficits causes us to overlook their strengths.

Conversely, the power of a strengths-based approach is the result of the simple fact that the greatest help we can give another person is the full dignity and respect that is due them as a human being. When we do so, we find that growth and learning occurs quite naturally, often by leaps and bounds. Even if we look at the situation strictly from the perspective of effectiveness, we can see the difference that our own approach can make.

Now we examine each of the six categories of collaboration with parents, exploring what the continuum between a deficit and a strengths perspective might look like within each. While some of these categories are more directly connected with children's literacy acquisition than others, we look at all six.

1. *Family support services and parent education.*

Obviously, a principal need faced by language-minority parents is English-language instruction. Yet too often, the quality of this instruction is unexamined. English-as-a-second-language (ESL) classes can embody either a deficit or a strengths approach depending on their design. As expertly demonstrated by Auerbach and her colleagues (1990), the ESL classroom can be designed to build on parents' prior knowledge and experience, validate parents' home language, and honor parents' abilities to think, create, and problem-solve.

While learning English is essential, the need for ESL classes must not blind us to the value of parents' home language for contributing to their children's cognitive, emotional, and ethical development. Likewise, it is crucial that we not mistake the lack of literacy skills as equivalent to a reduced ability to reason. Parents' problem-solving abilities and the wisdom they have gained from overcoming difficult life experiences often become invisible to us if we focus solely on their lack of English and literacy skills. Instead, a strengths approach seeks to bring together parents with limited formal education and their literate-bound children in a way " . . . that the parents will not lose face, and the children will respect and be proud of their language and cultural backgrounds" (Simich-Dudgeon, 1993, p. 199). A detailed example of a family literacy program based on a strengths approach is included in the section Practical School and Classroom Applications.

2. *Increased communication between home and school.*

Much emphasis has been placed on making the one-way communication from the school to the home more accessible to minority parents, for example, by translating materials to be sent home. While this is a laudable goal, greater awareness is necessary about the importance of two-way communication. It is true that minority parents can feel diffident and shy about speaking out as a result of the power imbalances prevalent in school-community relations; however, tremendous energy can be generated when conditions are created for parents to truly voice their hopes, fears, questions, and concerns (Shirley, 1997). These examples are discussed further in the fifth category, advocacy and decision-making.

Communication overlaps several other categories as well. Eliciting parents' voices is also an integral element of including parents in school curriculum and practice, our sixth category. In the section on practical applications, we explore how teachers can invite parent voices into the classroom through interactive home-learning activities. This form of two-way communication helps create classroom environments conducive to learning, where the richness of students' prior knowledge and experience is recognized and built upon (Developmental Studies Center, 1995).

Inviting dialogue and listening to parents is also an essential aspect of the strengths-based parent education programs explored in the first category. Two-way communication allows community concerns and cultural traditions to inform the content and design of ESL classes and family literacy programs (Auerbach, 1989).

3. *Parent or family participation in school-site activities and programs.*

While language-minority parents often have heavy work schedules, which make volunteering or attending school functions difficult, the quality of programs also makes a significant difference in parent attendance. When parents are invited to events in which they have no voice or they are lectured, the results are understandably low. Parents respond much more positively to events that celebrate their own cultural heritage or in which they see their children perform.

Parents also respond quite positively to opportunities for face-to-face conversations with each other about significant issues. Whenever time is created for such small-group discussions as part of an evening event, parents express deep appreciation for the opportunity to meet (Forest, 1994). This is especially significant because parent friendship networks have been shown to correlate positively to student's academic achievement, and some existing research has shown these networks to be less strong among minority parents (Muller & Kerbow, 1993).

4. *Parent or family participation in advocacy and decision-making.*

Schools often do not experience much success in recruiting minority parents for their school-site councils. Groups such as the Right Question Project (Rodriguez, Rothstein, & Santana, 1994), however, have shown that when parents are invited to work together in collaborative groups to brainstorm lists of their own questions about their children's education, a tremendous amount of interest and commitment can be generated. Similarly, Shirley (1997) describes the success of the Industrial Areas Foundation (IAF) in Texas, which built community support for school reform by holding meetings in parents' homes to identify their issues and concerns.

These examples point to a larger vision of collaboration between schools and families; one that includes not only the goal of improving student outcomes but also the goals of social integration of diverse populations, strengthening democratic participation among the public at large, and, ultimately, creating increased public support for education (Safran, 1996). To reach these goals, however, schools need to learn to truly share power with parents. Sarason (1995) offers a brilliant analysis of the challenges involved in doing so.

5. *Parent or family participation in home learning activities initiated by the school.*

The addition of the phrase "initiated by the school" is intentional as it signals a recognition that parents are already involved in a wide variety of learning activities with their children at home, although these activities may look very different from the kinds of learning we associate with schools. Indeed, some educators have offered a cautionary note regarding the danger of home learning activities when they are approached from a deficit perspective. The result can be a one-way transmission of school practices and culture to the home (Auerbach, 1989).

Home learning activities initiated by the school, however, can take various forms, corresponding to different places along the deficit-strengths continuum. From a strengths perspective, the most powerful home learning activities are interactive ones, based on the parents' own life experiences and stories, which encourage parents and children to communicate in the home language (Rich, 1987).

In addition, when home learning activities are designed to be followed up back at school, they can serve as powerful tools for including parent voices in the curriculum—our next and final category. An example of this kind of interactive home learning activity with a strong classroom component is the Homeside Activities/Actividades Familiares (Developmental Studies Center, 1995).

6. *Inclusion of parents, family, and community in classroom curriculum and practice.*

While a unit on the ancient history of Mexico may be a step in the right direction when we want to include Mexican-American children's experience in the curriculum, we must honor and respect the children's own families and communities, not just the past.

As mentioned earlier, interactive home learning activities that include classroom follow-up can be a simple way to start the process of validating children's families and communities at the school. In the Spanish-language parent video for the Homeside Activities program, we see examples of teachers using home activities for this purpose (Developmental Studies Center, 1997). Other approaches along the same lines were cited previously (Ada, 1993; Huerta-Macías & Quintero, 1993; McCaleb, 1994). A more detailed description of such a program follows in the next section.

In Table 10.2, we summarize the discussion of the six categories. In addition, we include the kinds of questions we might ask ourselves in assessing our efforts in each category.

TABLE 10.2

Categories of School-Home Collaboration	From a Deficit or Empty-Vessel Perspective	Towards a Building-on-Strengths Approach
Family support services and parent education	ESL classes taught from an empty-vessel approach Family literacy programs focused on English use at home	ESL classes using a "participatory curriculum" model (Auerbach, 1990) Family literacy models focused on parents as authors (Ada, 1988)
Questions for self-assessment	■ To what extent is our curriculum for parents built around parents' own ideas and experiences? ■ To what extent are parents treated as active and creative learners, with significant contributions and real choices to make? ■ To what extent do we help parents recognize home language skills as an asset to support their children's cognitive and emotional development?	
Increased communication	Focus on one-way communication from school to home on topics determined by the school	Creating conditions in which parents' real concerns can be heard: (Rodriguez, et al., 1994; Shirley, 1997) Inviting parent voices into the classroom through interactive home learning activities (Ada, 1993; Developmental Studies Center, 1995) Dialoguing with parents to cocreate content of parent education offerings (Auerbach, 1989, 1990)
Question for self-assessment	■ To what extent are we as educators listening to parents' stories to gain a deeper appreciation of their lives, their strengths, and their hard work?	
School-site activities	Activities planned with scant parent input; more reflective of school culture than community culture Parents seen as passive audience; few opportunities for active participation	School-site activities are culturally relevant Opportunities for parents to connect with each other (Forest, 1994) Activities are based on an inclusive, participatory model (DSC, 1996)

Questions for self-assessment	■ To what extent are our school-site activities inclusive, participatory, and noncompetitive? ■ To what extent are they reflective of the culture and traditions of the community? ■ To what extent do we provide opportunities, such as small-group activities, for parents to get to know each other?	
Advocacy and decision-making	Efforts to educate parents of rights/responsibilities limited to one-way transmission models	Parents work in collaborative groups to uncover concerns, learn to act effectively (Rodriguez, et al., 1994)
	Parents greatly outnumbered on committees; structural pressure to assimilate to prevailing school culture; token participation	Parents, organized as a community, collaborate with the school (Shirley, 1997)
	Appearance of "site-based management" and "partnering with parents" incongruent with real power dynamics	Schools look deeply at challenges of sharing power, both within the school and with parents (Sarason, 1995)
Questions for self-assessment	■ To what extent do we provide hands-on, collaborative opportunities for parents to learn participation skills? ■ To what extent do we work with community organizations on educational issues? ■ To what extent do we honestly address issues of power, both within the school and with parents?	
Home learning activities	Focused on getting parents to carry out school-like activities with children	Designed to elicit parents' views, life experiences, stories; promote home communication in home language (Rich, 1993); also to enrich classroom life by including parent voices (Developmental Studies Center, 1997)
	Few opportunities for parents to contribute own knowledge, experiences	
	Not designed for two-way flow back into classroom of parent voices, stories	
Questions for self-assessment	■ To what extent does the homework we assign promote communication and provide opportunities for parents to share their perspectives and experiences? ■ To what extent do we integrate the learnings from home activities back into the life of the classroom?	
Inclusive curriculum	Information on children's communities and cultural backgrounds presented without real respect or in stereotyped ways	Children's families and communities included as valuable resources for classroom learning (Ada, 1993; Huerta-Macías & Quintero, 1993; McCaleb, 1994)

(continued)

TABLE 10.2   Continued

Questions for self-assessment	■ In what ways do we invite parents to share their stories and life experiences to enrich children's classroom experience? ■ In what ways do we use the printed word and other technologies as a means of validating and celebrating children's families and communities?

Practical School and Classroom Applications

In this last section, we describe two examples of work with parents. The first is a family literacy program entitled "Parents and Children as Authors." The second is a classroom-based approach in which teachers write a simple book of their own as a way to introduce home learning activities and to create an inclusive curriculum.

Transformative Family Literacy: Parents and Children as Authors

In 1986, the bilingual program of the Pájaro School District in Northern California agreed to participate in an innovative project titled *Proyecto de Literatura Infantil* (Children's Literature Project). The original project (Ada, 1988; see also Brown, 1993) led to a series of replications based on a similar model and following the same set of principles.

1. Parents are the first and most constant educators of their children. Regardless of their level of formal education, all parents have a wealth of personal experience and family stories to share with their children.
2. Parents' home language is a valuable resource for children's oral language and cognitive development. Children's home language is also connected to their sense of identity and community.
3. Parents are valuable allies for children's emotional and social growth and development. Strong ties between parents and children, based on sharing a common language, help parents guide and support their children as they grow into adolescence.
4. Parents are more inclined to share books with children if they themselves have been able to experience the pleasure and relevance of reading. Giving parents the opportunity to listen to a story and discuss its relevance to their lives helps them to share that experience with their children.
5. Picture books are an accessible medium for parents. Even if parents are preliterate, they can retell the story to their children at home, using the illustrations as a support.
6. As parents and children are helped and encouraged to share their thinking, their writing, and their stories, their self-confidence grows in tangible and often surprising ways.

The format of the program consists of a series of monthly evening sessions, during which parents meet in small groups to listen to and discuss selected children's books. Parents are then given the books to take home and share with their children. At the sessions, parents are assisted in writing their own collective books and given blank books to take home for their own and their families' use.

The picture books shared with parents are carefully chosen for their literary and artistic merit and for their potential to initiate rich, thought-provoking discussions. Examples of books that yield excellent discussions include *Frederick and Swimmy* by Leo Leonni, *La conejita Marcela* by Ester Tusquets, *Arturo y Clementina* and *Rosa Caramelo* by Adela Turin, and *The Gold Coin* by Alma Flor Ada.

The dialogue following the reading is guided by the Creative Dialogue Process (Ada, 1991). This methodology is inspired by the work of Paulo Freire. Its basic premise is that reading, in its fullest expression, is a dialogic experience with the text for the sake of human growth and development (Freire, 1984; Ada & Campoy, 1997a).

The form of the dialogue consists of four phases, which in actual practice are often interwoven. During the *descriptive phase*, the content of the book is analyzed. The theme, conflicts, and development of the story are discussed, along with characters' motives and the consequences of the choices they made. In the *personal interpretative phase*, parents are invited to relate the story to their own life experiences, exploring how significant issues in their own lives may parallel or differ from those in the book. Next, the discussion is taken to a level of critical reflection in the *critical/multicultural phase*, as the participants are invited to offer their own perspectives, discuss what aspects of the book may or may not apply to their own culture, and examine other possible alternatives. The dialogue returns to parent's own lives again during the final *creative transformation phase*, in which parents are invited to reflect on their own present circumstances and discuss areas of potential growth in their lives.

Following the discussion, parents are helped to create their own collective books. The facilitators pose a generative, open-ended question to the group and record parents' contributions. Entries are read aloud for possible corrections or additions. Afterwards, the book is typed and bound, and copies are made to distribute to participants at the next meeting.

The collective books written by parents cover a wide range of topics. Sample titles include *From Yesterday to Tomorrow*, a collection of traditional sayings and proverbs and *Adivina, adivinador*, a collection of riddles. Other titles are *Celebrations of My Childhood, Our Grandparents, Our Dreams for Our Children and How We Can Help Them Come True, The Best Advice We Can Offer*, and *Things We Can Give Our Children That Can't Be Bought*. Facilitators have also offered simple sentence starters: books written in this manner include *Peace Is . . . , Friendship Is . . . , Family Is . . .* , and *Work Is. . . .*

At each session, parents are given blank books to take home. The number of parents with little previous schooling who have chosen to create books by themselves or as family projects, counts among the significant results of this simple yet profound process. Often, the blank books are used by the children to write their own stories. As parents bring these books back to the meetings, both parents and children are invited to share their books in front of the large group, and the family is celebrated as a family of authors. Later, the children's books are also typed, duplicated, and distributed to each family to add to their growing home library.

The following paragraphs contain some of the most salient results observed and documented in program sites (Anaya, 1995; Balderas, 1988; Gómez-Valdez, 1993; McCaleb, 1992; Murillo, 1987; Patrón, 1986; Reichmuth, 1981; Watts, 1988).

Parents who initially felt uncertain about their role in relationship to the school were able to establish a human, social relationship with teachers and administrators and experience firsthand their children's life at school. Once the gap they felt between home and school was bridged, parents were able to familiarize themselves with the content of their children's education, regain trust in their own abilities, and create an active role for themselves in their children's and their family's literacy process. The group discussions helped parents develop or expand their contacts in their community. Over and over, parents expressed their appreciation for having had the opportunity at the meetings to form closer ties with other parents.

Teachers participating in the program reported a greater understanding of the children in their classroom and of the challenges faced by those children on a daily basis. Teachers felt better equipped to serve the needs of each child. Teachers also reported that children who had the opportunity to see their parents recognized as authors by the school gained a greater sense of self-esteem and a new-found appreciation for the wisdom of their parents' words and their parents' life experiences.

Parents reported a greater interest in books and reading. Even more importantly, they reported that in the course of sharing their thoughts with each other, they had come to realize that their own personal stories are at least as important as those found in books. Parents also commented on the usefulness of books for inviting reflection and for promoting greater understanding of ourselves and of the world.

In addition to ethnographic research, other ways to assess the effects of a program of this kind include keeping records of the number of books written by the parents, the diversity of the subjects addressed in these books, and parents' willingness to read each other's books as evidenced by the books' circulation patterns. If the discussion sessions are videotaped, as was done in Pajaro Valley and other sites, the videos can be used to assess growth and development by observing parents' willingness to participate, their sense of ease in addressing the group, and the depth of their reflections.

In addition to summative evaluations, program planners must be involved in a continuous process of formative evaluation, using parents' direct and indirect feedback to create a climate of trust and respect. In previous implementations, the following have been identified as important contributors to program success: (1) offering an enjoyable program for children while parents are meeting; (2) presenting the family literacy program as an enriching cultural event, instead of as a remedial program; (3) offering to parents quality books with high aesthetic appeal and content that encourages reflection; (4) providing respectful and skilled facilitation for the small groups; and (5) including preparation time for facilitators to read the books and create discussion questions beforehand.

As mentioned earlier, the interest generated by the experience at Pajaro Valley led to the replication of the project in many other sites and under various names, including *Literatura Infantil* (Children's Literature), *Padres, Niños y Libros* (Parents, Children, and Books), *Padres y Niños Autores* (Parents and Children as Authors). Some of the schools in California where the project thrived for several consecutive years are Glassbrook School in Hayward, under the enthusiastic direction of Marcos Guerrero; Marshall School in San Francisco; and Project Even Start, at Windsor Elementary, under the efficient guidance of Jennifer Reynolds. The original Pajaro Valley program continues as *Literatura Infantil y Familiar,* under the auspices of the Migrant Education Office and the vision of its director, Dr. Paul Nava. In 1995, prompted by nationwide requests for information, the Migrant Office of Pajaro Valley sponsored the creation of a manual (Zubizarreta, 1996) that can be of assistance to those wishing to replicate the program.

Interactive Learning at Home and in the Classroom: Parents, Teachers, and Children as Authors

At various presentations on *Parents and Children as Authors,* teachers repeatedly brought up the question of what to do about children whose parents, for one reason or another, did not or could not attend the evening programs. Searching for an answer to this question brought us back to the following conclusion: by definition, authentically child-centered education needs to make children's home, family, and community a central part of the classroom curriculum.

While we advocate that parents and family members be included in the educational process on a daily basis, this does not necessarily require their physical presence at school. Of course, their presence is welcome whenever possible; yet, the presence of their thoughts, experiences, history, and words does not depend upon parents being physically on-site.

In the model offered by *Parents, Teachers, and Children as Authors,* a book is authored by the teacher to serve as a catalyst for interactive, dialogue-based home learning activities. The activities are designed to invite parents to share their life experiences, family stories, and words of wisdom. Parents' contributions are then woven into the classroom curriculum, as a way to honor and celebrate family and community (Ada, 1993).

Teachers wishing to follow this model do not need special training or materials. They do need to rethink their priorities to include (1) restoring parents' dignity as educators, (2) encouraging meaningful interaction between children and parents at home, (3) validating the home culture in the classroom, and (4) promoting the preservation of the heritage language. When we began working with teachers toward these goals, we invited them to send home, on a daily or weekly basis, oral or written questions and dialogue prompts. These dialogue prompts were created by the teachers themselves to elicit parents' thoughts, stories, and traditional knowledge.

As teachers explored how to make this kind of interaction between home and school a frequent practice, they discovered that authoring a personal book to share with families served as an excellent way to initiate teacher-family dialogue. By modeling the process of sharing their own life stories, teachers made it easier for parents to contribute their experiences. As we shared these earlier books written by teachers with others in subsequent workshops, we saw teachers become very inspired by the work of their own colleagues.

We found that books based on the teacher's own life or family are a good starting point. When teachers share their stories, they begin to bridge the formidable barriers of social class and educational status that may exist between them and the parents of their students. For example, a teacher who wrote a book about her mother and sent it to all the mothers of her students was able to convey a very strong message of equality and respect and elicited a strong positive response from the parents.

Many teachers have enjoyed writing a book about the story of their name. By sharing how their name was chosen, who else in their family carries that name, and what their name means to them, these teachers have sent the message home that there is a story in everyone's name and have modeled for their students the process of creating one's own personal book. Other books written by teachers include *I Was Not Always A Teacher* and *My Bed Is Not at School*. (Both of these books proved very popular with students, who are sometimes surprised to discover that teachers have a life outside of school.) For the most part, teachers have chosen to write books about their own parents and grandparents, children, spouses, or siblings to share these cherished stories with parents.

Once trust has been established, the process continues with questions and dialogue prompts that invite students to discuss with parents, in their own home language, any of the topics covered in school that day. Teachers show interest in parents' wisdom and experiences by recording the stories brought back by the students, by inviting students to create class books with the stories they have collected, or simply by providing students with the time and space to share their stories with classmates.

Students can also be encouraged to ask parents for memories of common human experiences: Who were their parents' friends when they were young? Did they ever have differences of opinion with a friend? How did they resolve the conflict? What do parents seek in a friend today? What would they be willing to do for a friend?

Or, parents can be invited to share their thoughts about universal values: What would they like to do to create a more just society? What would they like to change? What would they preserve? The teacher's role is to honor a diversity of opinions and model an attitude of respect. A variety of perspectives can be discussed, while maintaining the right of everyone to his or her own position.

Teachers who have asked students to collect their parents' thoughts are often happily surprised by the wisdom and insights they receive. When a group of parents in Windsor, California, was asked for their best advice to their children, Mr. Roberto Vargas responded by writing: "We are here to create a better world." Teachers decided to make a project based on this parent's words. They began by making a banner of the quote, properly credited, to display in every classroom. Next, each child was asked to create a page for a classroom book on how we can all make a better world. Needless to say, the response from the community was overwhelming. By treating parents as constructors of meaning, with valuable contributions to offer, we are indeed working together to create a better world for all.

Final Thoughts

By assessing what attitudes and beliefs about parents are embodied in our parent education programs, our parent outreach programs, and our classroom curriculum we can take the necessary steps to create more supportive conditions for children's literacy development. As we create parent education offerings that build on parent strengths, and as we create classrooms in which children can feel proud of their families and communities, we create greater opportunities for families to share the joy of learning.

DISCUSSION QUESTIONS

1. Because we have emphasized the importance of connecting academic learning with personal and family experience, this question invites you to consider your own parents' experiences. If you were to speak with your parents about how welcome they felt at your own elementary school when you were a child, what might they say?

2. In this chapter we've looked at how our limiting beliefs about language-minority parents can influence the design of our programs. Yet the very nature of our assumptions can make them difficult for us to identity. On the other hand, we tend to be very sensitive to others' assumptions about us. Think of a time when someone else held limiting beliefs about you. What were your feelings about the experience? What did you learn from it?

3. Any map, typology, or matrix is necessarily a limited representation of reality. What kinds of parent-school interactions can you think of that don't fit neatly into the matrix described in this chapter? How might you expand or accommodate the matrix to fit these experiences?

4. Think of a favorite elementary school lesson, on any subject. How might you create an interactive home learning component for that lesson that invites parents to share their own experiences with that subject? Once you have designed your dialogue prompts and activity, consider how you might alter or modify them to make them more inclusive.

5. Think of a favorite children's book. If you were reading that book to a particular group of parents, what kinds of discussion questions would you ask to help them connect the story to their own experiences? What do you already know about creating open-ended dialogue that you might apply to help parents feel more comfortable sharing their insights?

REFERENCES

Ada, A. F. (1988). The Pajaro Valley experience: Working with Spanish-speaking parents to develop children's reading and writing skills through the use of children's literature. In T. Skutnabb-Kangas & J. Cummins (Eds.). *Minority education: From shame to struggle.* Clevedon, England: Multilingual Matters.

Ada, A. F. (1991). Creative reading: A relevant methodology for language-minority children. In C. Walsh (Ed.), *Literacy as praxis: Culture, language and pedagogy.* Norwood, NJ: Ablex.

Ada, A. F. (1993). Mother-tongue literacy as a bridge between home and school cultures. In J. V. Tinajero, & A. F. Ada (Eds.), *The power of two languages* (pp. 158–163). New York: Macmillan/McGraw-Hill.

Ada, A. F., & Campoy, F. I. (1997a). *Comprehensive Language Arts.* Cleveland, OH: Del Sol Publishing.

Ada, A. F., & Campoy, F. I. (1997b). *Parents, Children and Teachers as Authors and Protagonists.* Cleveland, OH: Del Sol Publishing.

Anaya, A. (1995). *Empowering minority parents through the use of dialogic retrospection and participatory research.* University of San Francisco. Unpublished dissertation.

Auerbach, E. (1990). *Making meaning, making change: A guide to participatory curriculum development for adult ESL and family literacy.* Boston: University of Massachusetts.

Auerbach, E. (1989). Toward a social-contextual approach to family literacy. *Harvard Educational Review, 59*:2, 165–181.

Balderas, R. (1988). *Home language use and the attitudes of bilingual Hispanic parents and their spouses and the bilingual development of their children.* University of San Francisco. Unpublished dissertation.

Brown, K. (1993). Balancing the tools of technology with our own humanity: The use of technology in building partnerships and communities. In J. V. Tinajero & A. F. Ada (Eds.), *The power of two languages* (pp. 178–198). New York: Macmillan/McGraw-Hill.

Coleman, J. S. (1991). *Policy perspectives: Parental involvement in education.* Washington, DC: Office of Educational Research and Improvement, U.S. Department of Education.

Comer, J. P. (1988). *Maggie's American dream: The life and times of a black family.* New York: Penguin Books.

Cummins, J. (1981). The role of primary language development in promoting educational success for language minority students. In *Schooling and language-minority students: A theoretical framework.* California State Department of Education, Sacramento CA.

Cummins, J. (1989). *Empowering minority students.* Sacramento: California Association for Bilingual Education.

Delgado-Gaitan, C. (1990). *Literacy for empowerment: The role of parents in their children's education.* London: The Falmer Press.

Developmental Studies Center. (1995). *Homeside activities: Conversations and activities that bring parents into children's schoolside learning, Vols. K–6.* Oakland: Developmental Studies Center.

Developmental Studies Center. (1996). *At home in our schools: A guide to schoolwide activities that build community.* Oakland: Developmental Studies Center.

Developmental Studies Center. (1997). *Actividades familiares: Building on family strengths through conversations and activities in the home language.* 12-minute Spanish-language video. Oakland: Developmental Studies Center.

Dolson, D. (1985). The effects of spanish home language use on the scholastic performance of Hispanic pupils. *Journal of Multilingual and Multicultural Development 6*(2): 135–56.

Epstein, J. L. (1987). Parent involvement: What research says to administrators. *Education and Urban Society, 19*(2): 119–136.

Forest, L. (1994). Focus on parents: Making it easier to be involved. Interview with teacher Debbie Delatour. *Cooperative Learning, 14*(4): 14–17.

Freire, P. (1984). *Pedagogy of the oppressed.* New York: Continuum Press.

Gómez-Valdez, C. (1993). *The silent majority raise their voices: Reflections of Mexican parents on learning and schooling. A participatory research.* University of San Francisco. Unpublished dissertation.

Hewison, J., & Tizard, J. (1980). Parental involvement and reading attainment. *British Journal of Educational Psychology, 50,* 209–215.

Huerta-Macías, A., & Quintero, E. (1993). Teaching language and literacy in the context of family and community. In J. V. Tinajero & A. F. Ada (Eds.), *The power of two languages* (pp. 152–157). New York: Macmillan/McGraw-Hill.

Kerbow, D., & Bernhart, A. (1993). Parental intervention in the school: The context of minority involvement. In B. Schneider & J. S. Coleman (Eds.), *Parents, their children, and schools* (pp. 115–146). Boulder and Oxford: Westview Press.

McCaleb, S. P. (1992). *Parent involvement in education during early literacy development: A participatory study with Hispanic, African-American, and African parents through dialogue and co-authorship of books.* University of San Francisco. Unpublished dissertation.

McCaleb, S. P. (1994). *Building communities of learners. A collaboration among teachers, students, families and communities.* New York: St. Martin's Press.

Moles, O. C. (1993). Collaboration between schools and disadvantaged parents: Obstacles and openings. In N. F. Chavkin (Ed.), *Families and schools in a pluralistic society.* Albany: SUNY Press.

Moll, L. C. (1990). *Community-mediated instruction: A qualitative approach.* Paper presented at National AERA, Chicago, IL.

Montecel, M. R., Gallagher, A., Montemayor, A. M., Villarreal, A., Adame-Reyna, N., and Supik, J. D. (1993). *Hispanic families as valued partners: An educator's guide.* San Antonio: Intercultural Development Research Association (IDRA).

Muller, C. (1993). Parent involvement and academic achievement: An analysis of family resources available to the child. In B. Schneider & J. S. Coleman (Eds.), *Parents, their children, and schools* (pp. 77–114). Boulder and Oxford: Westview Press.

Muller, C., & Kerbow, D. (1993). Parent involvement in the home, school, and community. In B. Schneider & J. S. Coleman (Eds.), *Parents, their children, and schools* (pp. 13–42). Boulder and Oxford: Westview Press.

Murillo, S. (1987). *Toward improved home-school interaction. A participatory dialogue with Hispanic parents in Berkeley, California.* University of San Francisco. Unpublished dissertation.

Nieto, S. (1992). *Affirming diversity: The sociopolitical context of multicultural education.* New York and London: Longman.

Patrón, R. L. (1986). *Promoting English literacy for Spanish-speaking students: A participatory study of Spanish-speaking parents, their children and school personnel, using an innovative intervention model in Spanish.* University of San Francisco. Unpublished dissertation.

Ramirez, J., & Douglas, D. 1989. *Language-minority parents and the school: Can home-school partnerships increase student success?* Sacramento: California State Department of Education, Bilingual Education Office.

Reichmuth, S. (1981). *Hispanic parent empowerment through critical dialogue and parent-child interaction within the school setting.* University of San Francisco. Unpublished dissertation.

Rich, D. (1987). *Schools and families: Issues and actions.* National Education Association, Washington, D.C.

Rich, D. (1993). Building the bridge to reach minority parents: Education infrastructure supporting success for all children. In N. F. Chavkin (Ed.), *Families and schools in a pluralistic society.* Albany: SUNY Press.

Safran, D. (1996). Unpublished manuscript.

Sarason, S. (1995). *Parental involvement and the political principle.* San Francisco: Jossey-Bass.

Simich-Dudgeon, C. (1993). Increasing student achievement through teacher knowledge about parent involvement. In N. F. Chavkin (Ed.), *Families and schools in a pluralistic society.* Albany: SUNY Press.

Simich-Dudgeon, C. (1986). *Trinity-Arlington parent involvement project: Final report.* Submitted to the Office of Bilingual Education and Minority Languages Affairs under Grant No. G00B302061, Washington, DC: U.S. Department of Education.

Shirley, D. (1997). *Community organizing for urban school reform.* Austin: University of Texas Press.

Urzua, C. (1986). A children's story. In P. Rigg, & D. S. Enright (Eds.), *Children and ESL: Integrating perspectives* (pp. 93–112). Washington, DC: TESOL.

Watts, J. (1988). *A determination of parental expectations of and role in the educational process: Perspectives of African American parents.* University of San Francisco. Unpublished dissertation.

Zubizarreta, R. (1996). *Transformative family literacy: Engaging in meaningful dialogue with Spanish-speaking parents.* Cleveland, OH: Del Sol Publishing.

INDEX